GOD'S PROMISES for Teens

Ellen F. Pill

Marie D. Jones

Publications International, Ltd.

Louis Weber, CEO
Publications International, Ltd.
7373 North Cicero Avenue
Lincolnwood, Illinois 60712

Permission is never granted for commercial purposes.

Manufactured in China.

8 7 6 5 4 3 2 1

ISBN: 0-7853-9036-7

Library of Congress Control Number: 2003111427

Contents

You've Got a Friend in God

Hey—you're a TEENAGER, right? You've waited years to get to this point in your life. To have the respect, the privileges, the fun! You're cool. You're what it's all about. But what does it mean? What IS it all about? Sometimes it's tough to know exactly what's happening—both inside and outside your teenage self. It's a time of change, of emotion, a roller-coaster ride taking you from childhood to adulthood. It's a blessing and a curse, an incredible joy and a royal pain. It's being too old for this, too young for that, and sometimes feeling like you're never just right for anything! Then you turn a corner, and it's everything you imagined and so much more. Each day is filled with adventure, drama, challenge, life, love, and learning. It's all about being YOU—being a teen!

So how do I do this, you ask? What's the right way to act, to think? When do I assert my independence? When do I say "No!" How come my parents seem so clueless one minute and so wise the next? Why is life so hard some days? Where's God in all of this? The answer to this last question is *everywhere*. He's by your side when you head off on your first date, when you lose a friend, when you're giving life your all, or when you've fallen short of expectations. Whether times are good or bad, you've got a friend in God. That is his promise to you.

God's Promises for Teens is about it all—the highs and lows—and what they all mean. Inside you'll find stories for teens, about everything from losing a parent to learning to hit a fastball. Some of these stories might seem as if they were written just for you, while others will open your eyes to something new. At the end of each chapter, we've provided space for you to reflect on what's happening in your own life—to contemplate and meditate and pray.

Share these stories with your friends and with your parents. Doing so might make it easier to talk about some of the more difficult subjects. When life is getting tough and you can't seem to find God anywhere, turn to these stories. You're bound to discover—as the teens in these stories did—that he's been with you all along.

The teen years sometimes seem to go on forever, but if you ask anyone who's made it through before you, they'll likely say it went faster than the blink of an eye. So savor. Taste. Enjoy.

The road through the teenage universe may be bumpy at times, so fasten your seat belt. Remember that the destination is a whole new world of finally being old enough to experience life on your own terms, and the journey is all about having the adventure of a lifetime! Put on some music, sit back, prop up your feet, and dive in—you've got everything in the world to gain! And remember: You're never alone in this universe because you've got a friend in God!

Family Matters

A family is like a safe-deposit box—
it contains all your valuables and is always
there for reassurance.

Who knows us the best? Who's known us the
longest? Who spends the most time with us?
FAMILY! They are the people who love us when
no one else does, and they are the ones who
are always there no matter what. They drive you
crazy; they drive you to games; they drive you
to the mall. You like 'em, you hate 'em—but still
and always you love 'em! Besides, what would
you do *without* all that wonderful, maddening,
soul-soothing love?

From siblings to grandparents, from step-
parents to cousins, aunts, and uncles, family is
often at the heart of our deepest, most powerful emotions. Family is at the heart of our heart,
but sometimes we lose sight of what incredible
blessings family members are.

Dive into these stories about family, and
see what strikes a chord in you.

Generation Gap

When my dad told me his father would be moving in with us, I was not happy. My Grandpa Joe was an old-fashioned, conservative ex-Marine who was constantly on my case for how I dressed, the way I wore my hair, and the music I enjoyed. The thought of having Grandpa in our house 24/7 made me want to scream.

The day Grandpa Joe moved in, I helped carry his stuff into the guest room where he would be staying. I could tell by the look on his face that he hated having to move in with us. His heart condition was making it impossible for him to care for himself, but he was fiercely independent and made it clear to the whole family he would not be doted on. "Don't worry," I wanted to tell him, "I won't dote!" In fact, I planned to avoid him as much as possible.

As the days went on, Grandpa Joe became quiet and withdrawn. He had always been so outspoken and opinion-ated, but his lack of independence had sapped his spirit. I realized I actually *missed* his feisty personality. Now he was more like those folks you see in darkened hospital rooms, just sitting there watching TV with blank looks on their faces.

So I decided to light a little fire under Grandpa Joe. At dinner, I dressed in my wildest rock T-shirt and spiked my hair. I had bleached the tips, and my dad laughed, calling me a surf bum. Grandpa Joe didn't even respond. I decided to up the ante and talk politics, knowing Grandpa Joe hated my liberal views. Still, not even a click of the tongue or a roll of the eyes.

That night, I couldn't sleep. I really was worried about my grandpa. Difficult as he could be, I loved him, but I didn't have a clue how to reach him. I knew Grandpa Joe loved to read the Bible and decided maybe there was something in the Good Book, as he called it, that might help me. I opened it and read the first quote I came to, something about Jesus saying you had to be as a little child in order to enter the Kingdom. As I read on, something clicked inside my head. Then I heard a cough downstairs.

Grandpa Joe was sitting in the kitchen alone. I grabbed two forks and the apple pie leftover from dessert. Silently, we ate the pie. Then, I placed my hand on Grandpa Joe's. His hand was withered and wrinkled, but he turned his palm upward and gripped my hand hard. We made eye contact, and I could see he had been crying.

Grandpa Joe smiled and asked me how I liked having a useless old bum living in my house. I smiled back and told him that I loved having my feisty and opinionated grand-father around so I could pick his brain about the world. That made him smile even bigger, and I could see the twinkle come back in his eye.

"You mean I just might have a chance of changing you around a bit?" he asked, his voice sly.

"Definitely not, but won't it be fun trying?" I said. At that, Grandpa Joe started laughing, and I joined in. Before we knew it, we were laughing so hard we had disturbed the entire house.

I'm glad I reached out to Grandpa Joe. He is still very hard on me, but we have so much fun disagreeing!

Do not speak harshly to an older man,
but speak to him as to a father.

1 TIMOTHY 5:1

Lord,
Thank you for the older people in my life. I may not have much in common with them, but I know they are here to teach me what their eyes have seen and to help direct my feet on paths they have tread before. Help me to be kind to them and to understand that they were once just as wild and headstrong and energetic as I am now. Teach us to be friends, even if we can't always relate. Amen.

There is only one happiness in life,
to love and be loved.

GEORGE SAND

An Unexpected Christmas Present

"What'll it be for you folks?" the rolling-store man asked as Mama, Dad, and I stepped up to the back of the huge truck that had been converted into a miniature mobile general store. Two battery-powered lightbulbs dangling from the ceiling lit up the shelves where small dolls, toy cars, cap pistols, marbles, harmonicas, pocketknives, hard candy, apples, oranges, and a variety of other Christmas items were stacked in bins along with groceries and other merchandise.

The rolling store was well stocked on the last run before Christmas, and the sight of all those holiday goodies reminded me that I might not—probably would not—get the special present I wanted. And later, when the boys at school would ask what I got for Christmas, I'd have to hear them laugh when I'd mumble, "Oh, this and that." I had dreamed of being able to tell them about a two-key harmonica, an air rifle, or even a cheap guitar. I wanted something a 13-year-old boy could really be proud of.

The last rolling-store run before Christmas was almost as exciting as Christmas Eve for the children in our Appalachian mountain community. That was when the two-ton truck with a huge flattop box would make its rounds, loaded with as much "Christmas" as it could hold. And children, spying from windows and porches, would speculate wistfully on the contents of paper sacks and cardboard boxes carried to their house. There were some of us who could not expect much from the rolling store. But we all hoped anyway. I had hoped earlier that year, but, being the oldest of five children—with some understanding of the family finances—I didn't see any reason to expect much as Christmas approached. It had been a bad year, and all I could look forward to for Christmas was maybe a bag of marbles and some candy and oranges—certainly nothing special.

Dad had come down with the flu in January, and for two months there were no biscuits in my school lunch bucket, only corn bread, which I was embarrassed to eat in front of the boys whose parents could afford flour—some of the same boys who would ask what I got for Christmas. In late March a boiling pot overturned on the hearth, scalding the feet of my two-year-old sister, and my younger brother tasted some lye that had been left in a dish. Any extra money had to go toward their care. In May, however, our future seemed brighter when Dad got a job on the new state highway project. The three dollars a day he'd earn would put biscuits on the breakfast table and maybe buy us some new shoes to wear on Sunday. By June, Mama began to talk of some purchases she would like to make—linoleum for the kitchen floor, some cloth for new curtains, maybe even a radio someday so it wouldn't be so lonesome in the house when the children went off to school. That was when I began to dream of harmonicas, guitars, and air rifles.

But then in July, our fortunes changed again. The driver of the panel-body Dodge that took men to work on the highway project appeared at our door one day. He told us that Dad had been caught in the path of a sliding rock and had been taken 30 miles to a hospital because he had broken his leg. Mama hired a neighbor to take her to visit Dad and later to bring him home. In August Dad broke the leg again when he jumped from a runaway buggy going down a steep hill. Then in November he found a temporary job cutting logs, but he owed so much by then—for food, Mama's trips to visit him at the hospital, and medicine—that it was not likely there would be any money for Christmas.

But I still listened for the rolling-store horn when it topped the ridge that morning. I traced its progress as its horn signaled the stops along the main road, hoping against hope that I would somehow get the present of my dreams.

When Mama put our supper on the back of the stove, I realized that she, too, was expecting the rolling store. Around 7:00 she and Dad left my brother and sisters with Grandma and took me with them to the nearby gravel road where the rolling store made one of its scheduled stops. Seeing us waiting there, the rolling-store man gave a long blast on the horn. "Folks are sure buyin' lots of stuff this year for Christmas," he greeted us. Again I thought of the present I might not get.

Then Mama began to buy. Oranges. Apples. Candy. Two bags of marbles. Two packs of firecrackers. Three little cheap dolls. Two pairs of gloves. But no harmonica, air rifle, or guitar. She also bought some flour, sugar, yeast, chocolate, raisins, bananas, and bologna. As the rolling-store man put the purchases into paper sacks, I wondered if Dad would ask for credit, but to my surprise he handed the man a ten-dollar bill. "Been savin' this a long time," he said proudly.

But still no special present for me, I thought. At least not one from the rolling store. And where would another present come from now? Soon Christmas would be over, and I would have to answer "this and that" when the boys at school asked about my presents.

Christmas morning came cold and frosty with a sunrise that promised an afternoon warm enough for playing outside—if one had something like an air rifle to play with. Mama woke the girls, who screamed with joy when they pulled the tiny dolls from their stockings. My brother reached into his stocking and brought out gloves, firecrackers, and marbles. "My own marbles!" he yelled. "Big taw, too. Now I can get in the good games at school." While Mama and Dad looked at me, I slowly emptied my stocking and—just as I expected—found gloves, marbles, and firecrackers. I imagined all the wonderful things my classmates were

probably discovering in their stockings. Had one of them gotten the guitar I so desperately wanted? And here I was with a measly pair of gloves and some marbles.

Now the hoping and waiting were over, and Christmas would be a dull day—dinner with Grandpa and Grandma, playing marbles with my brother, and going with Dad to the field to shoot the firecrackers. Meantime, the other boys would be playing with trucks or wagons, trying out their harmonicas, or shooting at old cans with air rifles.

Later, as we gathered at the table for dinner, I felt a nagging in my heart. I looked around at my loving parents, doting grandparents, and smiling siblings, and it occurred to me that maybe, just maybe, I did have something special. I thought about some of those boys who were sure to flaunt their gifts, and I realized that I also had a really wonderful gift. There were the two brothers who were being raised by an indulgent, widowed mother. They might get air rifles, but they would not have a father or grandfather to teach them how to shoot. One boy was from a troubled home often filled with screaming, fighting, and cursing. I knew he wouldn't have a laughing, caring family joining him at his dinner table. Another boy had a drunken, abusive father who would certainly make Christmas a miserable day for his son, who might have to take refuge in the barn with his present.

I knew these boys might all receive wonderful presents, but I wasn't jealous anymore. I realized that as long as I had a loving family to spend the holidays with, I was truly blessed. After all, wasn't that what Christmas was all about?

As we bowed our heads to say grace I smiled, knowing I was part of a family held together by love, hard work, and hope for better things to come. And that was definitely something to be thankful for.

Home is the place where, when you have to go there, They have to take you in.
ROBERT FROST, "THE DEATH OF THE HIRED MAN"

Driving Us Crazy!

"Mooooooooooooooooooooooooooommmmmmmmmmmm!"
My brother's voice was yet again screaming from the backseat of our van. We were on the third day of our "family
vacation" and he was driving me absolutely, positively, most
certainly, and irrevocably INSANE!

*If he has to go to the bathroom again I'm going to
scream,* I thought to myself. Things were not going well.
Four kids, two parents, a broken VCR, and 3,000 miles did
not make for a fun trip in my book. At 15, I wanted to be at
the beach with my friends—*not* in the car with my family on
my way to see the United States.

Shall we just say that I was not a happy camper? Why,
oh, why weren't my prayers ever answered? Where was the
Lord when I needed him?

Just then, my mother screamed "Oh, no!"

Dad hit the brakes and prayed quietly and most unchar-
acteristically, "Lord help us . . ."

There were the horrendous sounds of metal hitting
metal, and then we came to a stop off the right shoulder in
an open field.

Dad turned around, "Everyone okay?"

There had been a collision directly in front of us, but
with God's watchful eye and Dad's great driving, we had
gone off the road and out of harm's way. We were all fine.

We drove along in silence for a very long time after
that. Finally, Mom broke the quiet. "I love you all so much.
Let's thank the Lord for keeping us all safe and together."

"Amen!" we all chorused.

The rest of the trip was pretty good. No more fighting. No more complaining. And I realized that God was indeed right there with me.

God,
Sometimes I wish I didn't have siblings. They are so annoying, and I constantly have to baby-sit them and be a "role model" for them. I feel like my parents favor them and think they can do no wrong, yet it always seems they are getting *me* in trouble. "They don't know any better," my parents tell me. But they do—I know they do. But even though I'd sometimes like to be rid of them, I also know I'd really miss them. God, I hope I learn to have more patience for them and understand that they really do just want to be like me.

Even though siblings seem like a pain,
as you grow older you'll learn they are actually friends
that never leave your side.

❖   ❖   ❖

Gotta Keep Rolling

It was totally freaky. I mean, I never expected my parents to get divorced. They were in love. I thought so, anyway. We did all kinds of happy stuff together. We went to the movies, bowling, and on long bike rides. We went to church every Sunday and always went out for brunch together afterward. We went on fun family vacations. But there I was on the couch having "the talk." Not *that* talk, but the one where they say, "It's not your fault, it has nothing to do with you." Well, if them getting divorced didn't have anything to do with me, how come they were making such a big deal about it? Oh, they were just ruining my life is all. No big deal. No big deal at all. It was just a horrible nightmare and any minute I'd wake up and all would be well. But I never did. Wake up, that is. And Dad started moving out the next day.

I hated them both. I hated myself and everyone else, and I really hated my life. I blamed everyone. I blamed God. I closed up. Didn't talk to a soul. Stopped praying. I sulked. Big time. Who was I gonna live with? Where would we live? Would we have enough money? Would this emptiness inside me ever go away?

Finally, one Saturday a friend convinced me to go to the mall with her. We wandered around, and she bought some stuff, but every time I'd see something I liked I remembered my mom saying how we had to cut back and watch our budget. I started to feel really sorry for myself—again. I saw families together. Laughing. Sharing the day. No way my life would ever be like that again. No way I'd ever get to be that happy. I was throwing myself a real pity party.

Then a girl about my age rolled by me in her wheelchair. A friend came running after her. They were laughing. I thought about how I wished I could laugh again. Then all of a sudden I felt so foolish. Those girls were so playful—so full of life—that I hadn't even realized that the one girl couldn't walk. *She couldn't walk.* I felt like someone had knocked the wind out of me. *I could walk. I could laugh.* I was blessed in so many ways that I never even thought about before. For some reason, that instant changed me. God had sent me a mes-

sage, and I had received it loud and clear. Sure, life can be rotten sometimes; but now, whenever I start to feel sorry for myself, I see that girl rolling by me in her wheelchair and laughing with her friend. She taught me that I can roll along and laugh, too. No matter what.

Dear God,
My family is going through a rough time right now. Please help us to make sense of what is happening and assist us in getting through. It's hard to know what is next, and the uncertainty is troublesome. Please shed light on the proper paths and bless my family with your love. Amen.

God is our refuge and strength,
a very present help in trouble.

PSALM 46:1

*Divorce may mean a physical separation between
family members, but love is not divided.*

God,
If there is supposed to be "no place like home," why do I
dread going there? My home is not the place of fairy tales.
My parents never seem to be talking to each other; they're
always picking fights with me or my siblings. It's a stressful
place to be. I wish my house could be more peaceful and
happy. I'm jealous of other families with their *Brady Bunch*
lives. Please bless my home with a love that can withstand
petty differences and troubling times.

Life is not meant to be easy . . . but take courage:
it can be delightful.

GEORGE BERNARD SHAW

Grandma's Kitchen

My grandma was around a lot. She didn't live with us, but we saw her so much that she might as well have. Sometimes it was kind of annoying. I'd want to have a friend over, but Grandma was there and always in the way. She talked with a thick Hungarian accent. I could understand her, but my friends couldn't. Plus she would intersperse her sentences with Hungarian words and Bible quotes. She had a verse for every occasion!

The kitchen table was her domain. Everything happened there. Good things and bad things. I had to do my homework at the kitchen table with Grandma's watchful eye looking over my shoulder. She also delivered soft, warm cookies fresh from the oven, which couldn't be so much as sniffed until a proper prayer was said. We all sat at the table when we learned that Grandpa had died. And we were all at the table when we heard that my sister was accepted to Harvard. "Grandchildren are the crown of the aged," Grandma exclaimed, quoting Proverbs 17:6.

As I got older, I found myself quoting Grandma and the Bible all the time. Now *I* seemed to have a phrase for every occasion. Yesterday, when my teenage son begged for a cell phone, I said, "My grandmother used to say that if you never had something, you can't miss it!" Grandma's not only a part of me, now she's a part of my children.

To quote Ephesians 1:16, Grandma, "I do not cease to give thanks for you as I remember you in my prayers." I think of you every time I bake cookies!

❖   ❖   ❖

Lord,
Thank you for blessing me with an extended family. Not all kids have the opportunity to grow up so close to a grandparent. And while sometimes I get frustrated that she can't just get up and out of my way, I feel fortunate to have the opportunity to learn from someone so experienced at life. I know I've said bad things about having her here, but please know she is a source of comfort and contentment for me. Please look after her both now and when she resides in your kingdom. Amen.

L isten to advice and accept instruction,
that you may gain wisdom for the future.

PROVERBS 19:20

*The best way to thank your family for their love and
support is to give them reasons to be proud.*

Lord,

Thank you for my loving family. I know not all kids are
blessed with a family that is so supportive and caring. My
relatives have passed on their values and morals to me so
that I can be proud of who I am. And Lord, I hope that, they,
too, can be proud of who I have become.

✣ ✣ ✣

More Will Come

I was walking down the main street of our little town with my older brother. I hadn't seen him in almost two years; he had been off in Los Angeles trying to become a professional guitar player. I'd never heard anyone play music like he did, yet he always seemed to be broke and without a job. Mostly I was just glad he had come to visit. As far as I was concerned, he was the biggest star ever—maybe the world just hadn't figured it out yet. He always had an aura of calm about him, too. Like he knew stuff the rest of us didn't. I sometimes thought he had a direct line for his prayers.

We were walking, and he was talking—sharing his worldly views with me on everything from organic food to sex to religion. I listened to some of it, and sometimes I just sort of basked in the glow of having him home.

I didn't really notice the blind man. He sat on his usual street corner with his usual bucket of pencils and his collection cup. I always just hurried by him, relieved that he could not see who I was. Rick kept talking as we walked past. Then, partway down the street, he stopped, turned to me, and smiled. "I think I need a pencil."

He ran back and emptied the contents of his pocket into the blind man's cup. He held the pencil up for a brief moment, then said, "No point in carrying all that change around. It just weighs me down. Besides, more will come." He tucked the pencil safely into his pocket. He didn't say another word about it.

Of all the things Rick was perhaps trying to teach me during that visit, the one thing I remember as clearly as if it were yesterday is the blind man. No sermon could have taught it better. I never walk away from someone in need anymore. And Rick was right. Whether it's love or money or goodwill and prayer, when you give away what you have, more always does come.

❖   ❖   ❖

I n all your ways acknowledge him,
and he will make straight your paths.
PROVERBS 3:6

❖   ❖   ❖

God,
Thank you for giving me older brothers and sisters. I never imagined they had so much to teach me about life. Even though we don't always get along, it's nice to know I can turn to them for advice. I can talk to them about things Mom and Dad would never understand in a million years.

❖   ❖   ❖

W hoever gives to the poor will lack nothing, but one who turns a blind eye will get many a curse.
PROVERBS 28:27

A Good Tree

I didn't want to help my aunt Helga. The thought of spending an entire week at a tumbledown farm in the middle of nowhere was bad enough, let alone having to spend it with my no-nonsense, German-to-the-core great-aunt.

"Please, Jen," my mom said, as though I had a choice. "I wish you'd give her a chance."

I frowned, picturing the prickly old recluse whom everyone said I resembled. Being the youngest branch on the family tree at 15, with no definite plans for the summer, it had fallen on my shoulders to help Aunt Helga clean her house. That's how I found myself waiting on the stoop the next morning, when her mud-brown Plymouth pulled to the curb at precisely 9:00.

After a long, hot drive (Aunt Helga thought air-conditioning was frivolous) we arrived at her farm. I glanced longingly at the creek. *How wonderful a quick dip would feel,* I thought. Aunt Helga had other ideas. She bustled about, assembling cornstarch, cleaning cloths, and a stack of old newspapers. "We start with the windows, okay?"

"Why me?" I grumbled, slapping my cloth at a streaky pane.

That evening, with the supper dishes drying in her now-spotless kitchen, Aunt Helga brought out a battered deck of playing cards. *How appropriate*, I thought. *Old Maid.* After five hands, I dropped into the four-poster bed in her guest room and was lulled to sleep by the whir of crickets and the sound of wind sighing in the trees.

The next morning Aunt Helga heaped my plate with raspberry pancakes. "Today, the floors," she announced as she set the plate before me.

When we'd beaten the rugs, scoured the plank floors, and polished the baseboards, Aunt Helga declared that it was time to rest. I rubbed my aching shoulders and carried the dog-eared copy of *Little Women* I'd found in Helga's bookcase to the shade of a weeping willow tree.

I sat for a moment, enjoying the mild June breeze. Aunt Helga stood at the clothesline, the hem of her housedress swaying as she pegged up a load of wash. A low, cheerful sound drifted across the yard, blending with the twitter of robins and the rumble of a tractor in a far-off field. To my surprise, I realized Aunt Helga was singing.

I read all afternoon beneath sunshine and clear blue skies. Finally Helga appeared carrying a pitcher of lemonade and two frosty glasses. She eased herself to the ground beside me, laughing as her old bones creaked.

"You must be thirsty, Jenny."

I sipped from my glass, savoring the cold, tangy liquid. Aunt Helga rested her head against the tree, closed her eyes, and sighed.

"It is a good tree," she said. "Strong and kind." Aunt Helga had a way of saying things that left me stumped for a reply. I couldn't imagine what made the tree so special.

"I heard him call to me last night," she said. "My Joe."

A chill ran down my spine as I thought of the picture on her mantel of a thin, smiling boy in work clothes. A boy who'd worked too hard, I'd heard it said, who'd died too young.

"He is with me always," she said, as if reading my thoughts. "In the skies and in the wind. But mostly here, in the trees."

I looked into her eyes, which were all at once soft and moist. "What do you mean?" I asked, setting my book aside.

She ran a gnarled hand along the tree trunk, then began her story. "I was teaching at the old brick school when the railroad came to town. The year was 1929. All day long the immigrant men worked to lay the tracks. Such loud men, swinging hammers, filling the air with good German folk songs. Every morning when I walked to school, Joe would be standing at the fence.

"'*Guten morgen,* schoolteacher. How are you today?' he'd say.

"Such a handsome boy. But girls were not so bold then as they are today. I held my chin high, but my hands," she made a gnarled fist, "I held them in my pockets so he wouldn't see how they trembled.

"Then one day, snow came. Such excitement! I had to let the children go home early. I was walking from the school when I heard a voice beside the fence. 'Children, watch! I am going to throw a snowball at the teacher!'

"I walked proudly, but my knees, how they trembled. SPLAT! I turned to see Joe, his eyes sparkling like the snow. Never was I so angry as then! I threw down my books and made a snowball. I chased him. Round and round the schoolyard I ran. When I caught him . . . splat! Ah, such pretty laughter he had. 'Now that we are acquainted,' he told me, 'I shall come and court you.' "

Her hand caressed the trunk. "He planted this tree that spring. 'When this tree is old and strong,' he told me, 'we will have loved each other for a very long time.' "

Aunt Helga looked into my eyes. "He never saw it grow. That summer he died with scarlet fever."

"I'm so sorry," I said softly.

"You take what the good Lord gives you," she said. "Nothing more and nothing less."

I took a good, long look at Aunt Helga. For the first time I didn't see a brittle old recluse. I saw a girl, not so much older than myself. A girl who, having once known the joy of true love, had chosen to live alone with her memories rather than settle for anything less.

"Aunt Helga . . ."

I don't know what I would have said, if anything. From out of nowhere, a fat raindrop splashed my cheek. Helga struggled to her feet. "My washings!" she cried. "They will be wet!"

I dashed across the yard, stopping when I lost my sandal. My aunt ran on ahead. She was halfway to the clothesline when the sky opened up, pelting us with shimmering beads. Aunt Helga stopped in her tracks. Laughing, she threw her arms open wide and embraced the rain.

The Fastball

I was afraid of the ball. Pretty embarrassing, huh? I considered myself an athlete—had been playing ice hockey since I could walk. I'd played every conceivable sport with my dad and my brothers, but I was afraid of that fastball. Seeing that ball coming at me was terrifying. I'd tried and tried to get over my fear. I'd even prayed about it. Nothing worked. So when my father died (when I was 14), I figured I'd just quit. I'd tried to hit one for my father. But now, why? I went to practice and had the speech all prepared for my coach. I was going to tell him I was already too busy with other sports.

I was about to deliver my news to the coach when I heard a familiar gruff voice call out from the stands: "Brad! Why aren't you dressed?" Why was my brother Jim here? Probably to tease me. After all, that's what he did best.

I hadn't worn my workout gear since I hadn't planned to stay. "I, uh, I can't stay..." I stuttered out my answer.

"Get your behind into some sweats, and get out there and hit that ball!" Uncertain what to do, I ran the block home to change and came right back. Jim was still there. I got to bat and started thinking my doomsday thoughts. I asked God why he had singled me out for such humiliation.

"Take a thick bat!" "Don't overthink it." "Hang in . . . Don't freeze." Jim's voice echoed in my batter's helmet.

It was like that for the entire season. We never talked about it. Jim just came to every single game and tried to advise me, reassure me, give me confidence. I didn't quit, but I didn't hit the ball either. Most games I didn't even get a turn at bat; everyone knew I was scared.

Then came a game near the end of the season. Several of my team members had come down with the flu. They put me in to hit. I heard Jim as always. "Take a BIG bat." I picked the biggest, thickest bat there was. "Work with the ball— don't fight it."

The first pitch came at me. I breathed deep and swung. CRACK! It fouled—but I'd hit it! Then the pitcher threw a crazy pitch meant to scare me. It was inside, and I had to step away to keep from getting knocked in the ribs. "That's okay," Jim yelled, "you're doing great. Just swing. Just swing."

The next ball was fast. It came at me like a blur. I locked my gaze on it, and everything started to happen in slow motion. I swore later that I could feel my father's hands on my arms in that instant—like when I was little and he was first teaching me to hit. I swung. CRACK! My line drive was shooting down the gap between right and center fields.

"Run! Run!" Dad shouted. Of course, looking back, I realize it must've been Jim shouting. But in my memory, in my mind that day, it was my dad's voice that I heard.

I took off and didn't look back until I hit second base. The outfielder had just caught up with my ball. Jim was grinning and pumping his arms up and down. I couldn't hear him, but I knew he was shouting, "YES! YES!" The entire bench stood up and cheered. I'm sure Dad was watching and cheering, too.

Baseball still isn't my favorite sport, but now I know that I can quit—*or* I can play and give it everything I've got. It's up to me. I believe in myself again. And I believe in something beyond myself that I had almost given up on.

I still haven't thanked Jim for everything he did. I wouldn't even know what to say. I guess I'd just have to thank him for being a brother—a really cool, supportive, patient, and kind big brother. Wow. What an amazing surprise to find in your own family!

Your family is the circle of people who serve as your haven from bad weather, your source of encouragement during times of fear, and your never-ending supply of love and support.

Whatever your task, put yourselves into it, as done for the Lord and not for your masters.
COLOSSIANS 3:23

The size of the family does not matter; it's the dimensions of their love that create a home.

The Power of Words

My mom was in the hospital. Yet again. Seemed she was always in the hospital for something. When I was little, I'd get so worried, so scared. She was always sick with one thing or another. And I was always praying as hard as I could that she wouldn't die, that she would get better and never be sick again. Then I got older, and I started to get angry at her. I got angry at God, too. I prayed less and less. It just seemed Mom was never home when I needed her. She would get moody and sullen, then sick again. Or she'd be out on a date or at work at my grandpa's store. I wanted her to be there for *me!* To help me make a cheerleading outfit for tryouts, to send me off on my first date, to make a real dinner. It never occurred to me that she needed me in any way. I sort of thought that it was probably a nuisance for her to take care of me.

It was no big surprise when, during my last year of high school, she ended up in the hospital yet again. I went to see her grudgingly, hurrying in and out so I wouldn't miss the dance at school. I sat at her bedside for a while and read an English literature assignment. At least I'd get something done while I was there. She dozed most of the time anyway. By now, I knew that my mom was "sick" because she had a mental illness, though my family didn't talk about it much. I thought that if you felt moody or sad, you should get over it and get on. I couldn't find any way to understand.

It was almost 7:00. I was hungry, and the dance started at 8:00, so I got up to leave.

"Leaving already?" her eyes popped open, begging me to stay.

"Yes, Mom. I've got to go." *Please let her go back to sleep,* I silently pleaded with no one in particular. I'd long since stopped asking God for any-thing.

"Wait!" She grabbed my sleeve. I figured I was in for the lecture on being a good daughter or the third degree about where I was going. "Would you just say 'I love you' before you go?"

"What?" I didn't think I had heard right. She repeated herself. In my self-focused confusion, I decided to stand up for myself and my own personal honesty. I said: "No. I can't honestly say that right now." She didn't say a thing, but the look on her face was the saddest I've ever seen. She simply turned her head, and I walked out. I was proud of my own integrity.

Then I grew up and had my own daughter. I realized how important it was to have a sense of religion in our lives. We went to church regularly and prayed together every night. I learned that "I love you, Mommy" were the sweetest words on God's earth.

But one day I called "I love you" to the young woman running out the door. I waited for the "I love you, too," but the door slammed. She had places to go, things to do. I knew she loved me. And I knew that she was growing up. Yet suddenly I saw my mother's face that day in the hospi-tal. And no matter what was wrong with her inside or out, I finally knew the pain I had caused.

I drove to the nursing home where she had become the little old lady I took out to lunch and for walks. She's fine now—thanks to new medicines. She's just getting old. She was surprised to see me because we had not made a lunch date. "I just wanted to talk for a minute . . ." I began. Those deep eyes looked into my soul. "Do you remember one day many years ago . . ." And I apologized. And I told her I loved her. That smile and hug and look of hope in her eyes will remain with me for the rest of my life.

I went home and told everyone else I loved how I felt about them. The power of our words is amazing. They can wound so deeply, and they can heal with miraculous power. We all have the ability to share God's love through our actions *and* our words.

L ove is patient; love is kind; love is not envious or boastful or arrogant or rude. It does not insist on its own way; it is not irritable or resentful; it does not rejoice in wrongdoing, but rejoices in the truth.

1 Corinthians 13:4–6

My family, like most, is not perfect. We have our disagreements, squabbles, and disruptions. We may not be the all-American mom, dad, two children, and dog family, but we're a family. I pray today to apologize for sometimes taking them for granted and also to ask you to look after them and bless them with happiness. Amen.

Working on Love

I got off the plane to meet my dad's new wife. Wife number four. He said he had married the teacher he'd been dating. I had met a teacher he was dating the summer before. She was okay. She had pretty red hair. So I scanned the crowd at the airport for that hair. No luck. My father came running up with a dark-haired lady holding his hand. We hugged. And then he introduced me to my stepmother. She wasn't the one at all! He must've broken up with the redhead and married someone else in between my visits. Jeez. I sure couldn't keep up.

We went home. They had bought potato chips and Twinkies—my favorite foods. And they had planned all sorts of fun activities: a trip to the local amusement park, a day at the water park. They had even bought tickets to see a boy band that I really liked. They were trying hard to make me feel welcome. But I didn't feel much like trying. I was disappointed in my dad. I blamed God for making my life so hard! I expected my dad to be Mr. Perfect. Expected my life to be like a storybook. Don't know why. It's not and he's not, never has been. But then I don't know anybody with a perfect life or a perfect dad.

So I unpacked my bag and decided to try. It wasn't easy, and it wasn't great, but it was okay. My dad was really happy. And each time I visit it gets a little better. Guess sometimes we have to stop blaming God and start appreciating, praying, and working at life and love.

Please help me understand and accept the wedge that has divided my family since the divorce. Help me to learn from my parents' mistakes and accept the changes that have resulted—like having a stepmom, stepdad, and especially stepsiblings. Remind me that they, too, are living through the same disruptions.

A family is a three-tiered construction built with love, respect, and pride.

Legacy of Song

"Listen to this one!" Dad would exclaim as he slipped a new LP onto our record player.

I was three the first time I clearly remember this. Dad propped me in a chair, switched on the stereo, and played one of the greats, Ol' Blue Eyes, busting his heart out for another old man, "Ol' Man River."

The memory resonates, not because of the particular song but for its effect on Dad. He came alive in a way I'd only imagined was possible, as though the music ignited his very soul and he just had to share the fire.

My father was not an emotional man. Displays of affection unsettled him. A history teacher, Dad was more comfortable in the classroom than at home. In class, surrounded by his books and chalkboard, he was in his element, and rapport with his students came easily. Rapport with his daughters did not. Dad simply didn't know how to interact with us. Awkward and distant, he floundered for a way to relate.

Music became his way. A bust at diapers, bottles, and toddlers' tears, Dad found his niche in lullabies. Night after night, he'd gather his girls at bedtime and croon to us. Sometimes the tune was "Fuzzy Wuzzy." More often, he sang of "Danny Boy," "Ramblin' Rose," or "Mack the Knife."

Judy Garland . . . Glenn Miller . . . Nat King Cole . . . one by one Dad introduced them to me, and one by one I fell in love, thrilling to the lyrics and rhythm that made Dad exclaim, "Isn't this grand? Doesn't it just send you?!"

Yes, more than Dad ever knew. The passion, the intense appreciation—these were the gifts he intended, but with them Dad bequeathed something else, something infinitely more precious.

Always just beyond my grasp, held away from me by a shy nature and a belief that real men concealed their emotions, my father was forever a mystery. He left the house each morning clutching his overstuffed briefcase and returned late each afternoon lugging the thick stack of papers that he would grade throughout the evening. During dinner he quizzed my sisters and me, challenging us to spell words like "Worcestershire" and "Schenectady." Whenever we traveled, Dad proved, to our dismay, to be an endless source of information. Each trip included a lecture on that place's history.

That side of him, the outside, I knew well, but of that other side, the inside, I had no inkling. I yearned to dance closer to my father's soul, to glimpse the part of him that was eternally obscured, the part where his essence—and his love—were hidden.

Music gave me that glimpse. It became a window into my father's heart. For Dad, it voiced the feelings locked away within him.

The summer I was 13 was memorable for little but the misery I endured, induced by the freckles and flat chest I despaired would be my permanent fate. My mother consoled me. My sister, older and more generously endowed, teased me mercilessly. Dad offered hope. He hauled me out of my bedroom, where I'd taken to brooding during the long afternoons, and made me listen to a record, a ritual by then as familiar as breathing. The album he chose was *Gigi*, a wistful medley of songs with lyrics that run in part: "She's a girl, a little girl, getting older, it is true, which is what they always do, until that unexpected hour, when they blossom like a flower."

Dad never could have put it into words. It would have embarrassed him. It would have embarrassed me, too. But he wanted me to know: In time, the freckles and flat chest would pass. Like Gigi, I, too, would blossom.

Better than any barometer, I learned to read my father by the music he played. If Tommy Dorsey filled the room, all was well, but Harry Belafonte meant life was pressing in on Dad and his mood was bittersweet. With Judy Garland he brooded. Her voice haunted him, rich with things he couldn't say but deeply felt. Nat King Cole was Dad's particular favorite, and Floyd Cramer, the "piano man" who coaxed magic from a keyboard, took Dad deep inside himself to a place that brooked no intrusion.

A few months shy of his 55th birthday, Dad died. To the end he remained a shadow of a figure, someone who loomed in and out of my life, ever at arm's length, ever hidden, except for those moments when music set him free.

It's often observed that few things separate the genera-
tions as much as music. This is true when Gershwin goes
up against the Grateful Dead or when Crosby, Stills & Nash
challenge Chopin. But it's also true that music is the univer-
sal language. For Dad and me it was our only language—a
language of the heart. Without it, I would never have known
my father at all.

The greatest happiness in life is
the conviction that we are loved—
loved for ourselves, or rather,
loved in spite of ourselves.

VICTOR HUGO

God,
Please help me to understand and appreciate my parents. I
get so angry with them because they are constantly bugging me for information. "Where do you think you're
going?"; "Who is going to be there?" "When will you be
home?" I know they ask questions because they care, but I
feel suffocated. All my friends are allowed to do whatever
they want and I have to answer to "Mommy and Daddy." I
want to understand how they feel, but I also want to avoid
feeling like a prisoner in my own home. Help me to peacefully coexist with my parents.

The Blue Nail Polish

I was 16 when my aunt Emmy finally became so crippled with arthritis that it was difficult for her to get out much. My mom suggested that I earn some extra money by doing her shopping for her. I was a busy teenager; I had more important things to do. I told Mom that Emmy could probably find someone older to help her. My mom tried explaining to me about families helping each other out, but it fell on deaf ears. I barely even knew Emmy. She and her husband had only moved back into town a few years before, and he had died suddenly.

I'm ashamed to admit that two of my best friends lived near Aunt Emmy, and I used to avoid passing her house when I'd go to visit them. That way she couldn't see me and call for me to help her. At the time, I felt absolutely no guilt about this. She was my mom's sister, and I hardly knew her. I had my own life to lead—she was simply not a part of it.

But later that spring, when the new fashions were coming out and I had no money to buy them, I asked Mom if Emmy had found someone to help her out. She said that a lady did her shopping, and she managed most of her cleaning herself with some help from Mom. I admitted that I needed money, so I offered to help out.

I went to see Emmy, and she had a list all ready for me. I did her shopping for a few weeks, sometimes taking a friend with me. Emmy always offered us coffee and said how grateful she was.

One day my friend Anna and I were at Emmy's house, waiting for her to finish her shopping list. Anna noticed my blue nail polish and remarked, "Oh, I wish I'd known you had that shade—it would have matched the dress I wore last Saturday!"

I shrugged. "You can borrow it whenever you want to."

My aunt said casually, "Why don't you girls share things like that to save money?"

We looked at her with interest. She continued, "You could keep your unusual nail polish at someone's house, and maybe shoes, too."

Anna and I talked about her idea while we shopped, and then we discussed it with another friend. It really did make sense. Anna had gold nail polish she didn't use much, and I had a new gold top; Janice had bright pink shoes that she only wore with one outfit, and Anna and I were both eager to borrow them.

Janice, Anna, and I went back to Aunt Emmy's with her groceries, and we were still buzzing about her idea. Emmy casually offered, "If you'd like, you could keep your things here. You live so close, it would be very convenient, and I have a spare room that you could use."

We accepted her offer and brought over our nail polish and shoes, then handbags and even some clothes. Before we went out for the evening, we'd all stop by Emmy's to try on various outfits and accessories. A full-length mirror appeared in the room, as did cans of soda. And whenever we brought back what we had worn the night before, Emmy would ask us about what we did. We began to confide in her, telling her things we didn't even tell our moms.

We soon got to know Emmy as a warm and interesting person. She told us about the crazy things she and her husband, Bill, had done when they were young. I confessed to her how I had been reluctant to help her at first and how I had even avoided going by her house. She understood, like she understood all of what we said. She put her arms around me and gave me a hug, simply saying, "At least you're here now."

When we all went off to college, we still kept in touch with Emmy, sending her postcards and always dropping by when we were home on vacation. Eventually, we could see that she was getting more frail.

One day, Emmy fell in her kitchen and was rushed to the hospital. She died the next day; the doctors said she'd had a heart attack. When mom called Anna and me to tell us the news, both of us cried at the loss of our friend.

All five of us girls who had used Emmy's as our "changing room" met for her funeral. It was the first great loss any of us had ever experienced, and it was awful. We went back to my house after the funeral, and my mom said, "I have something for each of you from Emmy." She handed out five identical packages. We opened them to find a bottle of blue nail polish and the same note in each.

"Don't be too sad for me. I still miss Bill so much, but you girls did all and more to help fill up my lonely years. I don't think I could have survived them without you. If it wasn't for the blue nail polish, all of us would have missed out on our special friendship. Love, Emmy."

That was ten years ago, and now I'm married with two children of my own. My husband, Eric, and I travel frequently, bringing back many lovely souvenirs and keep-sakes. But to this day, the special spot on my bedroom dressing table is home to my little bottle of blue nail polish. I have never opened it, and I never will. For me, it's a reminder to reach out to people. And it's a reminder of Emmy.

Making time for family might seem less than glamorous, but your family will never dismiss you for a fashion faux pas or a blemish on your face. The truest love is always found at home.

God,
Sometimes I am worried that my elder relatives won't be able to see the major milestones of my life—my graduation, my wedding, and the birth of my children. I know it's unfair for me to ask you to keep them here until I have accom-plished all my goals and it's selfish of me to want them to stay—especially if they're suffering. So, please, God, if you would, create a viewing area in heaven for my loved ones to sit and sneak a peek at all my happenings. It won't be the same as if they were here, but it will be comforting to know that they're happy—and watching. Amen.

The Tie that Binds

From my earliest memories, my mother was the only one there. It was just the two of us to comfort and reassure each other. My father left when I was very young, leaving my mother with the daunting task of raising a son on her own. I idolized her, looking up with sheer adulation. Of course, when I became a teenager, I developed a severe case of independence like all teenagers do. But it was then I realized just what held our small family together.

The year was 1974, the time when Nixon resigned, and it seemed that we all were losing a bit of our innocence. Being a fatherless child in those days was different than it is now. It wasn't nearly as common, and though we weren't mistreated, we weren't given much respect either. A mother and a child were more of an oddity, with few willing to lend us a hand.

That was how I grew to be so dependent on my mother. She was everything in my life. Not only my caretaker, but my guardian, my provider, and my comforter. She was both my mother and my father in a sense. She taught me all that she knew, how to treat others with patience and kindness. I learned volumes from her in my early years: how to get dressed by myself, how to tie my shoes, how to brush my teeth, and how to comb my hair. But when I reached 14, I discovered that, much to my surprise, there were some things she didn't know.

The week of my junior high school graduation had finally come. My friends and I were looking forward to our futures as high-school students, knowing that we would soon be involved in a rite of passage. We were no longer kids but soon-to-be adults. As such, we were to dress like adults as well. Our class adviser told us that the girls were to wear dresses and the boys were to wear suits with ties to the ceremony. *No problem,* I thought. But one of the other boys said that we were to wear real neckties, not the pre-tied, clip-on variety. "Dork ties" was what he called them. I had never tied a real tie before, but I assumed my mother would know how to do it. After all, she knew everything.

After graduation rehearsal, I went to a local store and bought a grown-up tie: a red, white, and blue striped one to stand out in the crowd. I waited with anticipation for Mom to come home from work that evening. I was anxious to learn how to tie a necktie. When my mother came home, I met her at the door with my tie and a look of expectation.

"What do you have there?" she asked as the necktie was thrust in front of her.

"I have to wear a tie for graduation, but I don't know how to tie it. Could you show me?" I never doubted that she knew how and that after some instruction, I'd know, too.

She held the tie in her hands, but her usual expression of self-assurance quickly dissolved. She didn't say a word; she just stood there in a moment of anxious frustration. She looked up at me and sighed. "I never realized you were growing up so fast," she said as I noticed a tear in the corner of her eye. "You're not my baby anymore; you're a grown man."

I was anxious to get back to the situation at hand. "Mom, I need you to show me how to tie a knot in this tie."

"I don't know how. Why can't you wear one of those already-made ties you have in your closet?"

I was shocked that she couldn't help me. She had always been able to before. It was then I realized that sometimes a mother can't be everything. And I could tell by the look on her face she discovered that, too.

"That's okay, Mom. I'll try it myself." I tied and untied, tied and untied, and each time the knot came out looking worse and worse. I feared I was destined to wear a boyish clip-on tie at my graduation.

The next evening came, and the ceremony was scheduled to start at 7:00. At 5:00, my mother came home from work with a surprise around her neck. I was so excited, I jumped for joy. It was my tie, done in a sharp double Windsor knot. Her boss had shown her how it was done, so now she could teach me.

The expression on her face as she came up the drive was one of happy accomplishment. She had faced another challenge and done what she needed to do for her son. The sight of her wearing that necktie over her dress made me realize that she must have gone through a thousand problems just like that one while raising a son by herself. Even though this incident was trivial in comparison to many others, it made me appreciate all her efforts. I realized that my mom doesn't complain when she reaches an obstacle—she learns from it and passes that knowledge on to me. Her determination and perseverance are what bind us together, and her love for me makes that bond unbreakable.

My Mother

Who ties the family together with strings of love?
My Mother.

Who puts the needs of everyone else before her own?
My Mother.

Who picks up my chin when it has fallen to the floor?
My Mother.

Who wiped my runny little nose when I was a kid?
Who else but my Mother.

Who helps pick up the pieces of my broken heart?
My Mother.

Who encourages me to chase all my dreams?
My Mother.

Who is an inspiration to all who know her?
My Mother.

Who still sometimes tries to hold my hand
    when we cross the street?
My Mother.

Who means more to me than any words could
    ever express?
My Mother.

Aunt Susan's Gift

Like most teenagers, I was often angry, scared, and emotional. To cover my anxiety, I developed a rather unpleasant front. I combined a sharp tongue with sarcasm and used it eagerly on the uncool. Aunt Susan was a favorite target. She *always* had a positive attitude and a smile, and she shared her deep religious faith continually. She drove me absolutely crazy.

My extended family was close and spent lots of time together. Holidays, picnics, and Sunday visits found me inventing snide comments to embarrass Aunt Susan or demean her ironclad faith. She either pretended not to hear or laughed them off. Despite my satisfaction, I felt guilty, though I worked hard to ignore that nagging feeling.

One super-cold day, my dad took a bunch of us out to get firewood. We used a wood-burning stove for heat, so gathering wood for winter was important.

When I saw Aunt Susan I hollered, "Great," and rolled my eyes. I'd made sure I pitched my voice in her direction.

Everyone climbed into my uncle's truck and headed to a building site where trees were being cleared. Kids were assigned to haul kindling, while the men began working with chain saws. Aunt Susan offered to help us kids.

An early frost had killed the grass around the site, which must have been fairly tall in August. Now it was a tangled mat that snagged our feet as we walked. I even tripped a few times.

Then, right in front of me, Aunt Susan got tangled and fell flat on her face. Of course, I took one look at her sprawled on the ground and just roared. I didn't even offer to help, I was laughing so hard. Finally, she managed to upright herself.

"I tripped over something," she said.

"Your own two feet," I snorted.

Aunt Susan saw something in the grass. She studied it with a strange expression, then handed it to me.

"You may need this more than I do," she said. It was a dark, slightly gnarled piece of wood. Some accident of nature, or perhaps some divine design, had shaped that piece of wood into a perfect cross. It was actually smooth, as if it were polished.

The cross felt heavy in my hands. I stared at it, then said, "Here, you take it," and tried to toss it back to her as if we were playing "Hot Potato."

"No, it's yours," she replied.

"Whatever," I muttered as coolly as I could under the circumstances.

I still have that cross. It traveled with me to college, an apartment or two, and even the home I live in today. Sometimes I get it out and recall that cold day when I learned an important life lesson about being "cool."

My Father's Love

They say you can't miss what you never had, but I say they're wrong. My parents divorced when I was just one, and growing up without a dad definitely left a painful void in my life. Even though I'd never known his face or the warmth of his hand taking mine, I still missed his presence.

When I was thirteen, some friends and I met at a church parking lot to shoot hoops. It turned out to be my first attempt to find the love I craved.

"Josh, don't go home, man," Michael urged, wiping sweat from his forehead after we finished our game. "Come to church with us. It starts in a few minutes."

At first I intended to say no, but something drew me. It wasn't a hunger for God or the hope I'd find something life-changing between those concrete walls, but more of a need to be included in whatever my friends were doing. It felt good to simply belong.

The pastor explained that they had a special guest that evening. A 17-year-old boy would deliver a personal testimony of what God had done in his life. I watched as the kid shook hands with the pastor and then took command of the microphone. He wore jeans, a T-shirt, and sneakers. His blond hair hung long and shaggy to his shoulders.

"My father loves me," he opened. "It took me 17 years to be able to say those words. My father loves me, and he will love me no matter what mistakes I make or what weaknesses I have. He will love me through every storm in my life and hold me in his embrace until the clouds clear and the sun streams through again."

The wounds I carried from my own uncaring father began to sting as if scoured with salt. This kid had a great dad who obviously loved him very much. I stared at him with envy.

"I'm not speaking of my mortal father," the young man said, scanning the congregation with his pale blue eyes. "My mortal father was incapable of love. He abused me throughout my childhood and beat my mom until she could barely stand. What meant the most to him was his vodka, which eventually caused his death."

My mouth grew dry. The people seated around me began to melt away, and all I could see was this boy, virtually the same age as me, drawing me into a world I knew too well. A world with a big puzzle piece missing.

"When I say my father loves me, I'm speaking of my real father . . . your real father . . . the father that will embrace you for all of eternity." He paused, pinning his gaze on me. "I'm talking about my spiritual father."

I thirsted for every word he said. He told of how God is our true father, the one who will never abandon us, turn away from us, or disappoint us. He said that knowing God and letting him into your life will bring you the most awesome parent/child relationship you could ever experience. By the time he closed with a heartfelt prayer, I had tears in my eyes as I bowed my head. I knew I'd never feel abandoned again.

I now attend Bible college. God is calling me to preach to inner-city teens, which I plan to do upon graduation. My dream is to one day stand in a pulpit, looking out into the eyes of lost young people, and say the words that changed my life just three short years ago: "My name is Josh, and I want to tell everyone that my father truly loves me."

Sometimes I feel like I'm all alone in the world. My parents are preoccupied with their own problems, and I feel like I have no one to protect me or to look out for me. Please help me to remember that I can always turn to your loving arms for the comfort and security I need. Amen.

It is better to take refuge in the Lord
than to put confidence in mortals.
PSALM 118:8

New Year's Eve with Grandpa

"But I'll be all right by myself! I promise!" Dora insisted.

Her mom barely paid attention as she put on her makeup in front of the mirror. Her dad was knotting his tie nearby.

"We're sorry, dear," Dad said. "We'd love to take you with us if tomorrow wasn't your big concert. And, besides, your mom doesn't want you to catch a cold."

Dora's mom closed her tube of lipstick and turned around. "I still think it was sweet of Grandpa to be willing to spend New Year's Eve with you," she said. "Besides, you two were always such great buddies. Why don't you want to be with him now?"

Dora knew it was useless trying to make them understand. To be alone at home on New Year's Eve was bad enough. But to have to put up with Grandpa and his boring jokes was simply more than she could bear.

It was true that at one time Dora thought the world of Grandpa and loved spending time with him. The things they did together—like eating pizza while watching Charlie Chaplin movies—were fun. Then.

But she was 13 now, and her idea of fun had changed. An evening of Charlie Chaplin and pizza with Grandpa no longer excited her. Obviously her parents didn't realize that when they invited Grandpa to come over and spend New Year's Eve with her.

The doorbell rang at 6:00. "Howdy, everybody," came Grandpa's cheerful voice when Mom opened the door. Dora sat playing with the TV's remote control and didn't get up to greet him.

"Okay, dears, we're off." Mom kissed Dora and Grandpa good-bye.

"Don't trouble Grandpa too much," Dad warned before closing the door behind him.

"So, after a long time we finally get to spend some quality time together," Grandpa beamed. He unwrapped himself from his layers of coverings and plopped down on the sofa beside Dora." "Don't you think this is great?" He poked Dora in the ribs.

"Yeah," Dora drawled. *He can't be serious,* she thought.

"Guess what," Grandpa chatted on. "I've brought a movie."

"Please don't let it be *Modern Times,*" whispered Dora as Grandpa took the cassette from his coat pocket. It was *Modern Times.*

"I've also ordered some pizza. It should be here in an hour." Grandpa smiled triumphantly, as if offering Dora the treat of her life.

Dora couldn't take it any longer. "Grandpa, I'm going to my room to practice for tomorrow's concert." Without waiting for his reply, she dashed away.

Once in her room, Dora started searching for an escape. She decided to give her best friend, Agnes, a call. Agnes sounded excited to hear from her. "Nick and I are going bowling with my sister and her boyfriend. Wanna come?" Agnes asked.

"Sounds like fun," said Dora. She was excited about joining them, mostly because she liked Nick. "Okay, pick me up in ten minutes." Dora told Agnes. "I'll get my bowling shoes."

Dora put down the receiver and looked in the hall. Grandpa was making hot cocoa in the kitchen. He came to her room and handed her a cup.

"I have to go to my music teacher's place for some final rehearsals," Dora lied. She pretended to put her music books into her bag.

"What a boring way to spend New Year's Eve," Grandpa said, sipping his cocoa.

"You don't mind, do you?"

"Well, I was looking forward to spending the evening with you, but if it's really important to you, go ahead."

Dora kissed him, took her coat, and hurried outside.

"Wait!" Grandpa called. "You're forgetting something." He went inside for a few moments and came back with her bag. He handed it to her.

"Thanks," said Dora, relieved. She was starting to feel a little guilty.

In the driveway, Dora waited for Agnes's car to show up. It would be fun to spend the evening with her and Nick.

It was freezing outside, and Dora hugged her bag. It seemed a little bulky. She curiously peeked inside. To her surprise, she found her bowling shoes tucked away in there!

"Who put these in here?" Dora asked herself aloud. She had forgotten all about them. No one but Grandpa had touched her bag that day. She suddenly realized the awful truth.

Of course Grandpa had done it. So he knew where she was going. He must have overheard her on the phone. And, yet, he didn't say anything. Grandpa had come this far to spend New Year's Eve with her, and then she had acted rudely and even lied to him. Dora felt ashamed.

Just then a car drove up. Agnes stuck her head out the window. "We're here," she called.

Dora could see Nick sitting beside Agnes. He was smiling shyly at her. She knew that this chance might not come again. But her mind was made up. "Sorry, guys, I can't come," she said.

Agnes looked surprised. "But it'll be fun," she pleaded.

"I know," Dora said, "but there's something at home I just remembered I have to do."

When Dora went back in the house, she found Grandpa watching *Modern Times*. He looked lonely. Dora felt sorry for him. She sidled up next to him and took his hand.

Grandpa looked up casually. "Well, that's the fastest rehearsal I've ever seen," he said.

Dora laughed. "I changed my mind, Grandpa. I really wanted to watch this movie with you." They sat in silence for a little while, and Dora could see that her grandpa was pleased. She didn't think about Nick and Agnes for the rest of the night. Instead, she ate pizza and watched a favorite movie with her grandpa. And there was no other way she would have preferred to ring in the new year.

What's on Your Mind?

Family. Close your eyes and say that word to yourself. See the word *family* written on a big blackboard. Then, take a deep breath, and write down the first five words that come to mind.

_____

Now, finish these two sentences.
—I wish my family would change . . .

_____

_____

—I thank God for my family because . . .

_____

_____

Look at what you've written. Would the changes you wished for truly be changes for the better? If so, how can *you* help bring them about?

_____

_____

_____

_____

_____

_____

Making Connections

T he only way to have a friend
is to be one.

RALPH WALDO EMERSON, "FRIENDSHIP"

Friends. Where would we be without them? We truly do need each other in this life. Friendship is a very precious gift. Sometimes it's as easy as can be, and sometimes it takes so much work we wonder if it's all worth it in the end. But the answer is always a resounding "YES!" We need friends. And we need to *be* a friend.

Relationships make it all worthwhile. Your friends can make or break your school day; later, the people you work with can sometimes make more of a difference than the job you do! It's all about people—how we connect with them—and sometimes, how we disconnect.

Check out these stories of friendship, romance, and more, and see how you feel about this incredible part of life! In fact, why not read this chapter with your best friend?

Too Cool for Sam

I was too cool to go out with Sam. He wasn't good enough for me. Sure, he was funny and nice and respectful. He was smart. He went to my church. He was even kinda cute. But I liked another guy. Someone who was "beyond my reach"— in another social circle entirely. I liked Steve, the football star, the lead in the senior play. Of course, he already had a girlfriend. Of course, she was a cheerleader. I didn't even know Steve, other than an occasional moment during calculus when he'd look at me while I answered a question. Or during a play rehearsal when he had to listen to my few lines to know when to say his own. Basically, he didn't know I existed, but I hoped and I prayed that suddenly he would come to me and ask me to go to the prom. I didn't see the irony of praying for something so superficial. Friends even told me that he wasn't very nice. He was always smoking after school, and he gave the younger kids on the football team a hard time. That didn't stop me at all. I still prayed for a "miracle"; I still wanted him to like me.

Sam asked me out over and over again. The poor guy just wouldn't give up. So finally I relented. We went to the movies. It was a film I'd been waiting to see anyway, so I figured why not? I had a really nice time with Sam. We talked easily about anything and everything. He had a great sense of humor. We even shared a love of theater; he was a wonderful actor. We talked about some of our church activities. We shared similar feelings about the importance of religion,

God, and prayer—something I seldom felt I could talk about with my friends. Then, when the movie was almost over, he tried to kiss me. I just couldn't. I mean, I didn't really want to be with him. In my heart, all I wanted was Steve. So I pushed Sam away and asked him to take me straight home.

After that date, Sam and I didn't talk at school anymore. He stopped asking me out. And Steve, my heartthrob, got in big trouble with the police after getting caught selling drugs. We all finished high school and went off to different colleges.

Last year, I came home for a visit during my junior year of college. I went to the pizza place where we all used to hang out during high school. Lots of kids were home from college that weekend—it was Christmastime. I looked around and spotted Sam. I almost bolted for the door in embarrassment, but I was too late. He saw me and came striding over. Sam wasn't cute anymore; now he was devastatingly handsome. He had grown taller, and his skin was clear. He smiled, took my hand, and asked how I was. We chatted for a while, and then I swallowed hard and apologized for being so rude the night of our date. He admitted that he'd been so confused about what went wrong that he didn't date anyone for more than a year after that. He felt he had done something out of line or hurt me in some way that he didn't understand. I was so relieved to have a chance to talk about it with him. He was still so easy to be with—even after all the difficulty I had caused him.

I was just mustering my courage to ask him if he wanted to stop by my house for lunch the next day when a girl I didn't know walked up and took his hand. "This is Jeanine, my fiancée," he said.

"You've got a good man, there," I told her and walked away. I vowed then and there to always give everyone a chance. No more surface judgments, no more rudeness, no more using prayer in a way that makes me lose track of what's real in my life. I'm not too cool for Sam anymore.

❖   ❖   ❖

God,
How do I know when I'm in love? Will there be fireworks and strange tingling sensations? What happens when I feel that way about somebody sometimes, but then at other times I'm not sure this person is right for me? I'm asking you to advise me in the area of love. I've never been "in love," and I'm not sure how to act. Help me to distinguish between true love and just plain lust. Help me to see when someone really cares and when they are just using me. Help me learn to love and be loved.

❖   ❖   ❖

A person's love is not a possession; it's a privilege.
Treat it with care.

Priorities

Tracy is my very best friend in the entire school, in the town, in the world, in the universe! We're great friends! Not too long ago, I sort of forgot that. But, luckily, we're such good friends that, with God's help, we were able to get through it.

It all started with Jamie, a cute guy (what problem doesn't?) we met at a football game. The three of us had a fun time sitting together. He bought us both hot dogs and popcorn and gave us each a gentlemanly peck on the cheek when we said good night.

Everything was cool. He was new in school; he had just moved here from England (so he had a really adorable accent!). We tried to include him after that when we did stuff as a group—movies and things like that. We all had so much fun together.

The trouble started when Jamie asked me out. It was a Saturday afternoon. Tracy and I were spending one of our usual marathon weekends together. We had just finished facials and were right in the middle of painting our nails. We had rented a pile of movies and purchased mass quantities of popcorn and candy.

The phone rang; it was Jamie. He asked me if I wanted to go with him and his parents to some kind of party at the lake. It was a once-a-year deal, and he had just gotten permission to ask someone. I jumped in and said, "Sure!" I told him I'd be ready in an hour, then hung up the phone and saw the reflection of betrayal in Tracy's eyes. It stunned me but only for a minute. I was so excited to hang out with Jamie that I didn't even think of Tracy's feelings. I didn't hesitate to blow her off even though we clearly had plans. The damage I did that day took months and loads of prayer to repair.

I didn't enjoy the evening. I couldn't stop thinking about that look in Tracy's eyes, and as the night wore on I became more convinced that I'd seriously erred in judgment.

I prayed about it in church the next day, but it took me a week before I had the nerve to apologize to Tracy and longer than that before she really trusted me and our friend-ship again.

Friends—there's nothing more precious—and I'll never ignore a friend's feelings again.

God,
I need your forgiveness and help. I am so ashamed of my actions. I blew off my best friend for a new boyfriend. We've always said that our friendship was more important than anything—especially some passing guy. Now the guy is gone, and my friend won't speak to me. I am truly sorry, and I miss her. Please forgive me, and help me find a way to win back her trust.

Keep your heart turned toward the Lord,
and he will guide it in the right direction.

Judging Others

I hated being rich. The other girls called me a "spoiled brat," and the guys made jokes about how I was born with a silver spoon in my mouth. So my parents had big bucks, big deal. I was no different than any other student, and I was getting sick of being treated like I was a snob when I went out of my way to be just like everyone else.

In fact, there was nothing I wanted more than to be considered "normal." I didn't shop in the expensive boutiques. I always tried to be friendly and inclusive and never gossiped. Yet no matter what I did to try and make friends, I ended up the outcast.

My parents were great, but the money made things so tough for me at school. When I tried to explain to my parents, they just laughed and told me to ignore the other kids. My dad said the other girls were probably jealous and the boys were intimidated. He said I shouldn't be ashamed because we were well-off. My parents had worked hard so that I could have everything, but what they didn't realize was that I wanted to have what other kids have: Normalcy.

I decided to ignore the remarks and insults, but one day at school I just exploded when a snooty cheerleader asked me if I was getting a Porsche for my 16th birthday. I flew off the handle and screamed at her that I couldn't help it if my parents were successful and her parents were losers. I saw the look on her face and immediately regretted what I had just said.

Here I was trying to make friends and be accepted, and I had turned a total stranger against me. I sat on a bench, trying to get my bearings. I even prayed a little, something I wasn't used to doing in public. But I really needed the help, and God had always been there for me before.

I saw the cheerleader later in the hallway. I don't know what made me do it, but I introduced myself and apologized for what I had said. Her name was Clarice, and she apologized back, shaking my hand. She sighed and told me that as a cheerleader she was often the target of remarks, too, and that she didn't know what got into her. If anyone should understand my situation, it should have been her, she explained.

We talked about how people always judged us from the outside in. I had judged her as being snooty and conceited, but she was really a smart, funny girl with a big heart. And she got to see that I was not little Miss Richy Rich after all.

We decided to do something about it and collaborated on a story for the school newspaper about how students shouldn't rush to judgment about others. Rico, the editor, loved the idea and gave us the entire front page.

The article came out, and we couldn't believe how many students told us they really connected with our story. Seems that everyone was judging everyone; we were not alone in our frustrations.

We can't say the article changed the entire school overnight, but it felt good to do something that would help others realize that we are who we are from the inside out. And it felt good making a great new friend in Clarice.

God,
You teach us not to judge others, but sometimes we do anyway. Please forgive us for judging, and forgive those who judge us in return. We are only human, but we are striving to be better all the time. Help us remember your golden rule: to do unto others as we would have them do unto us. Amen.

now join your hands, and with your hands your hearts.

WILLIAM SHAKESPEARE

It's impossible to love yourself until you accept yourself. Likewise, it is impossible for others to love you until you love yourself.

Mom's Date

My dad died ten years ago. It was really hard on my mom because they were like a storybook couple. It got really weird for me when I realized Mom was dating. Sure, she did stuff with her friends, mostly family friends from our church. I guess eventually my mom wanted to meet a man who shared our beliefs.

Anyway, this guy turned out to be the single dad of one of *my* church friends. Not only *that,* but he was the dad of my very best friend, Danielle. You can see that it's just weirdness upon weirdness.

At first, Danielle and I didn't even realize they were dating. The four of us were always doing stuff together. Then we saw *the kiss.* We were at a kite-flying festival. Mom and Danielle's dad were flying a kite together. And then we saw them kiss. It was kinda cool, very weird, and totally natural. All at once.

I prayed about it a lot and talked with my mom. I guess until I got to be almost old enough to date, it never occurred to me that my mom would want to have a guy around. Sometimes when we're all out together it's nice to feel like we're a normal family. Other times I really miss my mom and our "two-together" time.

I do know that when I start dating I hope it's as natural and right as it's been for my mom. Some of the older guys talk about kissing in the car or behind the bleachers at a game. That just seems gross. I want things to happen because it's right and I'm ready—like my mom talks about. Not because I'm looking to make something happen.

Oh, by the way, Danielle's dad and my mom are getting married soon. I'm the best man, and Danielle is a brides-maid. And you know what? I'm going to like having a best friend for a sister!

I know that, though I don't have a girlfriend or boyfriend now, you are a giving Lord and have a perfect companion in mind for me. I will try to wait as patiently as possible until you provide the opportunity for our paths to meet.

The New Kid

Changing schools in high school is really hard. I know. My junior year, my mom remarried, and we had to move. I was furious at everyone. How could God do this to me? I'd worked so hard to have a great life at my old school. I had lots of friends and was involved in a load of activities. I was sure the new school was going to be awful before I even got there.

Ridgewood High was everything I had imagined—and worse! Everyone just stared at me; nobody said a word. I certainly wasn't going to waste my energy by reaching out to a bunch of snobs. I didn't need the aggravation and humiliation of being rejected by a bunch of geeks who wouldn't even have been good enough to be in my group at my old school.

I was horribly lonely those first few months. I hated going to school. Then, second semester, I ended up in an advanced chemistry class where we had to work with lab partners. Turns out the teacher did the dividing up. I guess I was grateful for that, since I wasn't friends with anybody in the class.

I was paired with Shellie, this girl I'd seen around a lot. I could see her friends teasing her when her name was called with mine. But we had no choice. We started working on our experiment right away. At least she was as conscientious about school as I was. She was really nice to me; she actually treated me like I was a real person! I was amazed—and actually pretty delighted. I liked her, and we grew to be friends. I was so thankful that the Lord had finally decided to shine a bit of light down on my drab life for a change!

One day, after we'd been friends for a few weeks, we started talking about when I'd come to Ridgewood High. Shellie told me what she had thought of me when I first started at the school. Turns out she (and everyone else, I guess!) had thought that because I didn't talk to anybody, I was being really snobby! They all thought I was acting superior and didn't want any friends! When I told her the real truth—that I was afraid nobody would want to be friends with me—well, we had a good laugh about it.

That Sunday in church, as I was sending more prayers of thanks to God for finally finding me a friend, I started thinking more about what Shellie had said. It seems that it wasn't just their fault or God's fault that I didn't have any friends for so long. I hadn't really made any effort. In fact, I'd had my mind made up before I'd ever even started at the school. I'd decided that I would hate it, so I did.

I realize now that friendship is a two-way street. If we expect others to reach out and we try reach out, too, a connection is a whole lot more likely to happen!

I am truly blessed to have been sent such a special friend. She is my lighthouse in a dark harbor, my sunshine on a gloomy day, and my most dedicated confidante. I can't imagine what I did to deserve her friendship, but thank you, God, for believing I'm worthy of her love.

Do not neglect to show hospitality to strangers, for by doing that some have entertained angels without knowing it.

HEBREWS 13:2

In a Nutshell:
Six Ways to Make People Like You—

Principle 1:
Become genuinely interested in other people.

Principle 2:
Smile.

Principle 3:
Remember that a person's name is to that person the sweetest and most important sound in any language.

Principle 4:
Be a good listener. Encourage others to talk about themselves.

Principle 5:
Talk in terms of the other person's interests.

Principle 6:
Make the other person feel important—and do it sincerely.

DALE CARNEGIE, *HOW TO WIN FRIENDS AND INFLUENCE PEOPLE*

Wheels of Fun

I love to fly down the halls! But I hate getting detention, so I usually control myself and just go at a slow roll. That's how I met Theresa. Her locker is down the hall from mine, so I had to pass her every day. At first, she did the thing where she'd pretend not to notice that I'm in a wheelchair. I *hate* when people do that.

But then she started looking at me like I was a monkey in a zoo or something. So I started smiling at her. I'd roll by and smile and wave just to make her uncomfortable. One day, I got so preoccupied with my mission of smiling and waving that I dropped my books. Another kid picked everything up and handed it to me with the look I *really* hate: the pity look.

Then on Saturday we had a communitywide gathering of all the church teen groups. And guess who was there? Yup! My buddy, Theresa. I wheeled up to her and said, "Hi!"

"You, uh, go to church?" she stammered.

"Uh, yeah. Didn't you think we were allowed?"

"Huh?"

"Disabled people. Did you think we had our own church or something?"

"Jeez. I'm sorry. It's just that . . . well, it's just . . . I don't know what to say around you. . . ." She was totally blushing and stammering.

"It's okay. It happens all the time. I can't walk. Never could. It's part of who I am, and I'm okay with it. I wish everyone else was, too."

"It's not that," Theresa stammered. "It's that you're so . . . cute."

What? Nobody had ever seen *me* before. All they ever saw was my wheelchair.

"I've been wanting to ask you out for months, but I was just too shy," Theresa explained. "Would you like to go to the movies?"

We did go to the movies. In fact, we went out together for two years. I'd always thought I had things all figured out about being disabled. I'd found peace with myself and God. I wasn't angry, didn't feel cheated, and was thankful for all my blessings.

But I hadn't known that I was prejudiced. I made assumptions about other people based on my being in a wheelchair. I'm still thankful to Theresa for helping me to learn to see everyone as they are: a gift from God. Now I give people a chance to be themselves without any preconceived notions.

Cherish your first love; it will play
a crucial role in shaping your life.

Secret Crush

My love for you is a continuous flow,
How much you mean to me, you'll never know.

Each time I see you, my heart beats fast.
Each minute I spend with you, I pray could last.

I wish your love for me was clear,
I'd always want to have you near.

I love you so. Will you ever know?

❖ ❖ ❖

Sasha's Friends

I have one good friend. I pride myself on our friendship. It's really special and important to me, and I work at it. I'm so thankful to have Sasha in my life. She's about the best bud a girl could ever hope for. I thank God for putting our desks together in English class in seventh grade. We've been best friends for three years now.

During confirmation class one day, we were talking about friendships and how it's good to have not just one really close friend but to know all the people around you and in your community. We gave ourselves a "pop quiz" to see how we fared with the people in our own world. There were questions about talking with the postal carrier. There were questions about the people who collect our curbside recyclables, about the grocery checker, and the church cleaning person.

I failed miserably. Sasha knew all the answers. She knew the name of her mail carrier, Jenna, and that Jenna's husband has recently been ill. She knew that the checker at the grocery store has a new baby. She knew that the kid who serves our ice-cream cones has two older sisters in college. She knew—well, you get the picture—she knew everybody!

Well, I'm shy and she's not, I told myself.

But I started to notice. I noticed that the lady at the bank has a walker that sits next to her teller chair. I smiled at her instead of just hurrying off.

I noticed that the woman in the copy room at school has some really pretty jewelry. So I told her. She smiled and thanked me.

I came home as our mail was being delivered and said hello to the mail carrier. He smiled and said, "Isn't it a beautiful day?"

I guess I got the point that day. Every one of us is God's creation, and we all have a life and a story and need each other. I used to think that being shy was my excuse. I already had a good friend and didn't think there was any need to spend time on people who wouldn't ever *really* be my friends. But I guess friends are everywhere. All it takes is a smile and a kind word. And time. Now I understand that God always wants us to have time for each other.

Don't dismiss "bad" relationships as useless. Every encounter you have with someone brings you knowledge. Each relationship, good or bad, adds to your character if you simply look for what you learned.

Lord,
Today I want to thank you for my friends. I am so lucky to have such supportive people in my life who stand by me no matter what. Sometimes I can't believe I have been so fortunate to find friends that perfectly complement me and my life, but then I remember why they're a perfect fit—because you sent them to me. Thank you.

The Graduation Dance

Waiting in the school's parking lot with the windows down and the radio playing softly, I was enjoying the warm summer night. My son's face was beaming as he walked toward my car. I had to smile, too. I could see that Adam was brimming with news about the eighth-grade graduation dance he'd just attended. Adam always rushed home from school, erupting with stories before the screen door had even slammed behind him.

"I did the coolest thing I ever did in my whole life," he exclaimed as soon as he put one foot in the car. Very strong words from a person who's been in existence for just under 14 years.

The story just spilled out of him. "I was standing with Justin and Mark and Kristen and Britney," he began. "The music was loud and the gym was dark, and most kids were dancing and laughing. Then Britney pointed out a girl who was standing off in a corner, crying.

"So Britney goes, 'You should dance with her, Adam.'

"I told her no because first of all, I didn't even know the girl. I didn't know her name or anything.

"But then Britney started bugging me even more. She told me that as class president I had a responsibility to people. She said I should be a role model and that

I had a chance to do something really special if I danced with this girl."

"Did you dance with her?" I asked him.

Adam was not going to leave out a single detail. "No, Mom. Not then. I told Brit we didn't even know for sure why the girl was crying. That's when Britney said, 'Adam! Look at her. It's her eighth-grade graduation dance and she's standing alone in a corner. No one is going to ask her to dance, and she knows it. Maybe she isn't thin or beautiful, but she's standing in a room full of her classmates, and they're ignoring her. They only care about what they're wearing and how they look and who they're with. Just think about how long you spent trying to decide what you were going to wear here tonight. Well, she did the same thing. Only no one is noticing, and no one cares. Here's your chance to prove you deserved to be voted class president.'"

"So did you?" I asked. He looked at me with a not-so-fast-Mom frown, and I settled back into my bucket seat to listen to more of the story.

"No," he said. "I knew Brit was right, but I kept thinking all my friends would laugh at me if I danced with her. So I told Britney, 'No way, I'm not doing it.'"

"What'd she say to that?" I asked.

"Well, you know Britney. She wouldn't stop nagging me. She told me that if my friends laughed at me because I danced with the girl, they weren't really my friends in the first place.

"I knew she was right. But it was still hard to go over and ask the girl to dance. What if I walked all the way across the gym in front of everyone and she turned me down? I'd die right there. But Britney said, 'She won't turn you down, and even if she does, you'll get over it by tomorrow. But I promise you, if you dance with her, she'll remember this night 20 years from now. And she'll remember you for the rest of her life.'

"So, I went over to the girl, and I asked her what her name was. It was Janie. I didn't mention that she was crying, but I asked her if she wanted to dance. She said yes and as we walked out to the dance floor, I know my face turned red, but it was dark and I don't think anyone noticed. I had been so sure everyone would be looking at me, but no one laughed or anything and we danced the whole dance.

"Britney was right. It was three little minutes, but it made me feel really good. After that, a lot of the guys danced with her and with other girls who hadn't danced yet. It was like the coolest eighth-grade graduation dance. Everyone had a blast.

"I really learned something important tonight, Mom."

So did I, Adam, I thought. I learned that a 14-year-old girl can be filled with compassion. I learned that peer pressure can sometimes be a good thing. I also learned that my son doesn't need me to teach him all of life's lessons anymore. He was growing up.

Yes, that night my son did the nicest thing he'd ever done in his 14-year life, and I'm proud of him for it. The remarkable child, however, was Britney. With one push of encouragement she changed, if only momentarily, the lives of a lot of kids. She helped give one tearful girl a happy memory. She helped my son grow up a little. She challenged a bunch of teenage boys to reconsider what's really "cool." And she changed me, too. I always saw her as just another one of Adam's friends. Now I see her as his guardian angel.

Great dancing doesn't take skill.
It simply requires love.

L ove one another with mutual affection;
outdo one another in showing honor.
ROMANS 12:10

Three Cheers for Luther

I was sitting in the principal's office on Luther's first day of school. The office door opened slowly, and a small woman entered meekly, pushing a smaller boy ahead of her. The woman's clothing was clean but worn and frayed. The young boy standing beside her appeared to be about 12 years old. He wore a striped knit shirt, faded from too many washings, and a pair of blue jeans a size too small. Peering through wisps of unevenly cut black hair, the boy's dark brown eyes darted nervously around the room. He held tightly to a small paper bag, which obviously contained his lunch.

The woman and her son stood speechless. After a moment of silence, Mrs. Stemmons, the principal's secretary, asked icily, "And how might I help you?"

Glancing down at the boy, the woman said hesitantly, "I've . . . come to enroll my son . . . in school."

The secretary opened a desk drawer, selected a printed form, pushed it and a pencil across her desk, and said, somewhat brusquely, "Please fill this out. You may sit at the table by the window."

With obvious self-consciousness, the woman took the paper and pencil and moved quickly to the table. The boy followed her and stood silently at her side as she sat down and began to write on the paper. When she finished, she took a card from her worn, fabric purse and handed it, with the paper, to the woman at the desk. Mrs. Stemmons hastily glanced over the form and frowned as she looked at the boy's report card.

In a low, tremulous voice, the woman said, "Last semester was difficult for Luther. His . . . father . . . died suddenly. . . ." Her voice trailed off in a barely audible whisper.

Suddenly uncomfortable, Mrs. Stemmons stood and, with all of the uncharacteristic kindness she could muster, said, "I'm very sorry, Mrs. . . . Ramirez," hesitating as she scanned the paper for the woman's name. "You may leave Luther here. An aide will take him to his class."

Again looking at the paper, she added, "Bus number 15 is assigned to your neighborhood. The teacher on bus duty this week helps all new students find their bus. Luther will be all right."

The woman looked at her son as she turned to leave. For a moment her eyes seemed swollen with unshed tears. She tenderly touched his arm. His wide, dark eyes followed her as she quietly closed the door behind her.

I was back in class when an aide brought Luther to our room. Mrs. Miller, a warm and happy woman, was our writing skills teacher. She spoke briefly with the aide, and then she stood beside Luther and announced, "Class, let me have your attention. We have a new student who will be a part of our class. His name is Luther Ramirez. David, our class captain for the week, will help Luther find his way around the school. Each of you introduce yourselves to Luther. Since our writing assignment today is to tell something interesting about ourselves, share that with Luther. It might help him remember who you are."

Mrs. Miller assigned Luther to a vacant desk in the third row, across from Tommy Akin. She opened the supply closet and selected a spiral notebook, two pencils, and a copy of the handbook we were using in class, then took them to Luther. Tommy was the tallest boy in our class and was well built for his age. He was one of the campus bullies and was often in trouble for harassing the younger boys and making a general nuisance of himself. He liked all kinds of sports and told everybody he was going to be a professional baseball player one day.

Tommy turned sideways in his desk chair and glowered at Luther. He curled his lips upward in a disdainful smirk, sizing up Luther's small, bony, almost frail body.

"What kind of sports do you play, Luther?" Tommy asked, as he leaned closer to the new boy. In a loud whisper for all around him to hear, he said, "I'll bet you're good at hopscotch!" He laughed under his breath, and some of the other students sitting nearby began to giggle.

Luther did not acknowledge Tommy's insult. Concentrating on the handbook Mrs. Miller had given him, he pretended to ignore Tommy, though his face began to turn crimson with embarrassment and rage.

"What's wrong? Can't you talk?" Tommy sneered. He looked around at the students nearby who seemed to be enjoying his antics and said, "Whaddaya know! I don't think 'new boy' here can talk!"

About that time, Mrs. Miller glanced in Luther's direction. She saw that a disturbance of some sort was in progress. Because of Tommy's reputation as a troublemaker, she could imagine what was happening. She arose from her desk and walked slowly toward the row where Luther was seated. Tommy quickly pretended to be working on his project, and the other students who had comprised his audience did likewise.

When the class was over, Mrs. Miller called to me as we were about to leave. "David, take care of Luther. If there are any problems, let me know immediately."

I quickly caught up with Luther, introduced myself to him, and asked him his locker number. Luckily it was not very far down from mine.

In the days that followed, I noticed that Luther would always be near where I was on the playground, though he never approached me or initiated a conversation. I had not seen him in the school cafeteria during lunch, so I asked him one day if he brought his lunch to school. He answered that he did. The school menus were published in the local paper for the week. Occasionally when some particular food that I wasn't fond of was served, I would bring my lunch. I had seen Luther walking alone out toward the edge of the campus where a large oak tree grew. One day when I had brought my lunch, I followed him.

"Luther, mind if I eat with you today?" He shrugged his shoulders as if to say, "Whatever." We sat down beneath the tree. I opened my lunch, but noticed that Luther did not open his. I took out a sandwich, some chips, an apple, and several homemade cookies. "Aren't you going to eat?" I asked Luther. He said he wasn't hungry. I noticed that there didn't seem to be much in his bag. I pretended not to be hungry myself and said, "Here, Luther. Help me get rid of some of this lunch. I'm not very hungry either." At first he shook his head. But when I unwrapped the sandwich and offered him half of it, he quickly took it and, in two or three bites, wolfed it down.

I shared my chips and cookies with him also. After we finished, he opened his sack and took out its contents—a
single apple.

I told my mother about Luther, and I decided I would
take my lunch every day for a while. Mother would pack two
sandwiches, and she added helpings of other food that I
could share with Luther. We ate lunch together almost every
day and began to pal around. Gradually we became friends,
and soon my regular group of friends started to accept him
into the fold as well.

When ball teams were chosen during recess, Luther
was always chosen last, and he rarely got to play. One day
when I was a team captain, I picked Luther early in the
choosing. He had told me one day that he'd been the
pitcher on the ball team at his previous school. So I asked
him to pitch, over the loud protests of some of the guys. It
was soon obvious that Luther was a natural. After that, he
was the first one chosen every time. Once he was able to
demonstrate his skills, his confidence began to grow, and
even people like Tommy Akin had to admit that Luther could
really play ball.

When the school team was formed that spring, Luther
was top choice for starting pitcher. He was a standout
throughout the season, and that year our school won the
local championship. After the winning game, the team
hoisted Luther on their shoulders and carried him off the
field as a hero. I saw the sparkle in his eyes and the glow on
his face, and I recalled how different he seemed from that
forlorn boy in the principal's office who used to eat lunch
alone under an oak tree. He smiled at me, and I cheered as
loud as I could for my friend Luther.

No Greater Love

Ryan was my first best friend, and though many wonderful people have crossed my path since I knew him, not one has lived up to the example that he set. Forty years since our last meeting, my love and admiration for Ryan remains stronger than ever.

We met at school at the age of five and soon became best pals. Both of us were learning to play the piano, and it was our mutual love of music that brought us together. For the next seven years we were almost inseparable, forever hammering away at the keys of my mother's baby grand.

Ryan was a great piano player. I was small for my age and had trouble reaching the pedals, but his legs were just the right length for my mother's piano stool. We were supposed to be studying the classic composers, like Beethoven and Mozart, but Ryan loved to stretch his fingers toward the black keys and start jazzing around. Sometimes it was hard to figure out where Beethoven stopped and Count Basie began once Ryan really got going. I loved to sit with a glass of lemonade and listen to Ryan play. It was such a joy to be so young and carefree.

But those joyous, carefree days ended when we reached the age of 13. We were packed off to a new school, and we both encountered troubles when we got there.

I was still small and became an easy target for a fiendish pair of bullies. They stole my lunch and pulled my hair, but what hurt the most were the verbal insults. As soon as I got to school each day, the bullies would start teasing me about my height. I tried to argue back with them, but they were so much bigger that it made my protests seem comical. There I'd be, threatening to swipe them back after they'd hit me, when I barely came up to their midriffs. It wasn't much of a threat.

Ryan was the one who saved me. And considering what he was going through, his friendship and loyalty were all the more remarkable. At the age of 10, Ryan was diagnosed with hemophilia, a rare blood disease. When a victim of the disease is wounded, the deficiencies in the blood mean that it doesn't clot properly. Even the smallest cut becomes potentially life threatening if it doesn't receive immediate medical treatment.

Ryan and I were walking home from school one day when the two bullies jumped me from behind. They dragged me into some bushes and threatened to beat me up.

"You little worm," one of them shouted, shoving me to my knees. "Get down there with the other insects."

I didn't dare fight back, so I did as he told me. I lay facedown on the grass and felt a foot against my back. The other one had taken over now. He started to twist his foot against my body, like he was trying to squash me.

"Please let me go," I begged them, but to no avail.

"Quiet," the first bully shouted. I felt someone grab the back of my hair and start to rub my face in the dirt.

Soon I was crying, which the bullies loved since it signi-
fied their victory over me. At least they thought it did.

"Let go of him," said a voice.

I felt the hand let go of my hair and looked up to see
Ryan standing there. His hands were forming into fists, as if
he was readying himself for a fight.

"Buzz off," one of the bullies told him. "This is between
the three of us."

Ryan didn't budge an inch. "Let go of him, and go pick
on someone your own size," he said. He nodded at me, as if
telling me to stand up.

I didn't know what to do. All I could think of was Ryan's
illness and how dangerous it could be for him if a fight broke
out. I told him to run for it, but he clearly wasn't going to
leave me. He just stood there with his fists raised and told
the bullies what he thought of them. I'll never forget his
words. "Stephen might not be as big as you guys, but he's
50 times the person you'll ever be. If you ever lay a finger
on him again, I'll hit you so hard . . . "

It was amazing. He didn't even have to finish the sen-
tence. The two bullies just ran off. Since then, I've read
many times how all bullies are secretly cowards and will only
keep bullying until the day they're confronted, but at the
time neither Ryan nor I knew that. Ryan had stood up to two
of the nastiest kids in town and come out the winner. The
funny thing was that I shouted at him for it.

"You could have gotten yourself killed!" I screamed at
him. "One punch from them and you could have bled to
death, you idiot."

He just laughed. "Don't worry," Ryan said. "If either of them had thrown a punch, I'd have been out of there like lightning. You might be my best friend," he joked, "but I'm not crazy."

But even as a kid, I knew that he would never have run away and left me. Ryan would have risked everything for his friends.

We lost touch a year later when my family moved away. I hadn't seen Ryan for more than 12 years when I received a letter from his mother saying that the disease had finally taken him. He had passed away peacefully and had asked to be remembered to me.

Reading that letter, I felt like the kid that had known and needed Ryan all those years ago. I felt like a helpless 13-year-old again as tears poured down my cheeks and my heart longed for a friendly word.

Ryan, you will stay in my heart forever, and I will never stop praising God for the way you risked your life to save me. If I can be half the friend to others that you were to me, then I will know that I have lived a worthwhile life. And if I can be rewarded for my goodness with a place alongside you in heaven, then I shall live and die a happy man.

God bless you, Ryan, and thank you for being such a true friend.

The Heart of a Hero

The "putt-putt" of the little motorized cart rolling up and down the crumbling streets of our neighborhood announced that Owen was approaching. His twisted arms would guide the control stick as he smiled widely, exposing his big, crooked teeth.

Owen didn't go to school. Everyone assumed he was unable to learn. The neighbors all felt very protective of him and thought he should be allowed to live out his expected short life in peace and contentment.

I was nine and, to me, Owen was repulsive.

"Owen has a soul and is loved by God just like everyone else on this earth," Mama told me. "He's one of God's special lambs."

Special lamb or not, I thought he was revolting. "He's 16 and slobbers like a baby," I said. I cringed at the thought of Owen, his body sometimes jerking out of control.

"He's one of God's creations, and he's got a purpose here. For one thing, it's to teach the rest of us to be kind and loving to him."

I sneered, looking away.

"He's no different from you or me," Mama said. "He's a flesh-and-blood person, and he needs friends."

Perhaps that was true, but I couldn't imagine being friends with him.

Later that afternoon, I walked to Louie's Drugs for Mama's aspirin. Much to my disappointment, Owen was in front of the store in his cart, the motor humming as a few neighborhood boys gathered around him.

"Hi, Carrie," Christopher, an older boy, called.

"Hi," I answered self-consciously.

Owen made grunting noises and pointed his crooked finger in my direction.

"Carrie, Owen says hi," Christopher said. Christopher was always nice to Owen and didn't seem bothered by his disabilities. "He doesn't have any sisters, you know, and he'd like it if you'd be his friend."

I waved at Owen casually without looking at him. "I've got to get Mama's aspirin," I said, hurrying into the store.

I stayed in the drugstore, browsing through movie magazines and comic books, until all the boys outside were gone. Then I headed for home.

After supper, I sat beneath our catalpa tree to read a book. But my reading was interrupted by the familiar "putt-putt" of Owen's cart. I closed my eyes and sat very still, hoping he wouldn't see me. The sound grew closer, then stopped. I could hear the hum of the engine. Opening my eyes, I saw Owen's cart at the curb. He was making strange noises and looking at me. I felt my face flush.

Owen nodded his head at me. Saliva ran down his chin, and he made strange throaty sounds.

Old Mr. Joseph lived across the street from us and would pay me a couple of dollars to walk his dog. Shep was a medium-size dog of various breeds. He was a nice dog and liked me so I looked forward to walking him.

"Carrie! Carrie!" Mr. Joseph called from across the street. "Shep would like a walk."

I jumped up, happy my encounter with Owen was interrupted.

As I ran across the street, I heard the "putt-putt" of the cart fade down the street.

Mr. Joseph smiled. "You know Owen's mother is raising him all alone. Good woman, his mother."

"Why is she alone?" I asked.

"Didn't you know?" He put Shep's leash on his collar. "When Owen was born, and his mother wouldn't put him away in some home, his father took off."

He put Shep's leash in my hand. "She's done a lot to make sure that boy is happy for the short time he'll have on this earth."

We stood silently for a few seconds while I thought about what Mr. Joseph had just said.

"You and Shep enjoy your walk," he said, then went into his house.

Shep always wanted to run, no matter how hot the weather. Mr. Joseph had told me it was because he was penned up all day and needed to stretch his legs. I knew it was my duty to allow Shep to exercise, so I ran close behind him, hanging on to the leash.

When we reached Mrs. Blair's house on the corner, her old black cat zipped across our path, and Shep took off after him. I tried to keep up, but I tripped and fell on the sidewalk. The leash slid out of my hands, and I saw Shep chase the cat into the alley.

As I stood up, warm blood trickled down from my knees. I swallowed back tears and ran after the dog.

The cat darted across the alley into the open door of an abandoned garage, Shep yapping at his heels. I followed them into the garage and felt the stifling heat inside. The cat shrieked and jumped up on a shelf on the back wall, knocking over a can of liquid onto rags piled on the dirt floor.

Shep whined and sniffed. I started after the dog. As I walked around the pile of rags, the friction caused them to ignite. The flames spread to a stack of old newspapers, and the blaze spread quickly up the wall toward the rotting roof.

Within seconds, the fire squirmed across the ceiling to the opposite wall and divided into several fingers, then crackled in all directions. The cat tore by me, followed by the barking dog. Both of them ran out the door to the safety of the alley.

As I headed for the door, the blaze reached a shelf above it, and an old blanket fell, dangling over part of the door opening. I heard a loud "snap" above me and jumped back when I saw the rafter wrapped in fiery yellow and blue flames.

Smoke engulfed the garage. I coughed, and my eyes watered. "Help!" I screamed. "Somebody help me!" Frightened, I dropped to the dirt floor, prayed to God for help, then crawled toward the door.

Suddenly I heard the familiar "putt-putt" of Owen's cart. As I made my way to the door through the thick black smoke, I saw Owen's cart enter the garage. I could hear him muttering and was aware that the cart stopped. I climbed up next to Owen, and he drove out the door.

When we reached the safety of the alley, the doorway was covered in flames. I heard a loud bang and saw the roof collapse. My heart sank into my stomach when I realized how close I had come to not making it out alive.

Shep was sitting in the alley. He ran over to the cart and began nuzzling me apologetically. I patted him and assured him that all was forgiven, then looked up at Owen.

"Thank you," I said, suddenly feeling bad for all the mean things I had said about him. "Thank you, Owen." I realized for the first time that he was a real person. He had feelings and needs and concerns just like every-one else.

Owen smiled, and I took his hand in mine. It was warm and felt no different than any other person's hand.

"Are you all right?" Christopher appeared with Mr. Joseph close behind.

"Owen rescued me," I explained. Owen smiled.

"Owen's a hero!" Christopher shouted, beaming with pride.

Mr. Joseph scooped Shep up in his arms. "Is he the cause of all this?" he asked.

"Sort of," I answered. "He chased the cat—"

"I'm sorry, Carrie," Mr. Joseph said. "You're sure you're feeling okay?"

"I'm fine," I said. "Owen saved me."

I turned to Owen. "Would you mind driving me home?"

Owen's eyes shone with pleasure as the "putt-putt" of his little cart sounded throughout our neighborhood. I smiled, finally understanding that inside Owen beat the heart of a hero.

What's on Your Mind?

When you pray about friends and dating, what do you pray for?

_____

_____

_____

_____

Do you expect that people will want to be friends with you?

_____

Are friendships easy and natural, or do you have to work at it?

_____

What would you like to say to the Lord about dating?

_____

_____

_____

What would you like to say to yourself?

_____

_____

_____

_____

Sharing What's Inside

When I thought, "My foot is slipping,"
your steadfast love, O Lord, held me
up. When the cares of my heart are many,
your consolations cheer my soul.

Psalm 94:18–19

Everybody needs somebody to talk to. We're
just not made to hold everything inside, to keep
it all to ourselves. Prayer keeps us in touch with
God. And talking with each other keeps us in
touch with ourselves and the world around us.

Whether it's good news or bad, it's not
really news until we share it with someone else.
Have you ever rushed home with the most
exciting news—burst into the house just about
ready to explode—and then found no one was
home? Sharing what's inside makes the good
stuff even better and the sad times a little
lighter.

Remember, you can always talk to God
when it seems there's no one there. It's often
just the thing to keep us on track. God's always
there for us; he's always ready to listen, to
understand, and to comfort.

❖ ❖ ❖

My Tribe

I was new in town and painfully shy; I felt like such an out-sider at school. I went through my days in a sort of robotic haze, getting through each class and eating lunch by myself, trying to pretend that was just the way I liked it. The truth was, I wanted to make friends, real friends, but I just didn't have the social skills.

My brother, Mario, was the great social talent in our family. He was always trying to get me involved with some of his new friends, but the difference in our ages made it hard. I felt like such a freak.

I loved talking to Aunt Sophia. She understood about being shy. Hard as it was to believe, she had been shy when she was in high school! But she had broken out of her shell, and I was still trapped here in mine.

Aunt Sophia loved to pray about things. Whenever she was bothered or anxious about something she would medi-tate and pray. I had actually started doing it, too, and I admit it made me feel better. She suggested I take time each day to talk to God. She said I should ask him for help finding my "tribe"—people who were like me. She said they were out there, just as lost and alone as I was; all it would take for us to find each other was a little divine intervention.

So I decided to pray about my shyness and finding my tribe, asking God for direction. The first few times, I didn't really feel anything, but Aunt Sophia told me that sometimes God answers prayers in very strange ways. "Keep your eyes wide open," she said, "and your heart, too."

The next morning at school, I was walking by the message board when I noticed a flyer for an art contest. I loved to paint with oils, so I took the information down. I decided to enter a piece I had done a few months ago. The judges voted on more than 100 entries, and my painting won first place in the oil-painting category!

My parents took me to the awards dinner, but I ended up spending most of the evening with three other guys who had each won first place in their categories. We found out we had more in common than just art—we were all shy and quiet. We got along like we had been friends forever, and we decided to form a club of our own: the Shy Artist Club.

It started as a joke, but within a few months, we had 14 members, all shy kids who loved art and creativity. When we got together, we had a lot of fun, and it made it even easier for us to be more open and confident on the outside. That's when I realized that my real prayers had been answered. God had chosen a strange way to do it, just like Aunt Sophia had said.

I had found my tribe, thanks to Aunt Sophia and a little divine intervention.

❖ ❖ ❖

God,
Help me to find the people who are like me. I want so badly to have good friends to do things with, to laugh with, and to cry with. Give me the confidence to approach others with an open heart and mind and the courage to nurture new friendships when they do come along. Thank you, God. Amen.

❖ ❖ ❖

S ometimes when I'm lonely
Don't know why,
Keep thinkin' I won't be lonely
By and by.

LANGSTON HUGHES, "HOPE [1]," 1942,
THE COLLECTED POEMS OF LANGSTON HUGHES

❖ ❖ ❖

When no one else seems to be listening, be assured that at least one person is: the good Lord.

What's Eating Me?

I don't know why it happened. My dad had gotten married to this lady I wasn't too thrilled with. And we'd moved to a new town in the middle of my sophomore year of high school. Anyway, I was having a few cookies after school. Dad's new wife kept lots of junk food in the house. Nobody was home. I had three cookies while I was working on a huge project for school. Then I went back to the cookie jar and got three more cookies. Then I promised myself that I wouldn't have any cookies the next day to make up for it. It was like I'd "eaten ahead." I had it all worked out in my mind.

Well, this started happening all the time, to the point where I'd eat tons of food in one day. I wasn't hungry for it, I'd just eat it. It was something to do, I suppose, since I didn't really have any new friends. It also made me feel "full" inside and happy. The good feelings only lasted for a short while, though. Then I'd start to get really angry at myself. It got to the point where I'd go for two whole days without eating anything to make up for the days where I ate a lot. Sometimes I'd get dizzy or confused.

Nobody really noticed—except my poetry teacher, Ms. Allan. I had always loved to write, but during this time my poems got pretty weird and depressing. Ms. Allan was surprised by the change in my work. She asked me if something was wrong. I clammed up and was insulted that she might think something was wrong with me. After all, I was always perfect.

Still, I started hanging around after class. I'd help Ms. Allan erase the chalkboard or tidy up the desks. On Saturday, she worked at a shop downtown, and I went in there once or twice—just to say hello. I hadn't tried to talk to Ms. Allan about my problem, but I knew she was right. Something was wrong in my life. I didn't want to keep hiding. Either I was keeping how much I was eating a secret, or I was hiding that I wasn't eating at all. It was getting really hard to keep up all the lies.

I prayed for guidance, but I ate half a package of cookies while I was praying. As I was eating and praying, I kept thinking that there wasn't much of anything that rhymed with cookie. That made me think of Ms. Allan. Suddenly I realized that she was there for me—if I wanted her to be.

The next day after school I hung around to talk to Ms. Allan. She was really cool. We ended up going out for dinner. I was really self-conscious as I ordered a salad. Eventually, she helped me a lot. I went to counseling for a while. It was okay. I figured out that I was trying to fill myself with food to make up for the love I didn't get at home.

Counseling didn't magically make things better at home, but once I understood what I was doing, it was easier to get a handle on things. I'm okay now, though it's always day to day. I keep talking. And my poems are much happier now. My prayers allowed me to see that help was right in front of me—all I had to do was ask for it!

Lord,
I have a dark secret I'm hiding from my friends and family.
After I've eaten anything, I run to the bathroom to rid myself
of it. I thought I was so clever; I was losing weight, and no
one knew my secret. Now, though, I'm scaring myself. I
know I shouldn't be doing it, and I often feel tired and weak.
But I don't want to admit what I've done, and I certainly
don't want to gain weight again. I'm afraid for my life. I don't
want to die. God, please help me find a way to get help.
Amen.

Beauty is not found in a dress or pant size.
It's not related to name brands or a specific style.
It has nothing to do with wealth and status.
It is simply an attitude.

The Silent Language of Music

My dad played the violin. Not just as a hobby. It was his life. It was our life. He was first violin with the Cleveland Symphony Orchestra. When he died, my world went silent.

Music brought back the memories of losing him. I stopped listening to my stereo. I couldn't stand to have music on in the car. I didn't want to go to church because of the choir. I avoided football games because of the band. I totally cut music out of my life.

About six months after my dad's death, I headed for a hike in the woods by our family cabin. I walked for about two hours, then sat down to rest on the top of a beautiful hillside. It was a sunny day, and I loved the feel of the silence all around me.

Then I heard it. It was so faint at first that I wasn't sure it was real. Then it got louder and began to dance around my consciousness. Someone was playing the flute! The little valley had become a perfect concert hall, and the sound seemed to carry for miles. It sounded like the voice of an angel.

I listened. I couldn't *not* listen. The sound was everywhere. Finally, I couldn't hold out anymore, and I let the music fill my soul. I started to cry. At first, I was angry at God for making me feel it; I had done such a good job of holding everything inside. Then I was grateful. The music spoke to me, and I responded in a way that I hadn't been able to do with my mom, my pastor, my prayers.

I was feeling again. I had shut out life when I'd shut out music. Dad would never have wanted that. Never again will I close myself off to the bittersweet music of life.

Lord,
I would be happiest right now with my head in the sand. I constantly want to be alone; I don't want to be bothered. I have trouble getting out of my bed to face the day. Everything is difficult and brings negative thoughts about myself, your world, my friends and family. I don't mean to be so cranky and useless; I just don't feel like me. I don't know who I am anymore. Please help me to see that life is a gift and give me the strength to pull through my sadness.

Prayers to God are like small kisses upon his cheeks. He'll respond with a warm embrace that will pick you up off the ground and gently push you in the right direction.

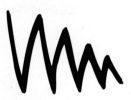

I Don't Mean to Be Mean

Sometimes I'd get mean inside. And then the meanness would just pop out of my mouth before I could stop it. I'm not a bad person, but all this ugly, bad stuff would get inside me sometimes. Usually the person I'd spew this stuff out on was Cami, my little sister. And then her big blue eyes would well up and oh, would I ever feel awful, like a horrid monster who made her sister cry yet again.

And I knew she wasn't doing it on purpose. She wasn't trying to be in my way or be annoying, but it was like I was possessed or something. I just couldn't stop myself.

I tried talking to my mom about it. But she'd just tell me that I had to be nice to my sister. Well of course I wanted to be nice; I just couldn't seem to master it. I began to think I was just going to explode if I didn't talk to somebody and find a way to stop. I didn't want Cami to spend the rest of her life being afraid of *me*!

I talked to God about it and prayed to change. But I knew that I needed to talk about it with someone else, too. I kept dreaming that I was sitting at a big table talking with God and someone else. I wasn't sure who it was, but the table was in the school cafeteria. I was telling them how I was angry all the time. In my dream, I could sense the bad feelings draining away.

Finally, I worked up my courage and went to the counselor at school, Mr. Bobson. He was cool. We went for a walk, and I told him about feeling so angry. I told him about my dream, too. He said it sounded like the answers had already come to me through my prayers. He helped me understand my image of letting the anger drain away. We visualized it, and I practiced letting my anger go and replacing it with healthier feelings.

He also told me that it's okay to get angry sometimes. He thought that maybe I was trying to *never* get angry and that's why I'd sort of explode sometimes. He was right, too. I had figured that good people didn't ever have bad feelings.

I know better now. And I have lots of ways to deal with the feelings I don't want to let out to hurt other people. I pray a lot. And I talk a lot. And I know that whatever I'm feeling is okay for me.

Why is it when you could use a friend the most, no one seems to notice? I haven't been telling anyone about my thoughts or showing anyone that I'm upset, but I thought my close friends and family would know something was wrong and volunteer to help. I know I need someone to help me, but I'm afraid. Please give me the strength to ask for assistance and not just wait for someone to realize something is really wrong.

Sometimes the most difficult thing to do is admit that you need help, but it's the simplest solution.

Dying to Be Me

Don't do it. Don't ever let yourself get this close. I wanted to die. I see now that I didn't even know what that meant, but I nearly took away the most incredible blessing we can each know—the blessing of life. And I nearly caused unspeakable pain to the people who love me the most.

I don't even know for sure why it happened—how things got so out of hand. I didn't talk with anyone about anything. I used to pray a lot, but then I sort of stopped talking to God, too. I can see now how important it is to keep talking; it helps you keep everything in perspective. I just kept it all inside, and one thing led to another. Things started looking darker and darker until it was as though I was enclosed in darkness. And instead of praying for the light, I pulled the darkness tighter around me. Like if I could make myself small enough everything would be fine. I felt so bad I was afraid to share my feelings with anyone.

I was incredibly blessed to have a good friend who would not leave me alone even though I asked her to over and over again (and I don't think I was always very nice about it). She persisted and finally got me to start talking and then I started praying with her again—and that's when the light started coming back.

I see a counselor now, so I know there's always someone there to talk to. Of course, I do know that God's always
there, too, and I've promised myself and God that I'll never
forget that again.

Lord,
Help me to understand why you test some of your children
with unfair situations while other kids don't have a care in
the world. I'm overwhelmed with sadness, and I often don't
want to live. I feel as though you hate me and shed your
blessings on everyone else.

I tell myself I can never be happy. I tell myself I must
not deserve it. Did I do something wrong? Why are some
people able to deal with bigger traumas and tragedies without thinking about ending it all? Please give me strength to
face my problems.

*Remember, the good Lord told us
he would always be with us.*

The steadfast love of the Lord never ceases, his mercies
never come to an end; they are new every morning;
great is your faithfulness.

LAMENTATIONS 3:22–23

In over My Head

Nobody would listen to me. I asked for help. Well, I tried to ask. Maybe if I'd been able to say it more clearly? Maybe if I'd known who to go to besides my mom and dad. I guess I didn't know I needed help. Not really. Though a couple of friends were worried. I just got really angry at them and accused them of not caring about me. Actually, they were the very best of friends. They were worried and scared. I started getting scared, too, near the end—too scared to listen and too scared to get help. I had lost my faith in everything: in myself, in my family and friends, in God.

Not only was I way over my head with the addiction, I was breaking the law. If only I'd talked to my parents, or my uncle, or my algebra teacher. He came to see me every day at the hospital. I could've talked to him early on. I tried. I hung around after class a couple of times. But he didn't get it. I expected everyone to read my mind, to hear my silent pleas. Though I now know that ultimately those unspoken prayers were answered or I wouldn't be here today.

Of course, I passed out on the couch at home a couple of times and my parents didn't get it either. They thought I was "overtired." They didn't know I was buying drugs (with money I stole from their wallets) from a guy who was probably selling to a whole bunch of stupid kids like me. I'm in the hospital now. It's been pretty bad. The police have been here, but I think if I talk to them it'll turn out okay. I guess if I'd talked to somebody long before this I wouldn't be in this wheelchair. Yeah. Bad news. They say I might not walk again. I jumped off the roof a week ago. I wasn't trying to hurt myself like some people think. I was high and just thought I could fly around for a while.

I never appreciated being alive before, but now I thank God every day that I got a second chance. I figure I'm still here for a reason, and I have more faith than I ever dreamed possible. Every day I pray that I'll walk again. I want to tell other kids not to be afraid to ask for help. And next time I have a problem myself? Well, I think I'll talk it over with the Lord and maybe with my parents. Just wish I'd figured all this out a little sooner.

The expression that "strength is found in numbers" is true. Challenges are easier to overcome with force.

God is faithful, and he will not let you be tested beyond your strength, but with the testing he will also provide the way out so that you may be able to endure it.

1 CORINTHIANS 10:13

A Gift of Love

Jane Nelms awoke the morning of August 29 at her parents' house in Denver, Colorado, with labor pains.

"It's time," she told her mother.

She knew what her mother must be thinking. She could hear the words echo in her mind to the same percussion of pain and guilt she had felt since she married Chad. "You should not have gotten married, and this baby is a big mistake. You've ruined your life."

Jane's mother didn't like Chad or the fact that he had moved out of the young couple's apartment when Jane was six months pregnant. And she didn't think Jane was ready, at age 19, to be having a child.

After Chad left, the company that employed Jane went out of business. She had no choice but to return to her parents' home. She knew she had failed her family by making poor choices. They loved her, but she didn't think she deserved their love—or God's. Not she, who had been rejected by her husband. She was unworthy.

After the labor pains began, Jane called Chad at the gas station where he worked.

"Please come to the hospital with me," she begged.

"It's your baby," he said. "I don't care about it."

Over and over, she pleaded with him to come. He refused. By the time Jane arrived at the hospital with her mother and sister, she was an emotional wreck. She was embarrassed to be there without a supportive husband. She felt like a failure, worthless, facing a future that looked completely hopeless.

After Jane was wheeled to the labor room, two nurses appeared. One of them was heavyset, middle-age, average height, with a calm, soothing voice. Her name tag identified her as Mary. She looked motherly and huggable, and her presence made Jane feel safe.

Mary soon dismissed the other nurse by saying, "I can handle things from here."

Standing beside Jane in a white uniform, her dark hair a contrast to her light complexion, Mary asked, "Have you taken birthing classes?"

"No," Jane replied, thinking that was one more thing she had failed to do.

Mary taught Jane how to breathe so she could deal with the pain. Jane loved her calm voice, so different than the raised voices often used by her family.

By 4:00 P.M., Jane's labor pains had intensified. About that time, Chad arrived with his parents, who had forced him to come.

Mary had to tend to her other patients, but she popped in frequently to check Jane's pulse and blood pressure. When the nursing shift changed later that evening, Mary didn't go home. She stayed to be with Jane.

By 11:00 P.M., Jane was fully dilated, so she went to the delivery room. Chad went, too. He stood on Jane's left side, and Mary stood to her right. She explained everything that was happening. She tried to get Jane to push. But things weren't going well. The baby's heartbeat began to weaken. Someone gave Jane an epidural. It made her sick, and she threw up. She needed oxygen, but she fought the oxygen mask, afraid she would throw up again and choke. Finally, Mary leaned close to Jane's face and said in her soothing voice, "You need to do this. The baby needs it." Mary's voice helped Jane calm down enough to accept the mask.

"Your baby is fine," Mary kept reassuring her. "You just need to keep breathing."

Mary didn't seem to care about the circumstances that had brought Jane to this place. She wasn't concerned about whether or not Jane had made a wise decision to marry and get pregnant right away. Her focus was on Jane and how she was doing. Mary continued to assure Jane that she would be all right.

"They don't think there's enough room for the baby to come," she explained later. "The doctors are trying to decide if they should take you up to surgery." Mary told Jane that a doctor had been contacted who could perform a cesarean section. Her calming voice helped Jane to relax.

When they wheeled Jane into the operating room, Chad was not allowed to go with her. But Mary never left her side.

Michelle was born at 1:30 A.M. on August 30.

After the other nurses had cleaned Michelle up, Mary asked Jane, "Do you want to see your baby girl?"

Jane looked into her daughter's eyes and examined her perfect features. "She's beautiful," Jane whispered. After spending some time with her new daughter, she handed the baby back to Mary and drifted off to sleep.

When Jane awoke in the recovery room, Mary was gone. Jane was in the hospital five more days, but she never saw Mary again.

After she recovered enough to return to her parents' house, Jane wrote thank-you notes to everyone who had helped her. She addressed Mary's thank-you note to Aurora Community Hospital, thinking it would be delivered to Mary. But several days later, it came back with a note that no such person was at that address.

Jane telephoned the hospital's maternity ward. "A nurse named Mary helped me through a difficult labor," she explained. "I would like to thank her."

"No one by that name works here," the nurse said. "But occasionally we do hire temporary workers. Perhaps she was just a temp."

After Jane got off the phone, she thought more about Mary. Could she have been an angel? *Impossible,* Jane thought. She had fallen too far from God, made too many bad choices. God couldn't love her enough to send an angel. There had to be some other explanation.

But the more she thought about it, the more Jane realized that she had truly been given a gift when her baby was born: a gift of love and forgiveness and the presence of a kind soul who walked with her through a troubled, frightening time in her life. Mary didn't judge Jane. She didn't criticize her. She didn't remind her of the mistakes she'd made or the distance she had put between herself and God. All she cared about was helping Jane and assuring her that she and her baby would be fine.

If God had orchestrated all of that, Jane decided, then he really did love her. He didn't judge her. He didn't blame her for making poor decisions. He didn't care about any of that—he just cared about her. He cared enough to remind her that she was worthy of love, that she had not been abandoned. And he showed her all those things through the angelic presence of a nurse named Mary.

I've always dreamed of having my own family with a loving husband who will help raise our kids to be well-rounded individuals. I always envisioned having a beautiful house with a white picket fence. Never did I imagine I would be a parent in high school. God, I'm sorry I made such a foolish mistake. Please help me to make the right choices for my future and my child's future. I know I can't turn back time and make things right again, but with your help maybe I can make better decisions in the months and years to come.

❖ ❖ ❖

What Are Friends For?

I've never had a whole lot of friends, but when I do connect with someone, we usually get really close. At least, I had always thought so. I just never knew how truly connected friends could be.

You see, I've always felt a bit different or out of it somehow. And I've found that when you don't talk with anyone, it's really easy to just go on feeling different. I've always talked with God; I pray a lot. I even write letters to God sometimes. Yet that wasn't enough for me to see that rather than being really different, I'm mostly just human in all the up and down ways that most of us are.

Anyway, I have this close friend Mark. And we are always together. We pretty much do everything together. We only date girls who like to double-date. Usually one of us meets someone and then we have that girl find a friend for the other one!

One afternoon, Mark and I were walking downtown. A new arcade had just opened, and we wanted to give it a try. We're really into video games. Anyway, Mark turns to me and says, "Don't you ever get disturbed by things?"

At first, I didn't know what he meant. Turns out, he had always wondered why I never really talked to him about my deeper feelings about things—like sadness, or God, or terrorism—all kinds of things. He really liked hanging out with me, but he always thought I was kinda shallow. Wow! That couldn't be further from the truth. I've always thought that maybe I worry about life a bit too much!

We hung out at the arcade for four hours that night as I filled Mark in on my thoughts about anything and everything! It felt great! And you know what? He didn't think I was weird or dark; he thought I was cool!

Learn to accept yourself and know genuine love for yourself, and others will follow.

❖   ❖   ❖

Growing Up Sane

At my house, a glass of spilled milk at the dinner table might've been met with a shrug and a smile, "No matter— no use crying over spilled milk." Or you could've gotten a screaming tirade about how clumsy you were or how stupid or how you'd better get it cleaned up this instant or else. . . . You just never knew how our mother would react. She was manic-depressive, which meant that she had mood swings and was terribly unpredictable. It also meant that she went through phases of abusing drugs and alcohol trying to feel better and then lied about it. She spent a lot of time going in and out of mental hospitals. Sometimes life was great fun, filled with the childish abandon of a home without anybody acting like a parent, and other times we all got farmed out to various relatives while Mom recuperated from her really bad depressive episodes.

It was a tough way to grow up. But I like to think I came through it okay. The more I've thought about it, I've come to the conclusion that I owe my sanity to one person. Well, not a person really. To my dog, Queen. When I was five, my mom thought we needed some protection, so we went to the animal shelter and got a beautiful German shepherd we named Queen. She quickly became more my dog than any-one else's, and I loved her so much I still miss her to this day. Queen listened to me. I could talk to her about my mom. I could scream, I could cry, I could laugh, I could talk about life. She was alternately my sister, my friend, my nanny, my mom, but she was never just a dog.

If I hadn't had Queen, would I have had the courage and the drive to talk with someone else? Whom could I have turned to? Would I have made it okay? Queen was my counselor, my teacher, my nurse, and my protector. Right before I left for college, she died.

Queen kept me sane. I believe that she must've been sent from the Lord to watch over me. She was my sweet, gentle, furry guardian angel.

Sometimes I wonder why parents don't have to take classes to have children. It seems as though, more often than not, I have to act as the adult in the house. How am I supposed to trust in people that have no sense of responsibility? No one takes the time to make sure I'm doing well in school and taking care of myself. If not for your love, Lord, I'd have no hope. Please help my parents to be less dependent on people and substances and more independent and supportive of us. I want tangible discipline and guidance in my life.

While it may not be clear today, or even tomorrow, why God has picked you to inflict with pain and difficulty, life's most valuable lessons are often learned during trying times.

Dear God,
I feel so alone and empty. I don't want to seclude myself from the world. Please help me to find the strength to seek help. Please help others to see that I am a good person even though I sometimes become depressed and bury myself in solitude. Please, Lord, send me a guardian angel to guide me through this.

❖ ❖ ❖

The righteous cry out, and the Lord hears, and rescues them from all their troubles. The Lord is near to the brokenhearted, and saves the crushed in spirit.

PSALM 34:17–18

❖ ❖ ❖

As I Sit

As I sit and stare,
I try to think of someone who cares.

As I sit and dream,
I'll be alone forever, it seems.

As I sit and cry,
I feel as though I'll die.

So I sit and pray,
And ask the Lord to send his love my way.

What's on Your Mind?

What would you talk about if you could say *anything* to *anybody?* Whom do you wish you could talk to? Try writing a letter in the space below and imagine saying and asking anything and everything on your mind.

_____

_____

_____

_____

_____

_____

Look over your letter. Pick one subject and discuss it with a real person, then write down your thoughts about how the conversation went.

_____

_____

_____

_____

_____

_____

_____

Doing Good in the World

How wonderful it is that nobody need wait a single moment before starting to improve the world.

ANNE FRANK, *THE DIARY OF A YOUNG GIRL*

Car washes, food drives, bake sales, mowing the neighbor's yard, feeding a friend's cat, smiling back at the lady who makes your change at the drive-through—these are all ways we help each other, help our church, help the community. The opportunities to do meaningful volunteer work are as limitless as your imagination. Everyone can find ways to help. Maybe these stories will spark your volunteer instincts. You might read about something you've done before, something you'd like to do, or something you've never even thought about doing. If you have a neighbor who is ill, you might be inspired to take this book over to his or her house and read the chapter out loud! Perhaps you'll give an extra smile to the grocery checker next time you run out for milk for the family.

As long as there are people in need—even if all they need is a kind word—there's a chance to do good in the world.

What Does the Music Say?

Rap, hip-hop, rock and roll? Is the music we love turning us into a bunch of violence-crazed kids? What does it say about us? What does it say about our world?

Everyone's entitled to their opinion, so hear me out on this. I know some music uses language that nobody needs to use, language that is not the way the Lord would like us to speak to each other. I know that. I don't argue with that.

What speaks to me—and I think what speaks to the world—is that there are a lot of artists out there today who are speaking from their hearts about their lives. And from the sound of things, they weren't great lives.

But stop and think for a minute. If you're hearing a song on the radio about someone who came from poverty or violence or abuse, do you realize what that means? It means that person had the strength to hang in there, to write a song, to get their song on the radio, and to make a pretty good living from their music.

I think that's a pretty cool message. To me it says, "I made the best of a lousy situation. I didn't sit around blaming God for what went wrong. I thanked him for giving me the courage and talent to pick myself up and make something of myself!"

It's just another way of looking at some of the entertainment that a lot of us enjoy. It inspires me to be the best I can be at whatever I do and to share my message, whatever it turns out to be. I'll never be a pop star, but I hope I can share a lesson with others and lead the best life possible.

I figure I've been incredibly blessed so far, and the least I can do to say "thanks" to God is to live a productive and helpful life.

❖   ❖   ❖

nobody

So many are homeless,
But people just stare.

So many are hungry,
But nobody shares.

So many are sick,
But nobody cares.

This world needs
More volunteers.

❖   ❖   ❖

The easiest way to make this world a better place is to practice good deeds often.

Mrs. Crimken's Smile

"Back in a sec . . ."

"Okay, Mom," I mumbled in between bites of chips. I figured she was going to Mrs. Crimken's house, though I really hadn't heard all she said. I was up in my room with the stereo blasting. I had a homework assignment that wasn't too distasteful, a big glass of iced tea, the cat on my bed, and the dog under my desk. Yes, indeed—life was good.

My mom seemed to go over to Mrs. Crimken's a lot since Mr. Crimken had died. She'd take her a bit of whatever we had for dinner or a few flowers that she'd somehow ended up with when she came home from the grocery store—things like that. My mom was nice that way. She'd give the shirt off her back to someone in need.

I liked helping people, too. I'd worked on a few Sunday school projects where we'd collected food or sung Christmas carols at a nursing home. It was fun. I just didn't have much time for that stuff now. I still went to church, but that was about the extent of it. I figured I probably got some points for all my mom's good deeds.

Anyway, that night at dinner, my mom said that Mrs. Crimken wasn't feeling very well. Mom looked a little worried, and we all said an extra prayer before dinner. We were about halfway through the meal when Mom blurted out, "Maybe some of the rest of you could drop by next door over the weekend?"

We went around the table in a chorus of excuses. Dad had meetings and golf and chores; my brothers both had games and homework and girls; I had a swim meet and a big school project. Mom looked deflated and didn't say much more the rest of the night.

At about 3:00 the next morning, I woke to the sound of sirens. There was an ambulance parked outside Mrs. Crimken's house. Mom grabbed her robe and slippers and hurried over. "I may go with them to the hospital!" she cried over her shoulder.

Mrs. Crimken came home three weeks later. She was much weaker and thinner than before. She'd had a really bad bout of pneumonia.

Something nagged at me for those three weeks. Sometimes I'd see my mother's face at dinner that night before the ambulance came. Every time I said a prayer, Mrs. Crimken's name or her house or her smile would creep into my consciousness. She had a great little old lady smile. She liked to sit on her front porch, and when I'd come and go (and I did a lot of coming and going), she'd wave at me and smile. She was always so friendly.

I thought about all the reasons I was always giving myself for not going next door. Mrs. Crimken could've died that night. How would I have felt then? I realize that I want to feel good about seeing her, not guilty and sad. My mom says, "There's always time to help people." She says that when you give, you get more in return one way or another.

I think I'll stop writing now. I'd like to go next door and maybe make a cup of tea for Mrs. Crimken.

D efend the poor and fatherless;
Do justice to the afflicted and needy.

PSALM 82:3 NKJV

Every day you make choices and change lives.
Whose life do you want to change today?

Father,
Please provide me with the inspiration and energy to help others who are not as fortunate as I am. I want to make a difference in at least one person's life. Give me creativity to come up with unique ways to touch a life. Helping others will make me feel better about myself. Amen.

It is often said that time is our most
precious gift. And to give your time to
something or someone else is an unselfish gift that
will be returned when you least expect it.

People Like You and Me

A poor teenage girl likely has little to offer our society today. So just imagine what it must have been like 2,000 years ago. Society was completely dominated by men. Women and children were relegated to second- and third-class status, just above criminals and prostitutes and sometimes just below livestock.

So, then, doesn't it seem strange that God would choose a poor teenage girl to bring his son into the world? I mean, it's odd enough that the King of Kings and Lord of Lords was born in a barn. There was no band, no hoopla, no pomp and circumstance. It was almost a nonevent. But to be born of an insignificant youngster, to top it all off?

This is, indeed, strange behavior for the God of the universe. But not uncommon. He has a history of doing the unexplainable. The unorthodox. The unconventional.

Remember Abraham and Isaac. Moses and Pharaoh. David and Goliath. Daniel and the lions. Jonah and the whale. All were chosen by God to perform Herculean tasks. All were miserably inept, horribly unprepared, too slow, too short, too scared, and too small-minded to know what they were about to get into. But they had one thing in common: They were available. And they trusted God.

Do you think Mary was scared? Probably. Do you think she was confused? Most likely. Was there a chance that she sometimes doubted what she had heard the angel say? I'm sure she did. So, how do you think she reacted? I think she continued to trust God. And she prayed a lot.

Has God called you to do something that you see as inconceivable? Has he asked you to perform the impossible? To complete the improbable? Do you wonder if the message is really from him? It probably is.

So, be strong and courageous. Remember, God used a poor teenage girl to bring the Savior into the world. He may use presidents, prime ministers, emperors, and kings to rule the world. But he uses people like you and me to change it.

Instead of getting angry when adults say teenagers are just trouble, prove them wrong and make a difference in your town, your state, or even your country. But most of all, do it for yourself—for the betterment of your own life.

I watched a story today on TV about two teenage siblings who collected food for their needy neighbors. I was inspired by their work and in awe of their dedication. Thank you, Lord, for showing me that teenagers can make a difference. Help me to find my own ways to make an impact. I want to help make the world a better place to live. Amen.

Catching Mom's Feelings

As a teenager who had just graduated from high school, I wasn't quite sure what lay ahead for me. I suppose, as my mother often told me, I needed to trust in God for guidance. One especially memorable lesson in faith began the day a letter came to our mailbox for Mr. Totten, an 80-year-old widower who lived down the street from us.

My mother looked at the letter. "It's from his daughter, Blanch. Marion, you'd better take it to him."

"Why, Mom?"

"I have a feeling we ought to get this letter to him."

My mother was always sending me to the old man's house for one reason or another because she had certain "feelings" that things ought to be done. I asked her about these feelings once, and she said they came from some heavenly source. "Someday you'll get these feelings, too," she assured me. "Then you'll understand what I'm talking about."

In a serious tone of voice, she added, "You can learn a lot from Mr. Totten. He's a man of faith."

I took the letter and went.

Mr. Totten was a very nice man. I remember when I got to his house, he was sitting on the steps of his front porch.

Handing the letter to him, I said, "This was in our mailbox. It's for you."

He took a big red handkerchief from his pocket and wiped his spectacles. Then he looked at the envelope. "Why, it's from my daughter," he said. "She doesn't write very often."

I noticed a frown come to his face as he read the letter. When he finished, he said, "Blanch says I'm getting too old to live by myself. She wants me to come and live with her."

For a moment he was silent. Then he looked at me. "Marion, would you mind answering this letter to Blanch? I shake so much, and my fingers are cramped with arthritis."

"Be glad to," I answered, a little curious as to what he was going to tell his daughter.

We both went inside. He got some paper and a pen from a desk drawer. He handed them to me, and I sat down at the kitchen table.

"Just tell Blanch," Mr. Totten began, "that I'm not aiming to leave here as long as I can do for myself. Tell her I trust the Lord for all my needs, and everything is okay except the roof needs to be patched with a few shingles. Tell her I have the shingles and nails, but I can't climb like I used to, or I'd do the job myself. Tell her I have faith that God will help me get the job done."

I had to write furiously to get it all down. When I saw he didn't have anymore to say, I handed the paper and pen to him. He signed the letter and stuffed it in an envelope.

"I'll mail this tomorrow," he said. "Thanks, Marion, for helping me."

I hurried home as fast as I could so I could tell my mother what old Mr. Totten had told me to write.

"He even told Blanch that God would help him get his roof repaired."

Mom looked at me, I thought quite sternly, then said, "Mr. Totten has faith. He believes in Hebrews 11:1, the Scripture verse that says: 'Now faith is the assurance of things hoped for, the conviction of things not seen.' The Lord will help people like that—people who do not doubt."

"But how?" I wanted to know. "God has never helped me or answered any of my prayers."

"Oh, yes he has," said my mother. "He gave you a good mind so you could graduate with honors. He gave you a healthy body. He's given you more blessings than you could ever count."

But I still didn't fully understand. I wondered if I'd ever have the same feelings about God that my mother did.

At the breakfast table the following morning, my mother said, "Marion, as soon as you have eaten, I want you to go back to Mr. Totten's."

"Why?" I asked, trying to shake the sleep from my tired eyes.

"I want you to repair his roof."

"What!" I exclaimed in disbelief. "I can't!"

"Oh, yes you can," Mom replied. "Didn't you help your father put on shingles when we reroofed our house last summer?"

"But who's going to pay me— and how much?" I asked.

"You'll get paid," my mother said emphatically. She went on to explain that the best kind of pay is not always money, and she promised I would never regret it. She said my pay would consist in a feeling that I had done a good deed, something I would always be proud of and would always remember.

It didn't make much sense to me then, but I put on a pair of sneakers, got one of my father's hammers, and started down the street to Mr. Totten's.

I remember Mr. Totten came out onto the porch when I walked up the sidewalk. I explained to him that my mother had sent me to repair his roof, and I told him about my experience in roofing.

"Your ma is a real Christian!" he exclaimed. Then he told me where I could find a ladder, nails, and shingles.

I was thankful that the roof wasn't very steep, and it was easy to see where I needed to place new shingles. Mr. Totten stood in the yard and watched as I worked.

"Be careful, and don't slip," he called. "God will help you if you put your trust in him."

I was about finished when Mr. Totten asked, "Did I ever tell you I was once a schoolteacher?"

"I don't think so," I answered.

"It's a noble profession," he said. "I have a feeling you'd make a good teacher because you're so kind and thoughtful of others. Children would really love you."

There go those feelings again, I thought, and from someone besides my mother. But he had given me something to think about. After graduation I hadn't been sure what lay ahead—but now I had an idea.

After I finished with the shingles, I put away the ladder and what was left of the nails and shingles. Then I started for home.

"Wait a moment, Marion," Mr. Totten called.

I turned and watched as he came off the front porch.

"What do I owe you?" he asked, fumbling in his pocket for his billfold.

"Not a cent, Mr. Totten."

For a moment he was silent, then in a shaky voice, he said, "What a wonderful Christian act. The Lord will surely bless you and your mom for this."

As I turned once more to go, he said, "I'll be praying that God will always guide your steps, Marion."

I guess he put it simply so a boy like me could understand, and now I did. As I walked home a lot of things that had been dim and far-off were now plain and clear.

When I got home, Mom asked, "Did you take care of the roof? What did Mr. Totten say?"

"Oh, he was real glad about the roofing. He said the Lord will reward us for this Christian act."

My mother was silent for a moment as though pondering what I had said, and then she asked, "Are you glad you repaired Mr. Totten's roof?"

"Yes, Mom. I feel good about it now."

And through the years I have. Both Mr. Totten and my mother have gone to their final rest now. Sometimes I walk  down the street to where Mr. Totten's house once stood. I stand in the street and think of the day I put shingles on his roof. I have always been certain that was the day I caught Mom's feelings. And when I start thinking of all the wonderful things God has done for me, my heart overflows with joy.

If a brother or sister is naked and destitute of daily food, and one of you says to them, "Depart in peace, be warmed and filled," but you do not give them the things which are needed for the body, what does it profit? Thus also faith by itself, if it does not have works, is dead.

JAMES 2:15–17 NKJV

I feel so sad when I see elderly people who are unable to do much of anything on their own anymore. I think about how it must feel to be robbed of the energy and abilities of your youth. I wish I could replace their rickety old bones and failing limbs with my younger, stronger parts. But since that is not possible, I pray, Lord, you will give them extra love and support and show me other ways that I can assist them.

Even a small gesture will leave a lasting impression on the heart of the recipient.

A Day to Remember

I'll always remember September 11, 2001. Everyone will. I was in school—seventh grade. The principal came to the door of our classroom with a look I'd never seen before. I was in my world history class with Mr. Carr. I saw Mr. Carr's eyes tear up as they spoke out in the hall. Then I thought maybe his wife had been in an accident or something. We all had our theories. But the truth of what was happening was beyond our imaginations.

Some kids cried. Some just stared off into space. A couple friends and I started praying. Even the class clowns couldn't laugh about this. It was too horrendous.

That night as my parents watched the news and I saw the towers collapse over and over again, I started to get antsy. I wanted to do something.

I called my mom into the kitchen where we'd be away from the TV. I didn't know what I needed or wanted to do. I just knew I couldn't keep sitting around. My mom wasn't sure what I meant. "You're too young to give blood," she told me. Yeah, I was always too young.

"There HAS to be something I can do," I insisted.

I spent the rest of the evening in my room. I fell asleep praying for the souls who were lost, for the families left behind, and that I might find a way to contribute.

"I'm going to have a bake sale!" I announced as I ran downstairs the next morning. My mom was a little skeptical, but I was very determined. I just knew in my heart it was what God wanted me to do. I called the city council and they gave me a spot at the farmer's market the next week.

I had my bake sale. I raised more than $300 and gave it to the Red Cross.

I'll always remember September 11, 2001. And I'll remember that by praying hard and listening for God's response, I did something that made a difference.

I the Lord test the mind and search the heart,
to give to all according to their ways,
according to the fruit of their doings.
JEREMIAH 17:10

❖   ❖   ❖

But you, take courage! Do not let your hands be weak, for your work shall be rewarded.

2 CHRONICLES 15:7

❖   ❖   ❖

God,
I know you are a powerful God and are responsible for all your children here on Earth. You look after us, assist us, and protect us. I want to help you with your mission of peace. Help me find ways to make the world safe from hatred. Show me ways that I can make a difference.

❖   ❖   ❖

I don't know what your destiny will be, but one thing I know: the only ones among you who will really be happy are those who have sought and found how to serve.

DR. ALBERT SCHWEITZER

❖　❖　❖

Learning Lessons
from a Child

I used to think there was nothing I could do to be of use to
anyone else.

But then a child came before me at a trying time and asked,
"Why do you have tears, and can I help you make them
go away?"

My sorrows seemed insignificant at the concern of this small
being. And I replied, "Why I cried is not important now,
and you definitely made my tears go away."

❖　❖　❖

And now may the Lord show kindness and truth to you.
I also will repay you this kindness, because you have
done this thing.

2 Samuel 2:6 NKJV

Feeling Like a Princess

I was 13 years old when my grandparents and I fled our Soviet-occupied country, Hungary, into neighboring Austria, with no possessions but the clothes on our backs. We were soon transported to a Displaced Persons Camp where we joined other refugees. The year was 1947.

Our new home, DP Camp Spittal, was a self-contained world of barracks lined up as far as the eye could see. Even though the camp was cramped and dismal, it was still an improvement over the life we had known in our war-torn country over the past six years. At least we had a roof over our heads, we were fed every day, and we were clothed from the donations of apparel that arrived regularly from the United States and other countries.

Since most of us in the camp had no money to speak of, we especially looked forward to the clothing distribution, which usually took place in the spring and fall. And if the clothes came from America, we fingered them in awe, for that is where most of us hoped to immigrate.

Of course the clothes were not new, but they were clean, and we were grateful to get them. Because we were equal in our hand-me-downs, no one eclipsed anyone else in the camp. Until the fall of 1950, that is, when providence allowed me—a teenage refugee resigned to not having anything nice—to shine for a little while.

We lined up at the distribution center as usual for our winter garments. The person in charge appeared with an announcement: "This year a rich lady in America donated something rare to the refugee effort: a beautiful multicolored fur coat in a young girl's size." He held up the coat so everyone could see it. "Oohs" and "aahs" could be heard throughout the crowd.

"Since we have only one coat and many young girls, we've decided to have a drawing for it. Girls can come up and try on the coat, and if it fits they will write their name on a piece of paper and drop it into this box. Then we will draw the name of one lucky recipient."

"That coat looks like it will fit you perfectly, Renie," said my grandmother, who was standing next to me in the crowd. "Go try it on and put your name in the box." I walked up and did just that. The coat was soft and plush and beautiful, and my heart ached to own it. Of course, every girl there felt the same way.

Finally, after a long wait, a small girl reached into the box and drew a name.

"Renie Szilak," the man in charge shouted, waving the piece of paper in the air. "Come up here, young lady, and get your coat!"

"I can't believe some girl in America gave up this coat," I said to my friend Piri on our way back to the barracks.

"Maybe it no longer fit her," Piri said.

"But it's so beautiful. I won't give it up even after it no longer fits. It will be mine forever," I vowed.

Piri, who was a couple years younger than I, had become the closest thing to a sister I would ever have. We lived in the same barrack, and because her father was ill and needed her mother at his side, she spent much of her time with me and my family. Since we had all applied for immigration to the United States, most of our time together was spent dreaming about our future lives in our new country.

The winter of 1950–51 was memorable for me. I turned 16, and whenever I wore my beautiful fur coat I felt like a princess. When I walked to school, the boys who usually ambushed the girls with snowballs let me walk by untouched. And whether the other girls envied or admired me, I knew they couldn't take their eyes off me.

Eventually spring arrived, and I reluctantly put my precious coat in a box and stored it under my cot. I hated to put it away, but at least I knew it would be there for me the following winter.

A short time later our family received the news we'd been waiting for. Our papers were approved, and in September we would board a ship that would take us to our new country, the United States of America! I hurried out to tell Piri the great news, assuming their papers had come through as well. I found her outside, her eyes red from crying.

"What's the matter?" I asked, sensing what was coming.

"We have not been approved. They say Papa is ill with tuberculosis. Only healthy people can go to America," she replied quietly, instantly turning my world upside down. We spent the few remaining months glued to each other, but inevitably, the day we had to part arrived too quickly.

On August 1, 1951, Piri and I prepared to say our last farewell before I boarded the transport truck already filling up with departing refugees. The truck was to take us to Salzburg, where our vaccinations would be updated before we'd go on to the Port of Bremen, Germany, to board the ship taking us to our new country.

"Don't forget me. Write to me," Piri said, holding on to me while tears rolled down her pale cheeks. Her mother, standing next to her, was crying, too. That's when it really hit me: We would never see each other again, and they were being left behind while we were starting a new life in a wonderful new country. I knew in that instant I had to do something to ease my best friend's pain. I broke away and ran after Grandfather, who was boarding the truck with a large box in his hand. I yanked the box away without an explanation and raced back to Piri's side.

"I want you to have the coat, and I want you to know I will never forget you. How can I forget the little sister that I love?" I said, shoving the box into her hands.

"But you said you would never give up the coat," Piri stammered.

"I'm not giving it up—I'm passing it on to my little sister," I said, tears welling up in my eyes. Then I ran to climb aboard the truck, which was about to drive away.

I will never forget the expression on Piri's face as she stood there teary-eyed, clutching the box, teetering between sadness and glee. It was the moment when I, a mostly selfish 17-year-old, discovered the joy of giving. I knew that the gift of a coat was trivial compared to the gift of liberty, but at the time it was the only thing I had to give.

It was mid-November by the time we had a permanent address I could send to Piri. I received her joyous reply a few days before Christmas 1951, and she also enclosed a photo. It showed a girl with long, curly black hair and a beaming smile. She wore a beautiful multicolored fur coat, and she looked just like a real princess in it. And that made my heart glad.

D o not worry about your life, what you will eat or what you will drink, or about your body, what you will wear. Is not life more than food, and the body more than clothing?

MATTHEW 6:25

A Hunch About Lunch

When I got to my high school, everything was really cool. It was a new building that even had air-conditioning! The teachers were great, the lockers big, and the homework small. There was just one thing that was weird. The lunch period was really short. *Really* short. I'm not a slow eater, and I pack my lunch, but I still didn't have time to sit down, relax a minute, say "hi" to a couple friends, and eat.

This frustrated me greatly, and I don't like to be frustrated. I have this driving need to get to the bottom of things. So I scheduled an appointment with the principal. My friends thought I was nuts. I just felt I was doing what was right.

My parents, my pastor, and my Lord have always taught me to speak up when I question something and to try and make a difference in this world. So that's become a part of who I am.

I felt a bit like the tin man in *The Wizard of Oz* walking down the corridor with Dorothy and the cowardly lion to see the Wizard as I walked the path to Ms. Johnson's office that morning. People rarely made voluntary appointments with her—usually it was more of a command performance.

But in I went. "Why is the lunch period so short?" She was surprised by my question. She gave me a studied look. She didn't reply for quite a while.

"Mr. Dawson, no one's ever asked me that before. I don't know!"

Turns out it was like that because no one had ever questioned it! I met with Ms. Johnson several times after that, and she agreed to lengthen the lunch period if I would agree to help with the rescheduling of some of the other activities that would be affected.

It was a little thing, and yet it was a big thing. It taught me once again that God helps those of us who speak out, ask questions, and help ourselves!

Maybe I didn't bring about world peace, but it gives me a good feeling to know that I made lunch at our school a nicer experience. And eventually, who knows? A little faith and a little courage can go a long way!

Life is what you make it. Customize it!

❖   ❖   ❖

Helping from the Heart

I wanted to make a difference. I asked the Lord to help me find the path in life where I could do the most good. There is so much hunger, homelessness, violence—so many problems that need to be addressed.

I was driving my mom absolutely crazy trying to come up with a volunteer activity. I kept trying things and quitting.

I worked at the humane society for a few weeks. Too many allergies. I worked at the food bank. The boxes of canned goods were too heavy. I worked at the soup kitchen, but I'm a lousy cook and the hours interfered with my homework.

I was hounding my priest for ideas. He kept telling me to be patient. That it was wonderful to want to help and that I'd know when I'd found my calling.

So I waited. And prayed. And waited. And prayed. I kept feeling that I wasn't doing enough. Meanwhile, my Mom had been going through this major spring-cleaning attack. She had piles of clothes and all kinds of things. She asked me to help her take it all to give away.

"Why don't we just have a garage sale?" I asked. There was a ton of everything, and a lot of it wouldn't be useful to the needy.

She was reluctant. "It's not right to sell it. If we're done with it, we should pass it along."

Finally, she agreed. I decided if I was to do a garage sale, I'd do it up right. I went around and asked all the neighbors if they had anything to get rid of. I asked everyone at church. I was really getting into it! I found some bricks and old doors to make tables for displaying everything. Father Mendez suggested I have the sale in the church parking lot as it was in a really good location for street traffic.

I put an ad in the paper; I handed out leaflets at the local grocery store. I loved it!

The day of the sale, I sold our stuff and everyone else's and made $2,345.75.

"What are you going to do with all your money?" everyone wanted to know. I smiled. I've always loved to shop at garage sales, and now I do just that. I hunt for things I think I can resell. I've been given permission to keep my treasures in the church basement and now I have my huge sales several times each year. I donate the money to different charity groups each time.

I've found my calling!

Each day, Lord, I try to assist someone in trouble, whether I tutor a friend or help a stranger with bags at the grocery store. I'm seeking your love and sharing it with others. I know these are not monumental achievements, but they make my heart glad. I think they make you happy, too. Please continue to help me find ways to assist others.

Personal wealth is an algebraic equation.
Kindness divided amongst good deeds leads
to two times the happiness in your heart.

Father in Heaven,
Hear my voice. I witness suffering every day in my neighborhood, my community, and my country. Since I feel insignificant, I am offering my prayers to you for the well-being of friends and neighbors. I may be only one person, but my prayers reach out to a world of hurt, despair, and loneliness.

He who oppresses the poor
reproaches his Maker,
But he who honors Him has mercy on
the needy.
PROVERBS 14:31 NKJV

The Paint Job

My whole confirmation class (well, there were five of us, anyway—we live in a small town!) decided to do something to help give back just a little bit to the church after everything they had done for us throughout our childhood. The classrooms were old and dingy, so we decided that we wanted to brighten the place up—make it livelier and contemporary. We went to the church board with our ideas to clean and paint the rooms. We presented a plan for repainting and then stenciling some Bible-related pictures as a border around the classrooms.

Although we were prepared to hold car washes and bake sales to raise the money for supplies, the board was so delighted with our offer that they volunteered the money. We were off and running. A couple of our parents planned to help, but we were determined to do this on our own. We set aside a Saturday to work. We put on the jeans we were anxious to splatter paint on (it actually looks pretty cool!), cranked up the radio so loud the Lord must've heard it, and we were off! We painted, and we painted, and then we painted some more! The walls! Our pants! Our hair! It was a lot of fun. By the time we got to the stenciling we were getting pretty tired and silly, but no one wanted to come back another day, so we kept going and just figured we'd do it kinda quickly. We also painted a big old cupboard that had been in one of the rooms probably since before the earth's crust cooled. Everything looked great when we stepped back and left it all to dry. We couldn't have been prouder of ourselves.

Sunday morning came, and we couldn't wait for Reverend Lynn to see our handiwork. We made him close his eyes while we led him into the room. He smiled . . . at first. Then we knew we were in trouble. His first comment was, "Did you think about your placement of the stencils?" Then, "And did you have permission to paint the cabinet?"

Basically, we had really screwed up. The stencils were supposed to depict the Bible, but they were horribly out of order. One of them was even upside down! (What were we thinking?) The cabinet, it turns out, was an antique donated by one of the oldest members of the congregation. She was not happy to hear about the painting.

At first we were angry. "They don't appreciate all our hard work!" "I missed a chance to go to the movies with Cory to do this!" "I can't believe they're complaining—we did it for free!"

Then we thought some more. We started with a good thought in our hearts, intending to do the Lord's work, but we'd gotten lost along the way with rushing, thinking just of ourselves, and wanting to have fun. I've got to run now; we're repainting today. I'm trying not to think about me, if I'm tired, or how I look. I think I'll concentrate on how the classroom looks, what God wants us to do, and why we're here doing it over again! By the way, I'm also looking for a good way to take paint off an antique.

*Don't make the mistake of setting
your goals too low. For once you accomplish a goal
you won't likely strive to reach beyond it.*

God,
I must apologize and at the same time thank you. I helped my wealthy neighbor with her yard because I thought she might pay me for it. I'm sorry for helping others only to obtain something for myself. It was wrong, and I feel guilty. But I want to thank you because she did pay me for my kindness—in friendship! She helps me with my history homework by telling me what it was really like, and she makes me homemade goodies to take with me to school each day. I am blessed to have her in my life, and I am thankful you showed me money is not the only source of payment.

✤　　✤　　✤

I've always been told to be kind to others and to do small deeds that will bring a smile to their faces. Well, today, Lord, I want to thank you for sending me the kind deed of someone else. I was the recipient of kindness and felt the warmth of it spread to my heart. I want to thank you for sending me such generosity. Please help me continue to spread joy to others in the future.

✤　　✤　　✤

To help one person with a minor task may seem like nothing to you, but it will mean the world to that one person and everyone else who loves them. Give freely, and give often.

Sharing

When I was growing up on a farm in north-central Minnesota in the 1950s, my family depended on gardening and berry-picking to supplement the family food supply. My parents, both immigrants, never had a lot of money, but our family always had plenty to eat. There were ten children in the family; I was the youngest. We all worked very hard, but our home was filled with love, so we had a rich life.

We had cows, hogs, chickens, and ducks, and we also had a huge vegetable garden. My father would sell cabbage, potatoes, and other produce to the local grocery stores and schools. Mom would can jars of berries for the winter, so we would have fruit during the cold months. We also sold some of the berries for extra money.

We grew some of our own strawberries and raspberries, but the best blueberry patch was about eight miles down the road, on government land. By the time I joined the blue-berry picking operation, most of my older brothers and sisters had moved on to other things, leaving only myself and two older siblings.

The berries were ripe during the heat of the summer. Once the regular chores were done, Mom and Dad would load us into the old family car and, during what seemed like the hottest part of the day, we'd head for the woods with big milk buckets. The berries grew best where the woods were covered with pine trees. On most days, the air would be still, and the mosquitoes would drive us crazy.

Like most teens, I got bored easily. The mosquitoes were irritating, and it was tiring trying to fill those big buckets with little berries. However, we didn't whine or complain; we just tried to fill up the milk buckets as fast as we could.

One day, after we'd been sweating and swatting and picking all day, my parents did what I considered to be a very strange thing, and it really bothered me at the time. My mother turned to my father and said, "I think we should give these berries to the family with all those kids. They're new in the area, and I think they could use them." My father agreed.

My mother was a kind, hardworking, religious person. At the end of each day, when all our work was done, she'd read to us from the Bible. She didn't speak English very well, but she taught herself to read it. Mother was always helping people. Not with money—we didn't have much of that. But she was always giving away eggs, vegetables, home-baked bread, and whatever else she could think of. Whenever we had company, Mother immediately brought out any pies, cakes, cookies, or bread on hand—even if it was just for strangers stopping by to ask for directions.

But giving away our hard-earned blueberries was another matter entirely, and it didn't sit too well with me. "Why can't they pick their own?" I asked stubbornly.

"Well," my mother answered thoughtfully, "because they're new around here. I don't think they know many people. And by giving them these berries, we'll make them feel welcome. It's important that we share our good fortune with others."

Of course later I realized just how much sense this made. But as a tired youngster who had just picked buckets of berries on a hot day while swatting a thousand mosquitoes, it didn't go over too well.

The people were shy about getting the berries at first. But they were quite poor and didn't even have a vegetable garden like we did. However, mother later saw to that, too. She shared all her gardening tips with them and even told them about the blueberry patch.

Later, my mother sat down with me and explained the importance of sharing. "All the wonderful things that grow and that we enjoy come from God's creation. It belongs to all of us. That's why we share whenever we can. I'm sure those good people we gave the berries to today would do the same thing for us with whatever they had."

Of course she was right. A few years later, my mother passed away. I was only 15 years old at the time. And those people she gave the berries to were some of the first to come over and offer their condolences. They brought some sandwiches . . . and some jam. It was made out of blueberries from the patch where, a few years earlier, we had picked berries for them.

When He saw the multitudes, He was moved with compassion for them, because they were weary and scattered, like sheep having no shepherd.

MATTHEW 9:36 NKJV

The Churn

During the sermon one recent Sunday, the pastor admonished us not to judge others by their appearances. I suddenly found myself transported back nearly 30 years before, when, as a young teenager, I used to go to town with my mother every Saturday afternoon.

Mother had gone into a grocery store to buy fruit, and I was waiting outside. I wandered off toward a nearby bookstore. Not wanting to worry my mother, I didn't go inside.

There was a large poster out front that read, "Famine in Africa. Please help."

I vaguely remembered hearing something about it on the news. I took 25 cents out of my purse and put it in a large old-fashioned milk churn provided for donations, thinking rather self-righteously that I was being very generous.

I then turned my attention back to the bookstore and started wondering if I had enough money for the novel I wanted, when a gang of youths approached.

They were dressed in motorcycle gear and carried their helmets as they swaggered along boisterously. Their hair was long and unkempt, their leather jackets were adorned with garish badges, and their jeans were patched and looked like they could really use a wash.

The boys were headed in my direction, so I made my way back to the grocery store, still watching them out of the corner of my eye. They stopped by the donation churn and seemed to take a great interest in it.

I was certain they were going to steal all the money collected for the famine victims. The churn was heavy, but eight boys would have no difficulty carrying it.

I thought about alerting the bookstore owners, but the gang stood in the doorway, and I wasn't brave enough to pass them to enter the shop. They were talking in an animated fashion, and I imagined they were planning to use the stolen money to buy drugs or alcohol.

Then one boy turned his pockets inside out, scattering a shower of coins into his hands. He dropped them all in the churn. One by one, his companions did the same, emptying their pockets into the churn. Looking satisfied, they sauntered off loudly, talking and laughing.

I felt so ashamed. I had completely misjudged them. They'd given all their money to the less fortunate while many well-dressed, respectable-looking shoppers had passed by the churn without a second glance. Even I had given just a meager donation.

On that Saturday many years ago, I learned a valuable lesson, and hearing those words from the pastor—"Don't judge by appearances"—brought it all back to me again. Those boys in the motorcycle gear made more of a difference than they'll ever know.

What's on Your Mind?

If time and money and people to help you were not a problem, what would you like to do to make this world a better place? Design your dream project. How would you organize it? What would it involve? How would it help your neighbors? Your community? Your country? The planet?

_____

_____

_____

_____

_____

_____

What can you do today to make this world just a tiny bit better? What can you do every day? How do you see yourself doing good in the future? Next summer? When you're an adult?

_____

_____

_____

_____

_____

_____

The Best YOU You Can Be

W ho in the world am I? Ah,
that's the great puzzle.

LEWIS CARROLL

Who are you? Do you like who you are and who
you are becoming? Being a teen can be tough.
There is so much going on! School activities,
extracurricular activities, after-school jobs.
Sometimes it just might feel like there are so
many yous running around that you're not sure
which one is the real and true you.

The important thing to remember as you
read these stories and complete the meditation
activity at the end of this chapter is that you are
an incredible creation. God has made you totally
unique; take time out to appreciate your special
gifts. Sometimes it's hard, but surviving the
tough times can help us appreciate and understand ourselves in new and better ways. So get
ready to start exploring an always-changing,
never-ending topic—being the best YOU you
can be!

The Real Winner

I was always the best—the best academically, the best in choir. And I'm the *very* best at clarinet. Last year, I won the all-state competition!

But when I got to high school there were a ton more kids, and lots of us were used to being the best.

The thing that matters most to me is band. I was determined to be first chair clarinet. My main competition was Sophie, a cute sophomore who was a really good player. I guess that's why I took an instant dislike to her. I had to play better than Sophie if I was to win first chair. So I practiced and I prayed. God helps those who play the best, right?

The audition took place during the third week of school. You can imagine how totally stunned I was when Sophie came over to me at lunch and offered to help me with the audition piece. I couldn't figure out why she would do that. I agreed to meet her after school, and we went over the music. I couldn't understand out what she was after. She did have some helpful tips for me, so I got together with her two more times.

The audition came and went. The results were posted, and, of course, I was the *best!* I won first chair over Sophie. YES! I was thrilled. The following Monday, we all came in and took our new seats. I was gloating away when Sophie came up to me with that cute smile and shook my hand. "Great job!" she said. "You really deserve first chair."

Jeez. Why was she being so nice? She seemed to be genuinely happy for me. I couldn't stand it and went over to her later, as she was putting her clarinet away. "What is it with you? I beat you out for first chair, and you're happy about it?"

She smiled that great smile again. "Hey, I wanted first chair. But it's okay, you know. You're really good. There are enough 'firsts' in the world for everyone. I just love to play my music."

I went home and had a long talk with God about that one. Seems that I might be first chair, but Sophie was the real winner in life. I prayed to learn to be more like her.

Please forgive me, Lord, I have become too self-absorbed. I have been so worried about myself that I have forgotten to care for others. Trivial things like tryouts and new clothes have taken precedence over family and schoolwork. I'm sorry. I want so badly to be good at everything and accepted by everyone that sometimes I get overwhelmed and lose track of what is important. Please help me to be a better person. Amen.

Don't worry about what others think of you. It's who you are in the eyes of the Lord that really counts.

Mask

I went through my early teen years wearing a mask. No, not an actual mask. In fact, unless you knew me really well—and it turns out there was only one person who knew me *that* well—you wouldn't have noticed. My family didn't know (at least I don't think they did). My mask was a smile. A constant, life-is-always-fine-with-me smile.

Maybe you think that sounds okay. It's good to smile and have a positive outlook. Well, yes it is. And I was very good at that. I always told everyone that everything was just terrific. I never wanted anything, and I never needed anything. The problem was that deep inside I wasn't usually smiling. I was really sad. I felt empty. I wasn't sure if what I was feeling was "normal" or not.

I wish I could tell you that I figured all this out by myself. About the mask and all, I mean. But it was really the youth pastor of my church, Nancy. One day during my junior year, Nancy was driving our youth group to a teen prayer group. I told her that even though I wasn't feeling very cheery, I'd paste my smile on. "Why?" she asked, "That's not real."

I didn't know what to say to that. I didn't want to be fake in any way. I just thought you were always supposed to be happy. Guess I didn't think people would like and accept the *real* me. The me that cries and gets upset and screams into his pillow. Of course, there's also the me that laughs until I think I'm gonna burst and is funny as can be. I'd kept him a secret, too, I guess. It's not always easy taking off the mask, and I still don't always do it with everyone. But always with Pastor Nancy. After all, she's the one who spotted the real me running away!

I am my own person. I will not become something I'm not just to get someone to like me. I will not sacrifice my values. I will not hurt others' feelings just to get a laugh. I will not disrespect my elders, and I won't be negative about myself. These are my own personal commandments, and though it may be hard, I ask you, Lord, to help me abide by them. Amen.

To love oneself is the beginning of a life-long romance.
OSCAR WILDE

Show passion for what you believe.
Express love to family members and friends.
Live honestly without hidden agendas or ulterior motives.
Live your life as YOU, not for or as anybody else.

The Dance of Life

I started dancing not long after I started walking, or so they tell me. When I was little, everyone said I was really cute with my little tutu and my shy smile. At my very first recital, I was the star of the show. I had the time of my life.

And it's gotten even better since then!

I used to always dance around. I got in constant trouble in Sunday school because I wouldn't sit still. After sitting all week in regular school, it was just too much. Finally, the minister asked me to dance on Sunday, and I was hooked. I'd "interpret" the week's Bible lesson in dance. I was a big draw for the Sunday crowds.

Then I got older and didn't want to do the cute stuff anymore. I got more serious about my dance study and about the spirituality connected with my passion. My parents took me aside one day and said that I needed to be more social. They wanted me to try some other activities. They were worried that I was too much of a loner.

That really made me mad. I quit dance totally. I participated in whatever sport they signed me up for. I tried gymnastics and especially liked the balance beam and floor exercise because they allowed me to use my dance training. Dance did help me in every physical endeavor. I have great balance and a good sense of timing from all those years of ballet.

Still it wasn't the same for me. When I'd get upset, I'd go to my room and put on music—any kind of music—and dance around. I have a giant stuffed panda bear who was my favorite partner.

I supposed my parents were right in suggesting I try other things. I've always known that I didn't want to be a professional dancer. But as I got to be a teenager, I realized that I needed dance. Ballet is at the core of who I am in some way I don't quite understand yet. It's like dancing is a form of prayer for me. It's the way I can get close to God and to myself. I find answers when I dance.

I don't go to dance class every day anymore, just on Saturdays. It gives me time to do my schoolwork and participate in other activities. Yet it's enough to keep me centered and on the right track. Whenever I have a problem, all I have to do is dance. It's like God flowing through me.

Praise the Lord for courage and strength. Thank the Lord for willpower and independence. Be grateful for support and guidance. For if it were not for these gifts from the Lord, I could not be the person I want to become.

May he grant you your heart's desire, and fulfill all your plans.

PSALM 20:4

Yours Truly

"You're not going to believe your eyes," one of my peer group members shouted, running to meet me before I could enter the student lounge. Everyone was laughing as she came behind me and covered my eyes with her hands, forcing me to walk blindly across the room. I was anxious to see the big surprise, and I was equally afraid that at any moment I would stumble into a chair, or even worse, a pole. It was just one more unplanned exercise in trust among this small group of people, and I forced myself to submit to her guidance though my hands were flailing and my feet were slow and unsure in their direction.

We had met only 11 days before, strangers to each other, but in that time, a bond had formed among us that we all knew would last a lifetime. It was an accepted fact that even if we lost contact with each other, the memories we shared would never be forgotten.

Summer Institute, or SI, as the participants affectionately dubbed it, was a type of summer camp. Yet it wasn't what most people envision when they think of summer camps; it wasn't swimming in the lake and classes in basket weaving or clinics in basketball or football. It was a place for learning and developing interests through courses not typically offered in high school. SI consisted of daily three-hour intensives in subjects including music video production, sign language, chemistry of the Rouge River, and creative writing. We traveled to the beach and museums, and we took introductory lessons in dance, American Indian folklore, and even Tai Chi. But the Institute helped us expand our knowledge and maturity in more ways than through classes and field trips. It gave us the opportunity to connect with different kinds of people—people we may not have usually associated with.

One of the ways we formed new relationships was through our "peer groups." These were groups of ten people who met each night to talk about school, love, friendships, and personal problems. These discussions were confidential arenas in which to reveal our true selves and get some support without being judged or criticized. Initially, I hated the idea of having to meet every night. I imagined the group would be therapy sessions filled with icebreakers and other "getting-to-know-you" activities. I soon learned, though, that our peer group meetings were not what I expected them to be. Many nights were devoted to playing games and laughing, yet just as many were filled with open conversations similar to the childhood game of truth or dare, in which we answered personal questions. It was okay to cry, it was okay to argue, it was okay to laugh or just to silently observe. Before the first week ended, we had already formed bonds through these conversations that would last far beyond the summer.

With my group, I was immediately comfortable and unashamed. I was able to act upon my feelings and express my emotions freely. I revealed more about myself than I ever had to most of my best friends at home. My new friends never failed to keep my trust, and they helped me feel perfectly at ease regardless of the situation.

So it was no surprise to me that night when my eyes were covered by Jenny's hands, and I had to depend on her to lead me across the room toward what could only be the unimaginable. Although I had only met her the week before, as with everyone else in our group, I felt that I had known Jenny all my life.

Much to my relief, we finally reached our destination, and I was allowed to see for myself what everyone else was laughing about. Standing before me was Eric, one of our peer group members, dressed in a skirt and blouse, sporting poorly applied makeup and painted fingernails. He had come up with yet another way to make our entire group laugh, just when we were almost ready to run out of things to tease him about.

Eric was short and wiry with a severe acne problem, and when he spoke his voice betrayed a telltale pubescent squeak. It was obvious by the way he constantly spoke in contempt of himself that he was too worried about his outward appearance and how people would react to his looks to focus on any of his good qualities. Yet it was difficult for our group to understand Eric's failure to acknowledge his own wonderful traits—how couldn't he know that he had a remarkable personality, great speaking abilities, and a sense of humor that appealed to everyone? He was such a wonderful person that we often forgot to notice his self-professed insecurities, and we made good-natured jibes about his quirkiness, his sense of humor, and his charmingly awkward personality.

But the night Eric came in with a dress on, and we began making fun of him again, I realized that we had all grown too accustomed to his outer actions and had forgotten that his inner self might be suffering. During previous conversations, we had learned how people at his school made fun of him for his looks and never treated him as a sensitive, feeling individual. Our group, on the other hand, had never considered his appearance an issue; through conversation, we were able to look at his personality first, and after that nothing else seemed relevant.

While we were teasing him about his wardrobe choice, though, I realized we had become so used to Eric as he appeared to us, we expected his self-consciousness to simply disappear. But of course nothing is ever that simple. There were times I could sense by the look in his eyes that he was uncomfortable and unsure. Even if he did things to make us laugh, sometimes our teasing went a little too far. And because we never meant our remarks to be taken as more than typical ribbing between friends, we didn't think Eric could possibly be hurt by our words.

Before I went to bed that night, I wrote Eric a letter. The words that flowed from my pen were almost beyond my control; they didn't seem to come from me at all. But I continued to write, sensing that this letter was important. I tried to allay the fears that Eric would never be loved, and I told him that if he allowed them to, more and more people would look past the thick lenses in his glasses and see him for who he truly was, the sweet, funny, clever person our entire peer group had fallen in love with.

As I wrote, I realized that the letter would probably never reach Eric's hands. My brilliant nighttime ideas usually didn't seem so brilliant when I woke up the next morning, so I assumed I'd probably just discard my scribbled sentiments the next day. But I finished the letter anyway, put it in an envelope, and sealed it up.

In the morning, when I saw Eric, the first words out of my mouth were, "I have something I need to give you. Come up to my room after peer group tonight and I'll get it." I had done it—I had to give him the letter now, there was no turning back. But why did I say that? I didn't usually follow through with my crazy ideas because they often involved the expression of my most personal feelings and, thus, a chance for me to feel foolish. It was always easier to simply not do something than to risk looking stupid.

I was scared. Now that I was speeding past the point of no return, I worried that I had only *imagined* Eric's self-esteem was in need of support. He was just a normal kid, and he probably didn't have as many problems as his stories implied. He couldn't possibly have that many worries or fears. But it was too late. I had already told him, and now I couldn't turn back.

That night, our discussion during peer group was about death, and it was the most serious topic we had ever tackled. The conversation opened a door for Eric, somewhere, and he was able to tell us about his battle with depression and attempts at suicide. Hearing about his struggles made me sure that he really did need to read the words of love and encouragement I had written.

My own concerns floated away after that, and I gave Eric my letter after our peer group meeting was over. The next day, I received a note from him, and I knew I had done the right thing. "Thank you for the great words of encouragement," he wrote. "I really appreciate your letter. It has already helped me in so many ways. I want you to know that the letter will always be with me and that when I'm low, I'll look at it."

Eric and I have been devoted friends ever since. If I hadn't risked my own embarrassment by writing the letter and then giving it to him, we may not have become as close as we are today, and Eric might not have realized how important he is to other people. He told me later that my letter gave him hope and renewed his self-confidence and that he wished he had been able to read those words before he had contemplated suicide.

This series of events helped me understand that every happening on this earth has a reason, even if we don't understand it. It made me recognize the importance of God's plan in every instance of my life. I also saw clearly that I have the ability to truly make a difference in others' lives if I let God work through me. God was the one who wrote that letter to Eric, through my hand. It was his insight in those words that streamed uncontrollably from my pen, and he was the force that spoke when I told Eric there was something I needed to give him. After I said that, I had no choice but to deliver the life-changing letter.

I can never know when something that seems trivial to me might end up meaning the world to someone else. Just as Eric learned to trust in the power of his true self that summer, I learned to put my trust in God and the plan he has for my life.

Simple Steps to a Happy Life:
Accomplish one small goal every day.
Forget your mistakes; we all make them.
Never hide your unique voice.
Always remember the importance of the words "I love
you," and never forget to use them.

Please, God, help me not only to think for myself but also to have the courage to make my feelings known and to stand up for what I believe.

not Such Great Expectations

I never expected much out of life. I'd made some decisions about myself and everything pretty much lived up—should I say "lived down"? —to my expectations.

I wasn't in the "in" crowd. I wasn't very good at sports or music. I just sort of squeaked by in activities and hoped no one noticed me. Sometimes I felt like the one thing I was really good at was being invisible!

I did do one thing, and I suppose I was good at it, because Reverend Glenn kept asking me back. Although maybe it was just that nobody else ever volunteered to do it! I taught the Sunday school class for the little kids.

Anyway, it was really a very simple and basic lesson that caught me that day and really turned things around for me over time. I remember quite well—the lesson was called "What do you pray for?" The idea was to get the kids to see if they ever pray with good expectations or if they are always just asking God to fix things that are going wrong.

It made me realize that I *never* prayed for anything with good expectations; I didn't feel I *deserved* good stuff. We asked the kids to do an experiment, and I tried it, too. It seemed so simplistic as to be almost silly, but it was quite revealing.

Every morning for a week, we were to pray when we awoke. Before getting out of bed! To say a prayer of thanks and then a prayer of expectation: expecting that the day would be terrific, filled with all manner of good events to help us lead a life of doing God's work.

I figured I should try it, so I'd be able to talk about it with the kids the next week. The amazing thing is that it made a difference! It was subtle at first, but I kept doing it and things kept getting better. It's become a basic philosophy of my life now, and I've found that God really does help those who expect the very best!

*Don't let the evils of laziness coerce you
into accepting less than your best.*

I'm at a loss, Lord. I want to do good by my family, friends and my schoolwork, but I don't know what I can do to make an impact in my environment. Please send me inspiration and energy to carry your ideas through. I want to contribute aid and assistance to your world—I'm just not sure how. Please help me to help you.

❖ ❖ ❖

Appearance Is Everything

We looked totally hot. Missy and I had primped for hours before heading off to the mall for an afternoon of recreational shopping. That's what we called it when we didn't really need anything—just wanted to shop for fun and to be seen by whoever else might be at the mall. Missy had done my hair with these cool beads she'd gotten for her birthday. I was really happy to be with her because we hadn't been friends for very long. I usually hung out with girls that Missy didn't really like. Her family had more money than most of the rest of us in my group. She dressed better than us and did a lot more things, like going skiing or taking family trips to Europe. I was surprised and pleased when she asked me to go to the mall today. We started at her house, and she did sort of a "makeover" on me. I was wearing more makeup than usual, but I did look pretty good. I was definitely planning to wash my face before I went home, though!

It was a rainy, yucky, early spring day, and we were hurrying across the parking lot from where Missy's older sister had dropped us off. I had my head down to make sure that I didn't step in a puddle and mess up the hem of the jeans Missy had loaned me. We walked about two steps before I heard Missy scream and the screech of brakes. A car of boys from our school sped through the huge puddle of water in front of us and came so close to hitting me that I fell backward.

"Oh, my God!" Missy came running over to me. I felt good that she was so concerned about me. "What have you done to my stuff?" She was going off about her CLOTHES! Her beads in my hair! She didn't even ask if I was okay. (Which I was, thank the Lord.) I was just happy to be in one piece. "I need a milk shake," I proclaimed. "Let's go in before they come back for a second run!" I was smiling and trying to lighten the mood.

"No way am I going into the mall with YOU. Just call your mom, and go home. And be sure to clean my stuff before you send it back." Missy turned on her totally cool heels and stomped off.

Wow. Obviously that friendship wasn't destined to last. I had never realized that in Missy's world, appearance really *is* everything.

I always feel like I'm the human version of the ugly duckling. I know I should be thankful for just being alive and healthy. But I can't help but get upset that other girls are so beautiful and perfect while I struggle to even feel presentable. My skin is far from clear, my hair does its own crazy styles, and I'm always so clumsy. I wish you could tell me why you make some of us so seemingly perfect while the rest of us awkwardly stand in a corner. But since you can't, I will have confidence that you will love me for who I am and reward me for simply being me.

Just a Little Job

I get straight As, I play saxophone in the marching band, I sing in the choir, and I help out enough at home that I always get my allowance. But I had been starting to wish I had more money. I wanted CDs and clothes and stuff for my room—things my parents couldn't or wouldn't buy for me. It's not that I needed anything. We're "comfortable," as Dad says. Not poor. Not rich. Just "comfortable." So when I kept complaining to my mom about all the things I couldn't afford, she told me I could get a job as long as I kept up with my activities and schoolwork. No problem! I'd heard that waiting tables was the best way to make money because of the tips, so off to work I went.

The first week I was exhausted! I wasn't used to the routine. I took whatever hours they wanted to give me. After all, I figured if I was going to work, the more the better, right? The money was great; I'd leave work with a pocketful of change. I continued to be tired, but I could buy whatever I wanted!

I stopped going to church so I could catch up on some sleep and then work on Sundays. I missed so many Sundays that I was asked to quit the church choir, which I'd always loved. I did notice that friends started asking to borrow money. Not my old friends, but suddenly I seemed to have new friends who wanted to go out when we should've been studying. They thought that since I had the bucks I should be buying beer and cigarettes. These new friends didn't go to church and didn't believe in God and prayer. Meanwhile, my old friends were too busy at home or with schoolwork or at band or church choir practice. It just wasn't working out how I thought it should.

But the other day, I came home from school, and my mom told me that my boss had called to fire me. ME? I was Mr. Perfect! I didn't get fired. Not from anything! Well, I'd sort of gotten fired from the church choir, but that was so I could work! My boss had told my mom I was too preoccupied with getting the most tips and not giving good service. He also didn't like the kids that had started to hang around when I was working.

I have to admit, I was sort of relieved. I mean, having a job can be a good thing. But only if you do it for the right reasons and keep your priorities straight. I like being with my old friends again. They even let me back into the choir at church. My old friends don't care if I have money or not. And you know what?

Neither do I!

Keep your lives free from the love of money, and be content with what you have; for he has said, "I will never leave you or forsake you." So we can say with confidence, "The Lord is my helper; I will not be afraid. What can anyone do to me?"

HEBREWS 13:5–6

Magnificence Within

As I wrap up my school years,
  I look back with both pride and regret.

I regret that I wasted so much energy
  on fitting in and being a carbon copy
  of my fellow students.

But I'm proud that I finally realized,
  after shedding many a tear,
  that I truly am magnificent.

Do not wish to be anything but what you are, and try to be that perfectly.

SAINT FRANCIS DE SALES

*If God wanted all of us to be the same,
he wouldn't have made us all so different!*

Raymond's Race

I first saw him in a crowded hallway at the high school where I worked. He was down on his hands and knees trying to pick up his books while a group of students were kicking them down the hall and laughing at him. Sadly, he was laughing right along with them. When he got back up, I noticed his right leg was disfigured. Before I could approach him, he disappeared into a sea of students.

I made it a point to try and find him. It wasn't hard. At lunchtime, he was eating alone in the corner of the cafeteria. We struck up a conversation and, soon after, we began a mentoring relationship. His name was Raymond Rice.

Raymond grew up with an abusive father. He contracted polio, which twisted his right leg inward at a severe angle and made it impossible for Raymond to walk normally. He was orphaned as a small child, passed from house to house, and eventually adopted by a family who lived in a predominately white community. His skin color was darker than most of the other kids, and that—in addition to his limp—made him stand out. Most of his life, he was the brunt of cruel jokes.

One day Raymond and I discussed the idea of life as a race and the importance of striving to win that race every day. Raymond confided that he didn't see himself ever running in such a way as to win. He didn't think he was capable of great things.

I'll never forget the day that everything changed. We were hanging out in his room. It was late August, and we were discussing what Raymond could do to make his senior year really count. He wanted to touch people, leave a legacy behind. We discussed some options, but none seemed valid. Then I mentioned the idea of him going out for the cross-country team. Silence. He stared back at me as if a knife had gone through his spleen.

"The cross-country team," he breathed, almost too low for me to hear. I couldn't tell if he was mad or just exasperated. "Yeah, right," he finally said. I dropped the subject.

Later that day I got a call from Raymond.

"I'm on the team!"

"What team?" I asked.

"The cross-country team," he said excitedly. "I just called the coach—I'm in!"

Raymond had told the coach that he didn't want to be an exception because of his disability. He would do whatever the rest of the runners had to do, no matter how long it took him.

A few days later, cross-country practice began. I knew several runners on the team and would occasionally run with the squad. I will never forget Raymond on that first day. He limped up to the other guys, smiled broadly, and introduced himself. I remember thinking that this couldn't be the same guy who, just six months earlier, had sprawled out in the school hallway collecting his books. The other runners looked curious but didn't say anything. The coach looked uncomfortable. Raymond smiled and began to limber up.

Raymond never missed a step of an assigned run. Day after day he was dead last in every workout—by a considerable margin. Pretty soon his teammates began to ask why he had joined the team. Raymond would just smile, shrug his shoulders, and keep right on running.

Gradually, the team's skepticism turned to respect. Not only did Raymond complete every workout, but he would also yell out encouragement to the other runners during each race. They seemed to get strength from him. If Raymond could do this with his disability, they could certainly do it without one.

On the last day of practice, the coach showed up with a grocery bag tucked under his arm. He loaded the team on a bus and drove them to a nearby lake. After the team stretched out, the coach called them together and announced that their last practice would be in honor of someone who had epitomized the spirit of the team. He pulled a shirt out of the bag and gave it to Raymond. It simply read, "Raymond Rice Day" and the date. In the center was a huge picture of Raymond with his trademark grin. The team applauded as Raymond put on his new shirt. When it was time to run, they insisted that he go to the head of the pack, and they let him lead the entire three miles around the lake.

Raymond had found his race and won the prize.

Self-confidence is the first requisite to great undertakings.

SAMUEL JOHNSON

Second Place

When I was growing up on a farm in north-central Minnesota, the county fair was always a big thing. Not just the rides on the midway or the cotton candy, but also the judging of the best pies, jams, and vegetables. My siblings always entered some things with the help of our parents.

I was the youngest of ten children, and I still remember the time when some vegetables I'd entered did not win first prize. I was disappointed, to say the least. But then my father told me a story that made me feel better.

My father and mother were Hungarian immigrants who came to America in the early part of the 1900s. (My father in 1912; my mother in 1921.) After working for many years, my father finally saved up enough money to buy a dairy farm in Pennsylvania. They worked hard on their farm, and they worked even harder after they started having children.

Since he had so much work, my father hired a teenager to work on his farm in the summertime. Jim was from a nearby town, and he worked on my father's farm to help supplement his family's income. As my father told me, "Jim's family didn't have a lot of money, but they were good, hardworking people. Your mother and I didn't have much money either, but we were able to pay Jim a little bit from the money we made selling milk and eggs."

One day my father had an idea about how to get Jim some extra money without affecting the work he was doing on the farm. "Jim," he said, "the county fair will be held at the end of summer, and they're giving prizes for the best vegetables. I've noticed you enjoy working in the garden, so why don't you register with the fair people and enter some of the vegetables?"

Both my father and mother were excellent gardeners, and they didn't get that way just because of the necessity of feeding their children. They actually loved working in the soil and seeing things grow. So Jim had good teachers.

The idea appealed to Jim, and since the pumpkins were some of the biggest items in the garden, he thought he'd enter them. "A fine choice!" my father said with a smile. "Pumpkins have always been one of my favorite things. Besides making good pies, they are one of the largest and most eye-catching items in any garden."

So, besides his regular chores (and there were plenty), Jim started giving special care to the pumpkins. He'd weed them more carefully, give them some extra water, and in general, give them a lot of love and care. And the pumpkins prospered.

"Jim," my father said one hot August day shortly before the county fair, "I honestly believe you've got some winners here. Those are some mighty fine-looking pumpkins. Especially that big fellow over there."

Jim beamed with pride. "Yes, they are nice, aren't they? I didn't realize they could get that big."

Well, the day of the fair arrived, and my mom, my dad, Jim, and my brothers and sisters (I wasn't born yet) headed for the county fair. My father pulled a small trailer behind his old Model-T Ford, and that's where Jim had his pumpkins. As he started setting up his pumpkins for display, he got to talking with a skinny young fellow about his own age.

"So what are you entering in the fair?" Jim asked.

The shy youngster answered softly, "Pumpkins."

"Why, so am I," Jim said with a smile.

"I have to win," said the young man. "My family needs the prize money."

"Yes, I could use the money, too," answered Jim. The skinny youngster in the patched clothes only nodded.

Now the prize money wasn't that much. Just a few dollars. But back in the 1920s even a few dollars went a long way. As Jim got to talking with the other boy, he found out that the skinny fellow's mother was to undergo an operation, which would further burden the family's finances. So this young man was banking heavily on winning some prize money.

As Jim began unloading his pumpkins, he noticed what the other fellow had. They were nice pumpkins, for sure, but Jim's huge pumpkin was without comparison and was certain to win first prize.

As my father came over to help Jim, he noticed that the big pumpkin was still in the trailer. Jim had placed a burlap sack over the pumpkin so no one could see it.

"What are you doing?" my father asked.

"I'll explain later, Mr. Kovach," Jim said softly. "It's just something I have to do."

And Jim did explain to my father later, after he won a second-prize ribbon for the pumpkins he entered. He got some prize money for that. But the skinny kid won first prize, and Jim smiled as he saw the ragged-looking youngster get the first-place ribbon and the prize money that went with it.

My father turned to me with a smile and said, "So you see, second place isn't always that bad." And he was right.

❖　　❖　　❖

Remember, it is rarely what you say that makes an impact. The actions you take are what make all the difference.

❖　　❖　　❖

Making a Life

Life does not just "happen."
You create life.
You happen to life.

Life is not just an existence;
It's a creation...
Your creation.

Every minute that goes by is a minute lost.
Don't sit back and wait for life to occur.
Get up and make your life—make a difference!

A good name is to be chosen rather than great riches, and favor is better than silver or gold.

ProVERBS 22:1

I want guts, Lord. I'm too shy. I won't raise my hand in class because I don't want to draw attention to myself. I walk with my head parallel to the floor. I couldn't even dream of looking directly in the eyes of my secret crush. I just wish I could be brave, just once, to know I actually have it in me. I'm afraid my teenage years will pass me by, and I'll have no interesting stories to tell my children and grandkids. I've never stirred up a debate in class or winked at a cute classmate. I've never smiled at someone just because I felt happy, and I'll probably never get up the nerve to try out for a sport or club. Please, God, surprise me with hidden courage that will prove my strength and instill me with confidence.

I hereby command you: Be strong and courageous; do not be frightened or dismayed, for the Lord your God is with you wherever you go.

JOSHUA 1:9

My Calling

I didn't want the job. The neighbor was a friend of my mom's. My dad thought I needed the responsibility and the money. I'd had the babysitting training class at the hospital, complete with infant CPR. But I just thought little kids were sort of annoying and yucky, not to mention dirty.

Of course I did it. The money was good, and my parents insisted. The kids weren't actually babies; they were five and seven.

I hated it at first. But it was easy and right next door, and I liked having the extra spending money. Then something really weird started happening. When I'd be outside, the kids would smile and wave, even run up to give me a hug. And I really liked that. I started going outside to play with them when I had really boring homework or there was nothing good on TV.

They say God works in mysterious ways. And I know it's true. I know he wanted me to realize how much I love little children. I thank God every morning for showing me that. I'm a pediatric nurse now. Every day I get to see those smiles and feel the glow of those precious hugs. Children are God's greatest gift, and I was so blessed to learn that helping them was what he meant for me to do!

The appetite of the lazy craves, and gets nothing, while the appetite of the diligent is richly supplied.

PROVERBS 13:4

Dear God,
I try to be kind to everyone, like my elderly neighbor next door and the "unpopular" kids at school. But my friends often make fun of me for reaching out to people they don't consider "cool." It makes me feel better to bring a smile to the faces of those less fortunate than it does to make my so-called friends happy, but I'm afraid to stand up to them. Please give me strength to be strong and stand up for what I believe in.

You can't change another person,
but you can change how you think about them.

❖   ❖   ❖

Sometimes, God, I feel as though my efforts go unnoticed. I try to be kind to all and assist others whenever possible, but when I do, it seems like no one is polite enough to even say thank you. I know I shouldn't do good deeds to receive recognition, but it's difficult to remember others when I feel neglected. Please release me from my need to be thanked, and help me continue to live the life you have in mind for me.

Since you are like no other being
ever created since the beginning of time,
you are incomparable.

BRENDA UELAND, *IF YOU WANT TO WRITE*

Secondhand Suit

On his way home from Clancy's Drug Store, where he worked part-time as a janitor, Kevin Swinney stopped off at the Community Thrift Store. He picked out a red tie and a white shirt, then tried on a tan linen suit. He wondered if anyone at his graduation would know this was a second-hand suit. It was made out of nice fabric, Kevin reasoned, even though it did have a hole in the inside coat pocket.

As he buttoned up the jacket and checked his appearance in the dressing room mirror, Kevin wondered if Rosemary would think he looked handsome in this suit. He smiled at his reflection. It was a modest smile that fit perfectly with his gentle blue eyes, his youthful face, and his blond hair.

Kevin was anxious to show his mother the new suit, but when he got home to his small, government-owned duplex, she wasn't there. Instead, he was greeted by a note on the dining room table that said she had gone to visit her ailing sister and had left Kevin's dinner in the oven.

Kevin hung up his suit, being careful to straighten out the wrinkles. Then he took a shower and shaved. He tried on his newly purchased white shirt and long red tie and then slipped his suit on again.

As he bent over to tie his shoelaces, Kevin noticed that something was inside the lining of his coat. He reached his hand down through the hole in his inside coat pocket and, after some effort, managed to pull out a partially sealed faded brown envelope.

Inside the envelope was what looked like a stack of brand-new bills, meshed together tightly with a band around them. At first glance, Kevin thought it was play money, but then he realized it was real.

Kevin sat down on the edge of his bed. He broke the band and ran his hand over a shiny $100 bill, and then another $100 bill, and then another. There was a whole stack of them.

"Oh, man! I can't believe this!" Kevin exclaimed. The bills were stuck together so tightly that he could hardly separate them. He was so excited, he couldn't concentrate long enough to count them. His hands shook as he began the count again and again. "Cool, man, keep cool," he kept reminding himself. Finally, Kevin concluded that there were a total of 100 bills there. One hundred pictures of Benjamin Franklin. "Wow, that's a total of $10,000!" Kevin shouted.

This is the answer to my prayers, Kevin thought. He could forget about applying for that student loan. He could pay his own way to college now.

"Money, money, money, I'm loaded," Kevin said. He had never seen so much money. He didn't know how to contain his joy. He could hardly wait to tell his mother, to tell Rosemary, to tell somebody. He rushed outside. He wanted to tell his elderly neighbors, who often sat on their porches in the warm springtime evenings, but it was the dinner hour, and no one was out.

Well, my life is arranged now, Kevin thought. If the Lord was willing, he was going to fulfill his lifelong dream: He would attend Castleberry University and study architecture.

He would marry Rosemary. And he would never be poor again.

He spread the bills out across his bed and counted them again. He picked up the bills and threw them high in the air so that it rained $100 bills all over his bedroom floor. "What luck! Oh, what glorious luck," Kevin shouted, as he slowly picked up the money.

But after his celebration, it occurred to Kevin that whoever lost the money would be looking for it. He could check the lost-and-found ads in the newspaper, or he could have the thrift store tell him who turned in the suit. Then he could return the money to the rightful owner.

Kevin took his coat off and searched the lining thoroughly, but he couldn't find anything else. Then he noticed the name Clarence J. Duggan, Jr., sewn on the inside of the coat.

Was this the brand name, or was this the name of the man who used to own the suit? "Oh, no," Kevin said, as a sinking feeling spread through his stomach. Had he discovered the owner? But he couldn't give the money back. "Finders, keepers" was his motto.

Was Clarence J. Duggan, Jr., a real person who lived nearby? Kevin had to find out. Still wearing his suit and tie, Kevin walked the short distance to the neighborhood grocery store. He checked the phone book and, sure enough, there was a listing for Clarence J. Duggan, Jr.

Kevin started to walk away but then went back and dialed the number. He could feel his heart pounding as he waited for someone to answer the phone.

"I'd like to speak to Clarence J. Duggan, Jr.," Kevin said when a woman's voice came on the phone.

"Clarence J. Duggan, Jr., is dead," she replied.

"Oh, I didn't know that," Kevin stammered.

"He died in an automobile accident in Las Vegas about six months ago. Who is this?"

"Do you know if he ever lost any money?" Kevin asked, nearly choking on the words.

"He bet on horses. He went to Las Vegas four times a year. But I'm not responsible for any of his debts," the woman said, raising her voice. "Did he owe you some money?"

"No ma'am," said Kevin. He hung up the phone.

Clarence J. Duggan, Jr., is dead, and no one knows about the money but me, Kevin thought. That settled it. He would keep the money and quit worrying about it. He went back home. He thought about eating his dinner, but instead he counted the money again.

In the eyes of the Lord, he was probably no better than a common thief, Kevin suddenly realized. This money didn't belong to him. The owner of the money was dead, but his wife was still alive.

Yes, but this money was an answer to my dream, Kevin thought. Only a fool would give it back. He could enroll at Castleberry University in the fall. This was the big break in life he'd been waiting for. *Nobody knows about it but me. That is, nobody knows about it but me and the Lord,* Kevin thought, correcting himself.

He looked at his watch. It was only 8:00 He put the money in his trouser pocket, combed his hair, and walked the two miles across town to the residence of Clarence J. Duggan, Jr.

It was a big house, almost like a mansion. He took a deep breath, adjusted his tie, and rang the doorbell. He could hear it chime through the house. No one seemed to be home, but just as Kevin turned to leave, a well-dressed, gray-haired lady answered the door.

"Hi, I'd like to speak to Mrs. Clarence J. Duggan, Jr.," Kevin said.

"Clarence J. Duggan, Jr., is dead, and he never had a wife. I'm Clarence Junior's mother. Can I help you?" she asked.

"My name is Kevin Swinney, ma'am."

"Are you the young man who called earlier in the evening?"

"Yes ma'am."

"How can I help you, Kevin Swinney?" Mrs. Duggan asked when Kevin seemed lost for words.

"Do you know if Mr. Duggan gave any clothes to the Community Thrift Store down on Main Street?" Kevin asked.

"Well, yes, after his death, I gave all of his clothes to charity," Mrs. Duggan said. "Why do you ask?"

"Do you recognize this suit I'm wearing?"

"No," Mrs. Duggan said, smiling. "Am I supposed to?"

"I found this down in the lining of this coat, which used to belong to Mr. Duggan," Kevin said, taking out the envelope and handing it to her. "It's all there, $10,000. I'm sure it belongs to you."

"Oh, my, come in," said Mrs. Duggan. Kevin followed her through the house, noticing its beautiful furniture and large chandelier lights, and he was invited to take a seat in the den.

"Are you sure that suit belonged to Jacob? We always called our son by his middle name," Mrs. Duggan said as she sat down opposite him.

"Look, ma'am," Kevin said, opening his coat. "It's got his name on it right here."

"Oh, my, this is Jacob's suit," Mrs. Duggan said. "I remember it now. That's the suit Jacob had tailor-made—he wore it to Las Vegas. And come to think of it, this is the type of stationery he always used," Mrs. Duggan said, taking out the money and examining the envelope.

"Oh, my, oh, my, this is hard to believe," Mrs. Duggan continued, "but it's so typical of Jacob. He always took a lot of cash to Las Vegas. And you found all this money in the lining of his coat that you bought at the thrift store?"

"Yes ma'am. I guess it fell through this hole in the inside pocket," Kevin said, holding the coat open for her to see.

"Oh, my," Mrs. Duggan said again. Her face turned pale, and her hands shook as she talked. "I was so upset at the time, I didn't go through his clothes very well."

"Well, I found out all I needed to know," Kevin said, standing up to go.

"This is great news," Mrs. Duggan exclaimed. "I've been wondering how I was going to pay the insurance and real estate taxes on this house, and now I can. I can keep my house, thanks to you. You're an honest young man," Mrs. Duggan said, walking Kevin to the door.

Yeah, Kevin thought. He often wondered about that.

I once was rich, but now I'm poor again, Kevin thought as he walked back home with his head down and his hands in his empty pockets. *But I have a clear conscience and the Lord Jesus in my heart, and that's worth more than all the gold in Fort Knox.* Kevin decided he wouldn't tell anyone about finding the money. He would let that be a secret between him and the Lord and Mrs. Duggan.

A week later, Kevin received a thank-you note from Mrs. Duggan with a check for $200 enclosed. Not long after that, Kevin received word that his request for a loan to attend college had been approved.

Kevin, dressed in his secondhand suit, graduated from high school, took Rosemary to dinner, and celebrated the news that he was going to college all in the same night. No matter what happened in the future, Kevin knew the Lord would always answer his prayers.

❖   ❖   ❖

All the days of the poor are hard,
   but a cheerful heart has a continual feast.
PROVERBS 15:15

❖   ❖   ❖

But the righteous live for ever,
   and their reward is with the Lord;
the Most High takes care of them.
WISDOM OF SOLOMON 5:15

What's on Your Mind?

If someone asked you to make a list of your special qualities—the things that make YOU you—what would you include? Think about the characters in the stories you just read. How are you like them? How are you different from them? You may be realizing more and more as you get older that life is a constant challenge. It's hard work to always do and say the right things. Sometimes, you might make mistakes, but as long as you're constantly trying to be your best, you're on the right path.

Use the space below to list some of your best qualities and some of your not-so-great qualities. Is there anything you can add to the first list? How can you change the things on the second list?

_____

_____

_____

_____

_____

_____

_____

_____

_____

Living with Loss

What we hold in our hearts, we can never lose, and all that we love deeply becomes a part of us.

HELEN KELLER

Loss is one of the hardest things to deal with in this life. Although some of us are so incredibly blessed that we grow into adulthood without ever losing a close family member, for others, it's a fact of life that has to be experienced very young. It's the price we pay for the incredible blessing of loving and being close to each other.

There are many types of loss. A good friend may move away, a new romance may end suddenly, a family pet may die. None of it is easy. We do the best we can to be there for each other and to maintain and strengthen our spirituality. We have to trust and have faith in the Lord. We have to believe in each other. And we have to believe there's more than this life we lead here on earth.

As you read these stories, remember that in loving and caring for each other we gain so very much that we will never lose. Each person, each creature that touches us remains within our heart—even if they pass out of our daily life.

Just Friends

I step onto the elevator in the hospital where my wife works and reach to push the button for the tenth floor. Someone yells for me to hold the elevator. I keep the doors open, and a young man steps inside.

"What floor?" I ask.

"Tenth," he says.

I push the button, and the elevator starts going up. I try not to stare at the young man but find it difficult. He appears to be in his teens, but he's very thin and completely bald. An IV in his left hand is connected to a bag filled with fluid. The bag hangs on an IV pole with wheels on the bottom. The young man glares straight ahead at the elevator doors, and I continue to sneak glances at him. I want to start a conversation but I doubt he'd be open to speaking with me, so we ride silently to the tenth floor.

The elevator stops, and the doors open. The young man makes his way off the elevator as I hold the doors open. I notice that his IV is leaking fluid.

"Excuse me," I say. "Your IV is leaking."

"So what?" the young man snaps. "I'm going to die anyway."

He exits the elevator, and I stand there in shock. After a few moments, I walk down the hall to the nurse's station where my wife is working.

"What's wrong, honey?" she asks. "You look upset."

"I was just on the elevator with a teenage boy, and I told him his IV was leaking. He said it didn't matter because he was going to die anyway. He looked so depressed—I just feel really bad for him."

"Oh, that must be Nathan. He has leukemia and needs a bone marrow transplant, but they're having a hard time finding a donor."

"What about his family?"

"His mother isn't a match, and he doesn't know his father or have any other immediate relatives. They're searching all across the country, but it's not looking very good."

"Can I talk to him?"

"You can try. He's not very receptive to anyone."

"I feel like I need to speak to him."

"Okay. He's down the hall in room 1013. Good luck."

I walk down the hall to Nathan's room and knock on the door. No one answers, so I step inside. The room is silent and dark. I can faintly see Nathan seated in the corner of the room.

"What do you want?" Nathan snaps.

"I was just in the elevator with you," I say.

"So what?"

I could see this wouldn't be easy. "I just wanted to come by and talk to you."

Silence.

"Is there anything I can do for you?" I ask.

"Yeah," Nathan says, "you can leave."

His harsh words ring in my ears. Even though I feel bad for him, it's clear he doesn't want to talk to me. I lower my head and slowly turn to leave the room. But in spite of my initial disappointment, I feel compelled to give it another try.

I turn back around and look at him. "Nathan," I say, "I was just hoping that we could be friends."

"What?" he asks, surprised.

I slowly take a few steps toward Nathan and notice he is crying. I open the curtain to let some light in and see that Nathan is holding a small book against his chest.

"What do you have there?" I ask.

"It's where I write down all my prayers. Every time I ask God for something I write it in this book."

"The book looks pretty thick. You must have a lot of prayers in there."

"Yeah. I was going to throw it away before you walked into the room."

"Why were you going to do that?"

"I was getting frustrated with God because he hasn't answered any of my prayers."

I'm not quite sure what to say next. It's easy to understand Nathan's frustration. I watch as he opens his book. He quietly flips through it, then stops on a page near the end. He stares at it intently.

"Are you still going to throw the book away?" I ask.

"No," Nathan says.

"What changed your mind?"

Nathan holds the book out toward me, and I walk over and take it. I glance down at the page and begin to read. The letter has yesterday's date at the top.

"Dear God,

I know I ask you for a lot of things. I'm not sure you're listening because it seems like none of my prayers have been answered. You know my situation and what I need, so I hate to ask again. There is only one thing I want right now. If you answer this prayer then I'll know you truly care about me. The only thing I really want is a friend.

Love, Nathan"

I look up at Nathan with tears in my eyes, marveling that God would use me as the answer to someone's prayer. "I'm glad we're going to be friends," I tell him.

"Me, too," Nathan says. "Me, too."

Dear Father,

I'm young, and I mistakenly thought I had my whole life ahead of me, but I was told recently that I may only have a few more years here. Cancer has invaded my body and is taking control. I don't understand how this can happen to me—I'm only in my teens. I haven't even graduated from high school. I try to be strong, but it's difficult when my friends start talking about the future. I don't want them to feel guilty, though. Lord, please give me strength to live each day to the fullest and bring happiness to others. I know it's tough on my family, too. So please provide them with comfort now and peace with my eventual passing.

Getting Over It

Emma, my big sister, had promised me. She had absolutely guaranteed it. But I didn't believe her. I just kept praying for things to be the way they had been. I didn't want to "get over it."

You see, when I fell for Steve I fell hard enough to break into a billion microscopic pieces. And when he broke up with me, that's just about what happened. To say that I was devastated is a considerable understatement. I couldn't fathom how Steve could possibly say good-bye and throw away everything we'd had together. As far as I was concerned, that was like saying good-bye to your eyes or your mouth or your... heart. It was as if molecules of "essence of Steve" had invaded every cell of my body. He wasn't just my boyfriend, he was my soul mate, a part of me. He was everything. We went to school together, went to the movies together, we even went to church together. It was as natural and right as a sunset, as comforting as prayer. I could talk to him about anything. He was my best friend. He was...

Okay, okay, you get the picture, I know. Maybe you've even been there yourself. If you have, then maybe you'll understand what I mean about Emma and her promise and why I didn't believe her. Why I didn't want to believe her. Every day since Steve broke up with me, he's been the first thing I think about in the morning and the last thing I pray about at night. Even though I know he doesn't love me anymore, he's still been stuck there in my cells, just hanging out, reminding me of what I had and lost.

Then today the strangest thing happened. I woke up. I showered. I got dressed. I ate breakfast. I went to school. I sat through calculus and Spanish and chem. And then somewhere around lunchtime, I suddenly thought of him. Steve. For the first time, it didn't hurt. But even more amazing, it took that long—five whole hours. I'd been awake for *five whole hours* without one single thought of Steve. He was vacating my cells . . . and my prayers had been answered in the best way for me to get on with my life. Emma knew what she was talking about.

Lord, I thought my boyfriend and I would be together forever, but he broke up with me today. I feel empty, lonely, and unable to face the world. Even though I know relationships don't work sometimes, I'm ashamed that he didn't want to be with me anymore. Please help me to know this isn't my fault and that someday someone even more special will grace me with his heart. Amen.

Flow, flow, flow, the current of life is ever onward.

KOBODAISHI

Callie the Cat

Wow. I miss her so much I can't even describe to you what it's like, but I'll try. Loving her has taught me a lot about life. I think it's helped me to grow up.

I've sure been praying about this. My parents and my minister say that loss is a part of life. That as you grow up you learn that it's the price you sometimes have to pay for love. It's a huge price, and for quite a while I just wasn't sure if it was worth it.

I found Callie when I was only four years old. Or should I say that she found me? I was at the playground with my dad and my big brother. They were roughhousing over by the blacktop when I heard the pitiful, tiny sound of mewing. I followed that sound all around until there she was! She was shivering by the swings. I could tell she felt small and scared, 'cause I felt that way sometimes too.

I knew I wasn't supposed to touch strange animals, but what harm could a little kitty do me? I scooped her up and carefully walked over to my dad. All I said was "PLEASE?" And Callie became a part of our family—a part of me.

I loved her so much. She was the cutest and the sweetest and the best blessing ever. When I thanked God for my blessings, she was always on the list.

We spent a lot of time together. Mostly on my bed, reading. We both loved to read. Well, I loved to read, and Callie loved to sleep on my feet!

She died three months ago today. I'm 16 now. Callie was with me nearly my whole life so far. The price I've paid for loving her has been to feel so incredibly sad and lost since she died. It's even harder because most of my friends don't understand; when they say, "She was just a cat," I want to scream. I've talked to God about this quite a bit. At first I was mad that I ever met Callie if she was just going to leave me. But the more I thought about it, I realized that what everyone was saying was true—it's a price, a trade-off, a give-and-take. If you never risk caring, you'll never know loss, but then again, you'll never know love.

I'm ready now; my dad brought home a new little kitten, and I wouldn't even touch her at first. But she's so sweet, and so small. I think I'm ready to love her. After all, it's so totally worth it.

An animal touches lives in ways
people never can. They sense sadness,
wiping tears with a gentle nudge.
And they never fail to greet you
in their unique way every day.

Glass Fragments

"I'm not sure if I can do it, Mom." I wasn't sure either. Being a pallbearer isn't easy for anyone, and it might be too much to ask of a 15-year-old. Sam's mother realized this and had reassured Mark she'd understand if he said no.

"Think about it," I encouraged. "You don't have to make up your mind right away. We can tell the Hewsons in the morning."

Although I didn't want to push him, I hoped that Mark would decide to be a part of the funeral. There seemed little else our family could do to share our friends' grief. Only a year ago, Sam's parents learned that his continual lethargic feeling was not typical teenage sleepiness but leukemia. Everything, even the bone marrow transplant from his sister Sarah, had failed to halt the relentless progress of the disease. In the end Sammy was so weak he could scarcely smile at the antics of Sox, his beloved hamster. Before his final trip to the hospital, Sam made his sister promise to take care of Sox. He seemed to understand and accept that he would not be coming home again.

"It isn't fair," Mark had said when he learned of Sammy's condition. Now Mark sat slumped in the living room chair, obviously trying not to shed the tears he felt like crying.

He glared at Wendy when she came cheerfully home from grade school.

I gently explained to her that Sam had died. Wendy started to cry.

"Oh, shut up, you baby," Mark snapped as he stormed out of the room. Lately, even when things were going well, it seemed impossible for Mark to be pleasant to his little sister. I even resorted to having Wendy sleep later so they would not meet at the breakfast table. Mark was convinced that she chose to annoy him at every opportunity. Even her attempts to please him were ignored. It seemed a stark contrast to the loving relationship Sam and his sister had enjoyed. I knew Sarah must really be struggling with Sam's death.

But obviously Mark was struggling, too. When I called him down for breakfast in the morning, he said he wasn't hungry. I'd heard him up several times during the night, so I knew he hadn't slept well. He looked worn-out when he came down for school. He'd made his decision: He would be a pallbearer.

When we drove to the church the following afternoon, Mark sat silently on the seat beside me. The gray November day did nothing to dissipate the despair we felt. The funeral director met Mark at the door and took him down the hall to explain his duties. The rest of us were led to seats near the center of the church. Sitting there as the soloist sang the first song, I could see the back of Mark's head. He was look-ing almost directly at the Hewsons on the opposite side of the church. I knew he could see Sarah crying. Even from where I was sitting, I could see her small shoulders shaking. At least she'd had time to show Sam how much she loved him before he died. Perhaps that would be a consolation to her later.

The priest's message broke into my meditation. He was talking about a beautiful stained glass window in a great cathedral. When a sudden, unexpected windstorm shattered the window, the scattered pieces of glass were carefully collected by the caretaker who placed them in a box in the basement of the church. There they remained until years later when the world's leading crafters learned of their existence and asked to reconstruct the window. The new window was even more beautiful than the old one. The priest went on to compare the reconstructed window to the glory of resurrection. I found myself wondering about the glass fragments that

might have been left behind when the caretaker originally cleaned up after the windstorm. Perhaps they were picked up and taken away by people who loved the old window.

Memories, like the fragments of shattered glass, were carried away by mourners who left Sammy's service that day. We carried the memories in our hearts as reminders of the special young man.

It has been several months now since Sammy's funeral. Winter is over. The bulbs buried last fall are sending new shoots upward through the spring ground. As the seasons have changed, so has Mark. Almost imperceptible at first, the changes seemed to start soon after Sammy's death, and now they're shown in a variety of subtle ways. Mark doesn't complain as much, and he's more enthusiastic about life in general. He says "thank you" more often, and I even get an occasional hug. But the biggest difference is in his attitude toward his little sister. Although they still tease each other and argue sometimes, a deeper, loving bond is developing between them. Last week, after Mark got his driver's license, he even asked Wendy if she'd like to be the first person to take a ride with him. Perhaps memories of Sammy, like fine glass fragments, have found their way into Mark's heart. And as he carries a bit of the vibrant glass, he's learning to let its light shine through him.

While we may not be able to control
all that happens to us, we can control
what happens inside us.

BENJAMIN FRANKLIN

Jesus said, "Come to Me,
all you who labor and are heavy laden,
and I will give you rest."

MATTHEW 11:28 NKJV

The Heavenly Bouquet

"Remember me . . ." she smiled and closed her eyes. I could almost see the bouquet beside her bed as she peacefully drifted off. She was already somewhere else. I stood there for a long time before it really hit me. My best friend was gone. My best friend was dead.

I still miss her terribly. Emily was the best friend I ever had. I'll never really understand why she was taken, but I've learned over time to accept it. I've talked to God about it quite a bit.

Knowing Emily changed me in so many ways. And watching her die affected everything I'd thought before about death. I'm not afraid anymore.

Let me tell you what happened. Emily and I were juniors in high school when she found the lump on her leg. It was an especially nasty type of cancer that spread quickly and killed her before the end of the school year. She was an actress, a singer, and a great student. She was beautiful—inside and out. And everyone whose life she touched was changed and made better somehow.

At first, Emily was really angry with God about the whole mess. I was, too. But somehow in her last few weeks, she began to find answers. Her eyes grew wiser, and her smile filled with peace.

"I've finished my work here on earth," she told me. "I just expected it to take another 70 or 80 years." Then she would laugh.

That last day she turned her head toward the sound when I opened the door to her hospital room. "Look!" she said excitedly, staring at the nightstand. "Aren't they beautiful? The daisies are my favorite—white and yellow. And the carnations—such a vibrant pink. Aren't they just heavenly?" She described a gorgeous springtime bouquet, but there was nothing there. "The angels brought them this morning."

I know that someday, hopefully a long, LONG time from now, there'll be a bouquet by my bedside. And I'm absolutely certain that Emily will bring it to me.

Dear God,
I pray today for understanding. I recently lost a friend. I'm still young, and I don't understand the logic of taking loved ones away, never mind someone so young. She was vibrant with life—an incredible source of inspiration. Her passing is a tremendous loss here on earth, but I'm sure her spirit will fill the heavens with laughter. Please take care of my beloved friend. Amen.

When sorrow seems unending, remember:
A friend lost here on earth is not gone forever.
You will joyfully be reunited in his kingdom.

✦   ✦   ✦

A Different Kind of Loss

My mom and I weren't getting along very well that spring. She was going through menopause, and I was going through adolescence; let's just say that most of our interactions weren't anything you'd want to witness! Then my brother, Ted, got called up for active service in the Army.

It was a strange thing. We had only three days from the time he got the call until he was halfway across the world, totally cut off from us. He had been living with us, working part-time and finishing college. He was engaged to be married, and his fiancée was at our house a lot, too.

When he left, there was an eerie silence in the house. My mom and I didn't feel so much like yelling at each other. I could see that she was both drawn to the daily news and terrified of it. I felt the same way, but I know it was worse for her. We all prayed a lot. At first, we'd just be on our own, but then we started extending our evening prayers and going to prayer vigils at our church. It was like God was moving back in with us after a long absence. His presence was comforting.

We sort of stopped yelling at each other, though neither one of us could totally stem the hormonal tides that welled up from time to time. We felt the loss of Ted's presence, even as we prayed for his safe return. It got us to appreciate each other more.

We made it through those tough weeks, knowing that Ted was in constant danger. He spoke the native language, and that made him essential on the front lines. It seemed that each day that passed we prayed that much harder, not only for Ted but for peace in a world where devastation has become all too common.

By summer's end, Ted was home. After all the celebrations were over, Ted went back to work and back to school. He never talked about anything other than what it was like to ride in a helicopter. He gradually became more and more active in groups working for peace. His fiancée left after a while. He didn't explain why. He just said it wasn't working anymore.

I knew why. It was because the Ted who had left had never returned. He knew too much. He had seen too much. My sweet big brother was gone forever. He had been replaced by a man who would never forget what he had seen people do to each other.

My mom and I never went back to our old fighting. We found ways to get along. We all were thankful to have Ted back, though we mourned the loss of his innocence.

Sometimes you don't physically have to lose someone to miss them.

For God has destined us not for wrath but for obtaining salvation through our Lord Jesus Christ, who died for us, so that whether we are awake or asleep we may live with him.

1 Thessalonians 5:9–10

All Part of the Master Plan

I was raised with two sisters in a happy Christian home by parents who taught us values and morals not only by telling us how we should live, but also through their example. My father was a hard worker and a man of strong virtues and beliefs. My mother was a beautiful woman who devoted her entire life to taking care of my father and us kids. We attended church faithfully, and both of my parents took active roles there: My mother played piano for the services, and my father was the song leader and the Sunday school teacher for the adult class. Our home was one of faith and unconditional love.

I was 16 when I began dating—and fell in love for the first time. Her name was Cheryl, and she was also a Christian. She had many of the same qualities as my mother, and that was exactly what I was looking for. She was a wonderful singer and was never ashamed to minister to our friends at school about the Lord. I loved her courage and watched with admiration as she talked to her classmates about God and invited them to church, even offering a ride to those who had no transportation.

It was Saturday, January 21, 1989, when all of our lives changed forever. Cheryl picked me up for a basketball game at 6:00 that evening, and I said my good-byes to my parents as I ran out the door.

We lived in the country, so most of the streets were pretty empty, even on a Saturday night. We came to a stop at an intersection that seemed to be deserted. But the next thing I can remember is waking up facedown in a ditch, alone and scared. I later learned that a drunk driver with a blood-alcohol content of nearly three times the legal limit had run the stop sign and hit our car broadside. He'd been driving in excess of 60 miles per hour and never hit his brakes.

Cheryl and I were both thrown from the car. I was thrown 185 feet into a ditch at the side of the road. Cheryl was thrown 165 feet into the nearby woods. She died instantly.

I was rushed by helicopter to Children's Hospital in Oklahoma City, where I underwent eight hours of surgery to try to repair or remove the organs that were injured and to stop the internal bleeding. I lost my left kidney and my spleen. Several of my organs were severely bruised. I suffered many broken bones—the most severe were my pelvic bones, which were broken into six different pieces that were found throughout my abdomen. Much to the doctors' surprise, I made it out of surgery alive, but in a very critical state.

Over the next three days, my body swelled to three times its normal size. I was on a respirator, and I had to lie on a plastic sheet because I was bleeding so badly. Twelve tubes going in and out of my body gave me blood, but with every heartbeat I was losing it through all of my wounds. In the end, I took 77 units of blood, which at the time was a record in that hospital. Infection set in, and my lungs filled with fluid.

Every day when the doctors arrived for rounds, they were surprised to find that I had made it through the night. They gave my family no hope, but my family had faith in God; they knew he could provide a miracle if it was his will.

My parents called on all their Christian friends to pray for me. We now know there were thousands of prayers being said on my behalf.

My father sat down by my bedside and prayed the most difficult prayer of his life. He said, "God, I love you, and I know you have a plan for everything that happens in our lives. I have had 16 beautiful years with my son, and I thank you for that. If it's your will that he come home to be with you, I will understand and love and praise you anyway, because I know your will is always best. However, if there's any way that I can keep him here with me, I'd be the happiest daddy in the world." I still get tears in my eyes when I think about that prayer. What a beautiful trust between a man and his Lord!

When I was taken off the critical list and was starting to awaken and remember what had happened, I began to ask how Cheryl was doing. My dad told me about Cheryl's death and comforted me as I cried over the loss of my first love. He told me he had attended the funeral to represent me and the family. He said when he passed the casket, he leaned down and told Cheryl how much I loved her and said good-bye for me.

I went through a variety of emotions over the next few months. I could not understand why God would do this to me. I had loved and served him all my life. Cheryl was one of the most devoted Christians I had known. Why us? I'm ashamed to say that, over time, I became bitter with God. I turned away from him, feeling that he had betrayed me in some horrible way.

I am glad to say that I've made my peace with God. And once I opened my heart back up to let the Lord speak to me, it became clear that he wanted to speak *through* me. God had given me a testimony that night. He had given my family and me a miracle, but I had been so clouded with anger that I could not see it.

My father once told me that God would never burden me with more than I could handle. When I think of it now, I feel honored that God felt he could trust me with this job. No matter what it takes, I don't want to let him down.

Making Memories Real

I was 15 when my dad died. Nobody expected it, but then again, no one was terribly surprised either. He was an older guy; my brothers and sisters were 20 years older than me. He drank too much, too, and that screwed up his liver and stuff. That makes me angry, you know. I sure would've liked to have him stick around longer.

The cool thing, though, is that because he was older, he retired when I was 14. Before that he mostly just worked all the time, either during the day at his accountant job with the phone company, or at night with a variety of odd jobs he'd pick up here and there to help make ends meet. So I hardly got to see him.

But that last year, we were always together. We did projects and played ball. We worked on the car and fixed stuff around the house. My dad had a gazillion projects that had all been waiting for his retirement. Mom was thrilled to finally see things getting done! He even went to church with us. It was kinda weird to see him bow his head in prayer. Made me feel like it was okay for a man to ask for guidance.

As we worked together, an interesting thing started to happen . . . something that had never happened before. We TALKED. My dad started telling me stories about when he was a young man. Not boring "I walked to school in the snow" stories—*real* stories about parties and friends and girls and the kinds of things you just don't picture your dad doing. Those talks were the best thing I remember about my dad. As we talked, I felt that I got to know a group of his friends. He described in detail the car one guy drove: a 1932 Chrysler that shot flames when he kicked it into high gear. I wasn't absolutely sure that everything happened the way Dad described, but it was very cool anyway.

Then Dad died suddenly of a heart attack one afternoon. As our tradition dictates, we held a wake, and all our friends and family came and sat with us for hours on end. I was pretty upset. How come God took a guy who had finally started going to church and praying every week? Just as the second and final day was winding down, a group of men I'd never seen before came in. They introduced themselves as old friends of my dad. I looked at the group and quickly began comparing their aging physiques with the descriptions my dad had given of his group of buddies way back when. It took all the courage my grieving, 14-year-old self could muster, but I went up to one of the men and asked if they were the friends who used to ride in the 1932 Chrysler. His mouth dropped open, and then he began to smile. "How'd you know THAT?" he asked as he draped an arm around my shoulder. So I explained about all the talks and all the stories—and much to my delight, I found out that they were all true!

I thank my dad and the Lord so often for those stories, for they brought me closer to Dad in a way I never had experienced before and allowed me to feel a part of him and his past. I am so glad I took the time to listen to my dad. I share my life history with my own son and daughter now and hope that one day they will do the same.

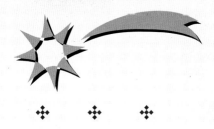

❖ ❖ ❖

A loved one's presence will never be replaced, but cherished memories will hold the empty spot in your heart.

I want the world to stop! No one understands what it is like to lose a parent. Everyone thinks they do. "How are you holding up?" they ask. Or they say, "Time heals all things." But it doesn't. They can still see their mom or dad. And everyone assumes I can do the same, but I can't. I'm so angry that my dad is gone and so frustrated that everyone thinks they have the answer. I know they are just trying to help, but I can't control my anger. Please help me to cope with this devastating loss and help me see that, maybe, someday I'll be able to smile again.

It's hard to understand why people we love are taken away from us. And there is no acceptable explanation for the loss here on earth. Just try and trust that in another time everything will make sense, and you'll be reunited again.

Wisdom at the Water's Edge

The summer I turned 12 had every indication of becoming the lowest point in my young life. However, thanks to the wisdom of a dear aunt and the beauty of nature, that particular summer provided me with a deep strength that I have drawn upon many times throughout my life.

Earlier that year, my parents had decided to end their 15-year marriage. The only home I had ever known would be sold, life with my father would be reduced to a weekend experience, and I would begin seventh grade in a new school. While all of these changes were terrifying to me, somehow that June, they didn't seem to matter that much. What disturbed me the most was forgoing our annual vacation to the mountains. Instead of spending the summer tucked away in the cool, verdant forest, I was going to spend the next ten weeks with my elderly aunt, who lived in a quiet seashore community. From what little I knew, the only friends I could expect to make were seagulls.

Needless to say, I did not want to go. I had never been a fan of gritty sand and salty surf, and though I loved my aunt, who was actually my grandmother's eldest sister, I hadn't seen her in nine years. I barely remembered her, and I sincerely doubted she would be much of a companion to me. But I had no choice in the matter. My parents were breaking up, not only with each other, but also from our home. The only thing they agreed upon that summer was removing me from the battlefield.

So despite my misgivings and protests, the very day school closed I found myself sitting on a train heading south. Beside me were two canvas bags that held my summer clothes, my books, and a daily journal I had been keeping since learning of my parents' impending divorce. My heart was so heavy with resentment, bitterness, and loss, I sometimes found it difficult to breathe.

When the train pulled into the station, I was the last passenger to leave my seat. The conductor must have sensed how desperate I seemed, because he patted my shoulder as if to assure me that things would somehow sort themselves out. But I knew better. My life would never be the same.

Waiting for me on the platform was Aunt Olivia. Demure, slender, and almost shy, she smiled at me, then hesitantly patted my shoulder in much the same manner as the conductor. I must have looked as forlorn to her as I had to him.

Poor Aunt Olivia, I thought. She was as much a victim as I was in this desperate situation. Her summer plans had not included a ten-week visit from a grandniece. I tried to force a smile for her, and I remember thinking how out-of-place she seemed at the station, almost like a young girl dressed in her mother's clothes. I was suddenly reminded of an old *Highlights* magazine from my childhood. Its theme was "what doesn't belong," and even to the most casual observer, Aunt Olivia seemed almost foreign standing in that station, like a baby seagull confined in a birdcage.

Hauling my canvas bags in the direction of the taxi stand, I trudged after Aunt Olivia, who moved with surprising grace and speed for an older woman. Fortunately, the line was short, and Aunt Olivia and I were soon seated in an old-fashioned Checker cab heading east toward the shoreline. In no time at all, the landscape started to change. With my face pressed against the window, I noticed that the city, with its tall buildings, traffic, and people, soon receded. Within a half hour, I sensed a hint of salty air and viewed a series of ramshackle bungalows bearing signs like "Bait and Tackle," "The Chowder Shack," and "Boating Supplies."

Three blocks from the ocean, Aunt Olivia directed the driver to stop in front of a small pink cottage. As I dragged my bags up the seashell path to the front door, I remember thinking that the house looked like Cinderella's coach, a transformed pumpkin. I tried to swallow the lump that was forming in my throat as I realized this would be my home for the next ten weeks.

Settling in with Aunt Olivia was much easier than I had anticipated. To her credit, she respected my privacy and sensed my need to be left alone. She didn't try to distract me with useless activity or engage me in meaningless chatter. Because the cottage was so tiny, my aunt had adopted a very simple lifestyle, which, looking back, was precisely what I needed at the time. Since the dwelling was so small, I slept in an open loft, tucked in the eaves. Every night as I climbed the ladder to my bedroom in the stars, I felt like Heidi. But unlike my storybook heroine, I had a view of the ocean, not the mountains that were so familiar to me.

During the day, I traveled using a rusty bicycle that had once belonged to my mother. For the first few days, I purposely avoided the ocean and beach, preferring to exhaust myself pedaling alone into the town. At the time I didn't think much about it, but in retrospect I think there was so much anger in me, I was unable to see, much less appreciate, the beauty of the shoreline.

By the fourth morning, I somehow found myself pedaling to the beach. It was a beautiful, clear sunrise, and while I had always been partial to the mountains, the seascape before me held a unique beauty. When I arrived at the beach, it was virtually empty except for two lone silhouettes—one feeding the  seagulls, the other fortifying a sand castle against the approaching tide.

Leaving my bike on the boardwalk, I ventured toward the sea. As I walked, I studied the figure feeding the gulls. There was something vaguely familiar about the stance. A natural grace, the fluid movements, almost an affinity with the sea. Then it hit me—it was Aunt Olivia. Dressed in worn jeans, a faded T-shirt, and a baseball cap, she resembled a young teenager from a distance. I recalled seeing her in the train station, stressed, strained, and out of place. Here, against the backdrop of the sea, pounding surf, and beach, she was home.

Although she did not turn toward me, she sensed my presence. "Have some bread," she said softly, handing me some crusts without taking her eyes off the pair of gulls she was feeding. As I crumbled the crusts, the sound of the gulls overhead, the scent of salty air, and the sight of the young boy defending his sand castle effected a calmness within me. I had not felt such peace since learning of my parents' impending divorce.

Long after the last of the bread was gone, Aunt Olivia and I continued to watch the boy. Finally, she spoke. "You have to admire his persistence," she said softly. "He's trying so hard to defend that castle. He's decorated it with beautiful shells; he's put his heart and soul into that project. But no matter how high the walls or how deep the moat he builds, the ocean is stronger and more powerful."

As she spoke, I watched the boy. The closer the tide came, the more frenzied he would get. His digging became manic, and his face was marked with apprehension at each wave. Finally, Aunt Olivia extended her hand to me, and together we walked down to the water's edge.

The boy looked up at us. At first, he seemed confused, but then I saw him smile. Aunt Olivia must have extended her other hand because the boy left his sand castle, stood up, and took her hand. As the three of us watched, a final wave crashed upon the castle, leveling it to the sand, destroying the walls, and flooding the moat.

As the seashells that had decorated the castle were scattered, Aunt Olivia released our hands. "Let's collect as many of these beautiful shells as we can," she said. "These shells were actually the best part of that castle. Let's gather them together. We'll use them to build a new castle in a more protected area." And that's just what we did.

Throughout my life, Aunt Olivia's words would guide me on many occasions. That day on the beach would help me countless times, as I fought to rebuild my life after forces beyond my control sent me into a tailspin. Years later, as I struggled to survive my own divorce, a corporate down-sizing, and the death of my best friend, Aunt Olivia's soft words often quieted my heart. And while attempting to rebuild my life, I tried to follow Aunt Olivia's example by taking the best of my previous existence with me, to ensure that each new castle I erected was a little bit better, a little bit richer, and a little bit stronger than the one before.

If we had
no winter,
the spring would not be
so pleasant;
if we did not sometimes
taste adversity,
prosperity would not be
so welcome.

ANNE BRADSTREET

I May Be Paralyzed,
but My Spirituality Isn't

In 1993 I dove into a lake and became an instant quadri-
plegic. I was 16 at the time. And to adapt to this new body
and life was the hardest thing I've ever done.

About a week after my accident I received a poster from
a friend. It showed a picture of a blue sky with a dove in flight.
And it read, "We cannot change yesterday, but we can
change what lies ahead." I loved that poster. My mom taped it
to the ceiling over my hospital bed, so it was
easy for me to see. Every morning when I
woke up, the first thing that came to my mind
was, "I'm still paralyzed. I can't believe this is
happening to me!" But the second thing I
thought, after reading the words on the
poster, was that my future was up to me.

It's essential to figure out a way to survive
when something happens to you that throws
your life off course. Some people choose drugs or denial,
and I didn't want to do that. So I continued to meditate on
the poster's message: Accept your life today because yesterday is already gone.

After months of physical therapy, I went home. My new
life as a person with a disability began. I finished high
school, made new friends, and reorganized what was important to me. I got used to being in a wheelchair instead of

walking. What was "normal" for me changed. And as the years passed, I began to think less and less about being paralyzed. Eventually, when I'd wake up, I'd think about what I was going to have for breakfast, not the fact that I would be sitting in a wheelchair while I was eating it.

Right after the accident, I prayed a lot. I asked God to heal me, to make me walk again. I specifically prayed that he'd heal me in the middle of the night. I wanted to be able to get out of bed, put on my soccer uniform, and walk upstairs to my mom's bedroom and surprise her. But that never happened.

Since God wouldn't answer my prayers, I finally stopped praying. I got sick of hearing about God and how he had a purpose for me. I decided I could take care of myself.

Over the next few years, I continued to feel better, move on, and adjust to my new life. I went to a private college where I did well in my classes, I learned how to drive

an adapted van, and I even had a girlfriend who didn't care whether or not I was in a wheelchair. But nearly eight years after the accident, I began to have more moments of pure sadness. Moments when I'd cry alone in my dorm. Moments when I'd become jealous of my male peers who had unbroken bodies. What was wrong with me? I thought I had come to terms with my disability and could live happily ever after for the rest of my life. But jealousy and self-pity were clouding my mind. At first, I figured it was just a downtime in my life. But the feelings didn't go away.

Then I remembered what that poster said: "We cannot change yesterday, but we can change what lies ahead." I knew I had to take charge of my future, but I realized I didn't have to handle everything on my own. God was just waiting for me to ask for his help.

I understood then that it was God who had inspired the poster's author to write those moving words. It was God who had given me strength and courage to make it through my ordeals and transitions. I'm not walking, but I am living. And I'm very happy to be here.

God did answer my prayers. He showed me ways to survive, and he was the one who comforted me when I was in doubt. He was there all along, pushing me in my wheelchair up that giant hill of life—I just didn't realize it.

When tragedy strikes, it's hard to believe normalcy will ever return. But have faith that with each new day the sun will shine a little bit brighter and the clouds will begin to fade away.

He heals the brokenhearted, and binds up their wounds. He determines the number of the stars; he gives to all of them their names. Great is our Lord, and abundant in power; his understanding is beyond measure.

PSALM 147:3–5

The Dance

"My dad wants you to tell your dad that he'll drive Friday night. Why take two cars when we're going to the same place?"

The words uttered by one of my classmates reached my ears despite the noisy chatter of three dozen other 13-year-olds rushing through the school hallway to their next class.

"Is your dad's car big enough for the four of us? I don't want my dress to get squished. We should . . ."

The second girl's voice trails off, and I know it's because my two schoolmates have noticed me standing by my locker. Their topic of discussion is the upcoming father-daughter dance, but I won't be attending. A father is necessary, and cancer claimed mine just a few months ago.

I pretend to be interested in my locker contents, thus giving the duo a chance to pass me by without comment. In this small, all-girl Catholic high school, I'm the only one who has buried a parent, and nobody, including myself, is exactly sure how to deal with this fact. Silence seems to be the acceptable solution.

Every year the school has a father-daughter dance. It's a fund-raising event to help pay for the extra supplies the school needs. The students pick a theme, decorate the gym, and solicit raffle donations from local businesses. There are committees for everything from setup to cleanup, and all students are urged to participate.

"I know how difficult this is for you, Jacquelyn," Sister Patricia says when she catches me gazing at a poster advertising the premier school event of 1967. "But life moves forward. In time you will be able to talk about your father without tears."

She's wrong! I cry myself to sleep every night, and I avoid the movie theater where Dad and I used to attend the cowboy extravaganza marathon every month. I worry constantly, too, but not about passing algebra. I fear I will forget the sound of my father's voice.

"Your father is gone, and you must make a life without him," Sister Patricia says as she points to the sign-up sheets tacked to the bulletin board beside the poster. "Start by helping out with some aspect of the dance. Sell raffle tickets or serve the lemonade."

I don't want a life without him! Why is this so hard for others to understand? I want my dad here with me now! We had plans, things we would do together...things that now will never be done.

Friday night I'm in my pajamas by 6:00. If I can force myself to sleep, I won't think about the dance. Then, on Monday, maybe I'll come down with some disease that will keep me out of school until the after-event talk becomes old news.

Suddenly I hear our apartment doorbell ring, then the sound of my Uncle Edmund's voice. Edmund is my father's brother, a bachelor by choice. Usually he stops by every

Sunday afternoon for a visit, but today isn't Sunday. Is something wrong? Filled with curiosity, I venture from my bedroom to investigate.

Uncle Edmund is dressed in his best black suit. At the sight of me, he smiles and remarks, "I hope you aren't planning to wear pajamas to the school dance. I believe something fancier is required."

All color drains from my face, and my throat tightens. I look to my mother for help, for her to tell Uncle Edmund I can't go to the dance with him. Yes, he's a wonderful uncle, and I love him, but this dance is for fathers and daughters.

"I figured you'd forget to buy the tickets, so I stopped by the school and picked them up." Uncle Edmund smiles at me. "I sneaked a peek at the gym, too. It looks great with all the flowers, rainbows, and stars. What's this year's theme?"

"Feeling Groovy." My mouth is as dry as cotton. Why didn't the clergy member who sold Uncle Edmund the tickets tell him what this dance is all about? "But I can't...."

"You're right," Uncle Edmund interrupts. "You can't begin to get ready until I give you the other ticket." From his front jacket pocket he takes out a small orange ticket, identical to the ones used at the movie theater. He hands it to me with the instruction, "Read what is written on the back."

I turn the ticket over, instantly recognizing my father's handwriting. On this ticket my father wrote: Good for one father event.

"Your father fought very hard to live, but when he realized he couldn't win the battle, he turned his attention to your future," Uncle Edmund softly explains. "He filled out more than a hundred such tickets and gave them to me to hold. I promised him I'd make sure you did with me all you had planned to do with him. That includes this dance. I spoke to your school principal, and she agrees with the validity of this ticket. Substitute dads are acceptable escorts."

Tears blind me. I can't move or think. Even though my dad is no longer here, he is still taking care of me.

Reaching out, my uncle uses a fingertip to wipe away my tears. "Hurry now. You get ready while I go pick up your corsage. Your mother says the dress you wore to Vincent's wedding is perfect for tonight." He clicks his heels together. "We don't want to miss the dance contest. I do a mean tango."

Uncle Edmund and I attended the father-daughter dance that night, and in the years that followed we used tickets that were good for one Broadway show, good for one prom dress shopping spree, and good for one high school graduation dinner. Eventually Uncle Edmund learned to like Roy Rogers movies; I learned to tango. In time, as Sister Patricia predicted, I could even talk about my dad and smile.

I don't think any child ever gets over the death of a parent. However, I consider myself lucky that my father loved me so much he unselfishly helped his only brother to become my hero. Because of Uncle Edmund, I was able to do many of the things my dad and I had planned to do. And even though Dad wasn't actually there with me, he has always been there in my heart.

A parent is supposed to care for and protect children. I am not supposed to be left behind. Why, God, would you take someone so important away from me? I don't know if I will ever understand. I'm jealous of other kids who have both their parents. I wonder what it must be like. I hope that someday you will be able to explain to me why all children shouldn't grow up with the comfort of two loving parents. Until then, I will do my best to make my dad proud.

Nothing can replace the heartache of a lost loved one. The only thing that will even come close to filling the void are memories. They will swirl around in the vacant space and prevent your heart from crumbling.

Our loss is our loved one's gain.
They walk in the meadows of heaven.

Many waters cannot quench love, neither can floods drown it.
SONG OF SOLOMON 8:7

Balcony Seats

I stand numbly as the shower water
>blends with the tears streaking down my face.

I try to move on with my life
>as if nothing is different,
>but once again my everyday activities
>have, without reason,
>brought about a flood of memories.

I remember when he'd sit Indian style on
>the floor to check out my new game
>or how he used to be the last at the
>dinner table because he talked so much.

How can I move on
>knowing that he is nowhere
>on this earth?
>How can I act as if nothing is
>wrong when my mind
>constantly wanders to
>his sweet face?

The only way to live with the hole
>in my heart
>is to always remember
>that he is happier now with his balcony seats.

God,
I must ask you this favor. My loved one has just been taken from me, and I'm trying not to be selfish, but it just seems so unfair. Please promise there will be no more pain, sadness, or discomfort for them. Shower them with the happiness they spread to everyone who is now left behind. Life as I know it will never be the same, but knowing that you will watch over my loved ones until we meet again makes the days a little easier to handle.

When two hearts are connected by love,
a physical separation of bodies
cannot erase the bond.

The pain is so sharp, Lord, I feel as though I am dying, too. The wound is so deep, the loss so final. Please help me to heal from this devastating blow. Show me that I can be happy again. Help me believe there is life after death. Amen.

Make Every Day Count

The county fair! We waited for it at the close of every summer. And the best time of all was "kids day," when all school-age kids through high school were given a free admission ticket! This year I'd gone with my family: my mom, dad, and younger sister. I'd wanted to go on my own, but my mom insisted we have a "family day." YUCK! Nobody ever went to the fair with their family—except little kids and me! I felt like I had a horrible burden to bear, like everyone was looking at me and laughing. Why ME, God? Pity party, big time! At least my sister and I got to go off on our own a little bit in the evening. We took Mom's cell phone and headed off to the midway. Sheri wanted to go off on her own, and at 13, I figured it would be okay for a little while. She wanted the cell phone, though, and I said "no way"; I was the oldest, I kept the phone.

We were to meet Mom and Dad at the gate at 9:30. Sheri never did. My baby sister left the fair for some reason. We'll never know why for sure. Outside the fairgrounds, she was kidnapped. That fight I had with her over the cell phone? It was the last time I ever saw her.

I miss my sister so much I can't even tell you what it's like. Now I ask, *Why Sheri, God? Why did you take her?* It's so hard to accept that she's gone. I talk with God about it a lot. And I will tell you that when my friends say they can't come to the movies or the mall because they're doing something with their family, I'm the first one to say "Cool!" I believe in family now in a deeper and more meaningful way than I ever could've imagined, and I sure do pray a lot more. I just wish my sister was here to share our family times once again.

God,
I pray not to be angry or place blame. I know we're all here for an undetermined amount of time. I've realized I must be happy with the time we spent together. But I must admit I fear for my loved one. I do not know what goes on after death, and I pray that heaven will be more wonderful than I can even imagine. Please promise you'll take care of my family departed from this earth and reunite us again when it's my turn to join you. Amen.

Give ear to my words, O Lord; give heed to my sighing. Listen to the sound of my cry, my King and my God, for to you I pray.

PSALM 5:1–2

New Year's Eve Prayer

New Year's Eve is a time for celebration, reflection, and new beginnings. My birthday is five days later, on January 4, so I have always seen New Year's Eve as the start of a celebratory week.

In 1974 I was 17, and I had just finished my first semester of college. My father, a retired coal miner who had never learned to read, was 75. At first, he didn't want me to go to school, but he eventually resigned himself to the idea. Every day, I came home and told him stories about my courses and my classmates. I filled him in on my projects and told him about the papers I was working on. Even though he didn't come out and say it, I got the feeling my father was proud of my accomplishments. His health was failing, and we seemed to have resolved some of the conflicts that had plagued my high-school years. Maybe both of us knew that our time together was growing short.

On New Year's Eve 1974, we spent the day watching television. I ordered a cake for my upcoming birthday and talked to some of my friends. That evening, I sat on the arm of the vinyl recliner and looked wistfully out the living room window. Nearby, my father sat up in his hospital bed. Due to an old mining injury that affected his legs, as well as the progressive deterioration caused by black lung, he could no longer climb the stairs to his bedroom. He was able to get from the bed to his wheelchair, but that was the extent of his mobility. I spent my spare time taking care of him. Sometimes I felt as trapped as he did in his chair.

I sighed as I watched passing cars go down the street. "Maybe you'll get to go to a party next year," my father said.

"Maybe," I answered sadly.

We stayed up until midnight, then I kissed his cheek, wished him "Happy New Year," and went upstairs to my bedroom. In my room, I got on my knees and asked God to help my father and ease his pain.

About a year later, on December 27, 1975, I went to visit my father in the hospital. He could barely talk, but I was able to make him smile. As I left, I kissed his cheek. "I love you," I said. "See you tomorrow." He waved weakly as I left his room in the ICU.

That night, my father died. Due to black lung and pneumonia, his lungs could no longer get rid of the fluid and coal dust that had infiltrated them. His funeral was on December 31—New Year's Eve. It rained all day, and the ground was wet as he was laid to rest next to my mother, his wife of 50 years. After five years apart, they were back together again.

Even though friends and relatives offered to stay with me that night, I wanted to be alone. The house was still alive with my father's essence. When I saw the monogrammed cup I had gotten him, his favorite drinking cup, I started to cry. I looked out the living room window and thought about the conversation I'd had with my father the year before. There was no party this year. Instead, there had been a gathering of family and friends, people coming together to say good-bye.

My mother had died when I was 13, and I was an only child. So now I was all alone in an eight-room house, facing my 19th birthday. I looked at the watch on my wrist, the watch that I had bought my father in September for his 76th birthday. He was wearing the watch when he died. When the hands showed midnight, I got on my knees and prayed. I prayed for my father, who was now out of his misery. And I prayed for my future, asking God to help me make it alone.

I woke up the next morning filled with hope. It was a new year and a new beginning.

A year later, on December 31, 1976, my cousin and I had a New Year's Eve party at my house. We laughed and danced and had a great time celebrating with our friends and relatives. At midnight, I stopped to pray, thanking God for this party, which I had wanted for so long, and thanking him for giving me the strength to survive the most difficult year of my life.

Now every year at midnight on New Year's Eve, no matter where I am, I thank God for all that he has given me. I thank him for my parents, who adopted me as a baby and gave me opportunities I would not have had otherwise. And I thank him for helping me make it through another year. When I was little, my mother used to say that she prayed every day upon waking because "so many people that went to bed last night didn't wake up this morning." No matter what I have experienced during the year, I am thankful for the gift of life. And I'm always thankful for the promise of a new year.

Do not fear, for I am with you, do not be afraid,
for I am your God; I will strengthen you, I will help you,
I will uphold you with my victorious right hand.

ISAIAH 41:10

Finding God

I still remember the moment you came into my life
It seems so long ago but, yet, just like yesterday.
We've been through a lot since then, and without you,
I'm not sure I would be where I am now.

You were always there to carry me
when I was too weak to walk.
You were always there to comfort me
when I had bruised my confidence.
And you're the only one
I'd want beside me when I succeed.

Life without you—
I can't imagine.
You're forever in my heart
And always on my mind.

Surprise!

I found my old diary the other day. The burgundy, imitation-leather one. The key had disappeared years before, so I used a paper clip to break into my long-ago secrets.

I got the diary for my 11th birthday—the last birthday I celebrated in the house where I was born and where my brothers and sister and I had spent most of our childhood.

Dear Diary, I'd written, *the past looks better than the future.*

It sounds a bit grown-up, so I suspect it was a phrase I'd overheard from one of the adults who were ruining my life that summer by breaking up our family. We kids were to go with our mother, while our father was set to remarry three weeks after the divorce. The future looked grim, no matter how you put it.

Worst of all for me was having to leave my best friend, Amy. We were born the same month, and our mothers were best friends. We had grown up on the same block and considered each other soul mates. We "belonged" to one another's families.

I thought leaving her was the worst thing that could happen, until we moved from our spacious old house into a stuffy third-floor apartment. And if that wasn't bad enough, I had to go to a new school. But it was all made bearable, as my diary well knew, because Amy still lived close by. We spent nearly every weekend together, sometimes in her familiar house that I'd loved as much as my own and sometimes lost in the exploration of my new apartment complex.

With Amy nearby, it was as if everything hadn't ended for me. She was the connection, the link to all that was good and familiar and what might yet be. She was just "one removed," as we used to say, "from the real thing."

Then Mom fell in love.

"Yuck!" I told my diary and Amy.

"Double yuck!" Amy echoed, crossing her eyes and holding her nose.

This is a good thing, people tried to tell me.

But why didn't it feel that way? I asked my diary. Amy said it just wasn't fair that kids had to do what adults told them to. "And they never even ask us what we think."

Amy was wise that way.

And then the final blow: another move, this time out of state.

New friendships were slow to form, the town seemed strange, and our house was way out on the edge of town. I knew, as I complained to my mother, that nobody would want to drive that far out to see me. *If only,* I wrote in my diary, *Mom hadn't made us move.*

One particularly glum Friday, I walked down our wooded hill toward the house, feeling sad, angry, and lonely.

Mother greeted me at the door, her arms full of clean laundry. She loaded me down with shirts to hang in my closet and prodded me upstairs. She refused to argue when I protested about child labor, and she just laughed when I grumbled.

Still scowling, I opened my closet to hang up the shirts.

"Surprise!" Amy yelled, jumping out and hugging me. "I'm here for the weekend. Your mom flew me in."

Forty years later, the memory of Mother stashing my best friend in the closet still serves to ease the inevitable transitions that life brings. As I reread my diary, I realize now what I could not see then: that Mom did what she thought was best for the entire family, and that she was not—as I suspected at the time—immune to the pain it caused me.

Today is moving day again. This time for my mother, who's just moved into a retirement community.

Alone now, having lost her lifetime companion, my beloved stepfather, she needs someone to lift her spirits. That's why I'm picking up mother's best friend—Amy's mom—at the airport and taking her to see an old friend.

I've lost all my friends. Not because I was untrustworthy or dishonest. After years of laughter and bonding with my close-knit group of friends, my parents decided to up and move. Now the only comfort and stability I had is gone. I need your help, Lord, adapting to my new life. I can't imagine living without them—it's like life without air, romance without love, and happiness without smiles. Please help me to make new friends. Amen.

What's on Your Mind?

We've spent a lot of time in this chapter talking about death, heartbreak, and sadness. Why don't you take some time now to think about LIFE! Use the space below to make a list of the family and friends (yes, pets count) that matter most to you. What do you love about them? Once you're done, choose someone from your list and tell them just how lucky you feel to have them in your life.

_____

_____

_____

_____

_____

_____

_____

_____

_____

_____

_____

_____

_____

_____

Lead Us Not into Temptation

God is faithful; he will not let you be tempted beyond what you can bear. But when you are tempted, he will also provide a way out so that you can stand up under it.

1 CORINTHIANS 10:13 NIV

So many temptations! You may be facing more temptations now than at any other stage in your life. There are drugs everywhere. Kids might have parties where alcohol is served. Dates might pressure you to have sex. Your peers may pressure you to look like they do and act like they do. You might be tempted to fit in by using profanity. This is the time when inner strength is a virtue you can't afford to be without!

Remember, God is there for you when the temptations seem too great. His presence is within you—just take a moment to look deep. God has great faith in your ability to make it through these years without giving in to things you know to be wrong.

With the power of prayer and the support of family and friends, you're sure to come through your teen years a winner—led not into temptation but into renewed faith!

Not Really Me

I couldn't believe the resemblance. The ID card Josh gave me belonged to his 21-year-old brother, Rick, but the picture looked exactly like me. Josh assured me that we would have no problem getting into the club that night.

I had never been in a 21-and-over club before, since I had just turned 17. But tonight was something I couldn't pass up. My favorite rock band, The Sign, was in town, and Josh had scored two tickets—and now these fake IDs. There was nothing standing in my way of getting in and maybe even having a beer. Nothing but my nosy parents and a small, nagging feeling in the pit of my stomach.

My mom and dad had already given me the third degree about where we were going. I hadn't really lied, just bent the truth a little. I told them we would be at a club for kids under 18 and that Josh's brother, Rick, was getting us in. So the club was for 21 and up—I'd told a little white lie about that. At least I'd told the truth about Rick getting us in, well ME in. I'd just left out the part about the ID card. The nagging feeling that I was doing something that would backfire came back, but once again I ignored it. I really wanted to see The Sign.

Josh would pick me up at 7:30. My homework was done, and my parents were being pretty cool about letting me go out on a school night. In fact, they offered me money for something to drink at the club. I doubt beer was what they had in mind, but I took the money anyway.

We got to the club a little after 8:00. The Sign was playing at 10:00, so we hung out, drinking sodas at first. Then Josh got us a couple of beers. I felt like a real adult, swigging a beer, and these two great-looking girls even started making eyes at us. The night seemed to be going perfectly, until I heard the shout behind me.

I heard the gun go off before I saw anything. Suddenly, the club erupted into mayhem as Josh and I tore for the main exit. On my way past the bar, I saw a body lying on the ground. It didn't look good. The guy with the gun was screaming and waving the gun around. I felt sick to my stomach, wishing I had listened to that nagging voice inside me earlier.

The main exit was blocked with people trying to get out. Josh pushed me under a table, and we huddled there, waiting for the cops, or somebody, to rescue us. I couldn't move, so I just prayed. I asked God to forgive me for lying to my parents, and then I asked that God get us out of there alive, so I could gladly accept the consequences of my actions.

I don't really know how much time went by, but eventually the bartender found us and hustled us outside just as the police arrived. We got in the car and left; when Josh dropped me off, I could tell he was just as shaken up as I was. I went in the house, and my parents saw the look on my face. I told them everything and asked them to forgive me. I had learned my lesson and would never do anything so stupid again.

Something in my parents' eyes told me they believed me. They grounded me anyway, but I actually felt relieved. I didn't feel like going out for a long, long time.

Lord, lead us not into temptation, and keep us in tune with that voice within that never leads us astray. Only when we refuse to listen to your guidance do we get into trouble. Remind us of your constant presence in our lives and your constant wisdom, too. Amen.

Life is like a video game—
except without the extra lives.
Choose wisely.

Lately, I've been tempted to disregard the words of my parents and rebel. Friends invite me to all-night parties and to have alcohol or drugs, and I think, *What could be the harm?* I'm sure my parents weren't angels as kids either, but I know there must be a reason they want me to stay away from such environments. Even though I want to give in, God, I need you to supply me with strength and maybe with creativity to come up with other ways to have fun that will be more acceptable to everyone in my life—even me.

Being Addie

My middle name should be "straight." Anna Straight Smith. I've never cut a class, never lied to my parents (well, not about anything important), never stolen so much as a gum ball, never missed church unless I was sick or out of town with my family. Maybe that's why Addie held such a fascination for me. She was a "bad girl"—in detention three times a week, failing half her classes, and smoking in the girls' room at lunchtime. I used to watch her, wondering what it felt like to be her.

My best friend, Cara, was just like me but with one difference: her big brother, Louis. Louis was cool. He was into all kinds of things I didn't even want to know about. This sounds crazy, I know, but Cara actually looked up to Louis. And I guess I wasn't the only one who wondered what it was like to be a bit of a rebel, because when Louis offered Cara a joint, she took it. "It won't kill you," he said.

"You're not going to let me do this alone, are you?" Cara pleaded the next day.

I hesitated, the role-playing moments of all those DARE classes running through my head, the voice of our pastor during all those youth ministry sermons. I was supposed to say, "No way." Instead I said, "Okay, just this once."

Cara smiled. "Just this once," she agreed.

We decided to walk back to my house to smoke it. Both my parents would be at work. We were halfway through the park when I saw Addie. She was standing by the pond, talking to herself and waving her hands wildly.

Before we could say a word, Addie spotted us and sprinted over. "Sammie says yeah-yeah," she said. She stopped in front of us, blocking our path. "Sammie says yeah-yeah-YEAH!" She grinned with a crazed sort of look in her eyes.

Cara started to push past Addie, but I stopped her. "Addie?" I asked. "You okay?"

She did a little dance. "Sammie says yeah-yeah," she repeated the nonsensical words.

"Who's Sammie?" Cara asked.

"He's the MAN! He gives me the STUFF! The GOOD stuff!"

Suddenly Addie's expression changed, she looked at us suspiciously. "Are you NARCS? LEAVE ME ALONE!" And she was off, running wildly toward the road. An SUV came around the corner. Cara and I screamed. Addie looked straight at the car and LAUGHED as we heard the sickening sound of brakes screeching as the car hit her.

It was a miracle that Addie wasn't killed. I'll never forget the sound of her laughter. That day taught me more than a billion sermons and DARE classes. It taught me to keep my faith in myself and my beliefs—and to respect myself and take care of my body—no matter what.

When we got to my house we flushed that joint down the toilet.

I don't think I want to know what it feels like to be Addie after all.

It's Not Always
What They Think

I didn't really want to do it. But my girlfriend did. Well, I thought she did. I don't know exactly how it happened. My parents had given me all kinds of lectures. I'd sort of listened with one ear and nodded my head and thought it was all kinda stupid. I wasn't going to do anything wrong.

But it seemed like EVERYONE was doing it. Sure, we talked about it in my confirmation class at church. I even prayed for the strength and presence of mind to keep my hands to myself when I was with my girlfriend.

Then we ended up at her house one night when her parents weren't home. I was just dropping her off from the movies. She expected them to be home, but they were having dinner with friends and were still out. She invited me in, and we went up to her room.

Things started to get out of hand—and then I remembered my promise to myself. I remembered all my prayers and talks with God. I told her I had to leave.

Just then her parents came home—as I was running out of her room. They got REALLY mad. They assumed the worst. She got grounded and was told not to go out with me again.

Maybe it's for the best. I don't know. What I do know in my heart is that I did the right thing. For her. For me. For our families. I'm proud of myself and of my strength and my faith In what's right. It doesn't matter what anyone thinks.

I've learned that sometimes you don't get the chance to explain yourself. And I've also learned that the good feeling inside me can't be changed by anyone. I plan to keep on doing the right thing.

Dear God,
I know I shouldn't even be thinking about sex at this age, but everyone in school seems to be talking about it or doing it. I feel ashamed for wanting to save myself for that special person because my friends think it's "uncool." But I know it won't mean as much if I'm not ready, and I know you want me to wait until I'm married. Please guide me to make the right decision so that I won't regret my actions and can be proud of myself in the days and years to come.

It is a wise person who knows
right from wrong. But it is a brave person
who chooses right over wrong.

*In life, unlike school, it's not important
to know the questions you're going
to be asked. It's the answers you
give that make the difference.*

There is a voice inside of you
  That whispers all day long,
'I feel that this is right for me,
I know that this is wrong.'
No teacher, preacher, parents, friend
Or wise man could decide
What's right for you—just listen to
The voice that speaks inside.

SHEL SILVERSTEIN

❖   ❖   ❖

Listen Up!

I'm not usually allowed to get in touch like this. But this message is so important and so hard to get across that I got special permission from my Boss. Pay attention, though. I doubt that I'd be allowed to talk with you a second time—unless it was in person, of course. And then, it would be too late. Way too late.

I want to tell you about one day when I was a junior in high school. It's hard to tell how long ago that was. I still haven't figured out the whole space-time continuum thing up here.

Anyway, a bit of background on me. I'd been a pretty good kid. Got grounded once for hitting my sister, but I hadn't meant to do it. Her nose sort of got in the way of my angry gesturing. Other than that, I did okay. Got decent grades and had some really good friends. I listened to my folks about stuff and figured I'd never do anything stupid. I went to church regularly and had my own ways of chatting with the Lord. I used to take long bike rides and discuss everything that was on my mind. I volunteered a couple times each week at the animal shelter, too, though my mom wasn't too happy when I kept coming home with new pets!

Well, I just got told I'd better hurry it up. I've got to go in a minute. Here's what happened. I was at a party. I knew the friend having the party but didn't know her parents weren't going to be home. Some other kids found out that the 'rents were gone and brought over some beer. I didn't drink anything. I knew I needed to go home. A whole bunch of kids were leaving. The problem was that I didn't call my parents for a ride. I took a ride from another kid who lived near me. I didn't realize that he'd been drinking before he got to the party. He seemed pretty okay to me. He wasn't. We got in an accident just a block from my house. It was so close, in fact, that Dad heard the crunch and came running. I think he even saw me lying there. I wanted to apologize to him, but I couldn't. I was killed on impact. There were six of us in the backseat, so we hadn't buckled ourselves in, and I was thrown from the car.

I didn't drink. I was a good kid. I had a lot of faith in myself, in God, in everyone. But he doesn't control our free will, and I made a mistake. Could've been a little mistake, but it turned out to be big. Just please don't come and see me anytime soon. Even good kids sometimes make bad choices.

I've got to go.

❖   ❖   ❖

Choice is a gift; it's not a right.
Don't be foolish with decisions.

I am so frustrated and torn in different directions. I'm constantly in fear of something or someone. I'm afraid I will disappoint my parents by making bad choices, but I'm afraid that if I don't do what my friends do, I'll no longer be accepted in our group. I fear I will never be loved for who I really am because I can't be me and still please everyone. Sometimes I want to take drugs, or drink, Lord, because everyone says it's an escape, but I know that is not smart. Please help me to stand up to my friends and to explain to my parents that I'm doing the best that I can. I know deep down that I am a good person—I'm just afraid that no one else will think so. God, I ask that you give me the courage to believe in myself and the strength to let it show. Amen.

*It's easy to be sucked into drugs
or alcohol by constant peer pressure,
but it shows more courage and individuality
to convince others that the best way
to be cool is to be yourself and
accept others as they are.*

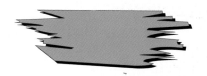

My Best Friend's Girl

Neither one of us had dated much. We spent most of our weekends playing basketball, working on our bikes, and just hanging out. Then one weekend, Ben went off to the lake with his parents. He invited me, but my mom was singing a big solo at church that Sunday, and I knew it meant a lot to her for me to be there.

Come Sunday night, I got a phone call from Ben. He just couldn't wait until Monday morning to tell me about Jenny. He said he'd met this great girl—beautiful, smart, funny, nice—and she actually liked him!

They started going out. I saw a bit less of Ben on the weekends, but Jenny went to a different school so we still hung out during the week. He talked about her a lot, and I was glad that he'd found someone he really cared about.

Then it happened. Ben and I went to a game at Jenny's school, and I met her. POW! I thought I was instantly in love. She was everything Ben had said and so much more. I wanted to go out with her more than I'd ever wanted anything. I passed her my phone number on a scrap of paper when Ben was getting hot dogs.

She smiled and tucked it in her pocket.

The next day the phone rang. "Why did you give me your number?" It was Jenny.

"Because I think you're incredible! Didn't you feel the electricity when we met?"

"Of course I did, but I'm with Ben and he's your best friend. I can't go out with you. What I *will* do, for your sake and Ben's, is just forget we ever had this conversation at all. Okay?"

I'd finally met a girl—and what a girl!—and she'd flat out rejected me. Even though she agreed she'd been attracted. Why me, Lord?

I prayed quietly for a while. The next thing I knew I was reciting the Ten Commandments to myself. And it hit me. "Thou shalt not covet..." Not only had I wanted Ben's girl for myself, I had totally disregarded his feelings. I would've felt like a total louse if Jenny hadn't been such a class act and said no.

I put my hand on the phone to call and thank Jenny, then thought better of it. I sent the thank you via God. I'm sure she'll get the message.

God,
I'm not sure why you flaunt temptations in the faces of naive teenagers. Is it to test our ability to make it in the "real world"? Or just a test for ourselves? Either way, I think I came out on top, and I want to thank you for your guidance and love, which helps me stay on the right path.

You will be "tested" throughout your life and there might be some multiple-choice questions, but remember there will be no grading scale. You either pass or fail.

I can understand how some of the kids at my school get sucked into drugs and alcohol and other pressures. The teenage years are not really so simple. I'm juggling homework and classes, work, family life, and personal relationships. I feel like I'm under so much pressure—pressure to finish all my homework before work; pressure from family squabbles and from friends to go to secret parties and hangouts; and then, of course, there is pressure to have a serious boyfriend or girlfriend. I don't know how much more I can pile on my shoulders before I give up. God, please, all I ask for is strength.

Making friends is not more important than making a life for yourself.

This above all: to thine own self be true,
And it must follow, as the night the day,
Thou canst not then be false to any man.
WILLIAM SHAKESPEARE, *HAMLET*

✜   ✜   ✜

The Kid

I know you don't think I could ever be real. You don't think I could happen to you. You think that if you keep your faith it doesn't matter what you do. You figure you are immune to all the little quirks of nature.

But you are wrong.

Sex is a God-given gift meant for older, married people. I'm the whole point, you know. But God never meant for kids to have kids. You need to pay attention to the real messages. You think you'll be "safe." The thing is: The only way to really be "safe" is to wait. Until you're older. Until you're married. Until you can deal with the possibility of a baby, whether planned for or not.

What would happen to me? Your parents could raise me, which is about the last thing they want to be doing in their retirement. You could give me up for adoption and spend the rest of your life wondering where I am and who I am and if I'd love you and forgive you. None of the choices are great.

And baby makes three. Or more likely two, because a silly young boy is never going to stick around and be my dad. And would you even want him to?

I hope that your friends get the message, too. Listen, be smart, be safe—don't think that faith will erase the consequences if you make poor choices. If you truly listen to your heart, I'm a gift from God, and I'll tell you to wait to have me until we're all ready.

Do you not know that your body is the temple of the Holy Spirit who is in you, whom you have from God, and you are not your own?

1 Corinthians 6:19 NKJV

Please, Lord, help me to be strong. Every day I'm bombarded with people who want things from me: homework, help, sex, money, good grades, good work habits. Sometimes I'm so overwhelmed and afraid of making bad decisions. Please guide me along a path that will lead to memorable teen years but also keep me from a wrong path.

Two roads diverged in a wood, and I—
I took the road less traveled by,
And that has made all the difference.

ROBERT FROST, "THE ROAD NOT TAKEN"

I feel like an elastic band being stretched to the point where it's just going to snap. How am I supposed to prioritize my life when everyone is telling me to focus on different things? My friends want me to be with them; they want me to sneak out of the house and go to parties. Even though I know it's wrong, it always seems intriguing and fun. And of course, my parents want me to get good grades so I can get into a good college and get a job. Meanwhile, my boss seems to forget I'm still in school, and I have six hours of homework to do every night. How am I supposed to please everyone and not make myself crazy? I know you can't actually answer me, God, but please guide me through the sticky web of "teenhood" without becoming tangled. Amen.

Be strong in the Lord and in the power of His might.

EPHESIANS 6:10 NKJV

Do not imitate what is evil, but what is good. He who does good is of God, but he who does evil has not seen God.

3 JOHN 1:11 NKJV

Temptations will never go away, but as your faith in God grows stronger and stronger, they will become easier to avoid.

A Debt Forgiven

I could blame Martha Maude for leading me into temptation, but I know it was really my own fault.

Martha's dad drew a small pension, so her family had cash money. All the cash my family had came from the crops we sold. We lived on a few acres called a truck farm, except we had no truck. In season, we hauled produce to town in a two-horse wagon.

Although it was the 1940s, the Depression of the '30s was still with us. Every spring, Dad borrowed money from the bank to buy seed and fertilizer. Each winter, if crops were good, he paid the money back. If crops failed, the debt remained on the books. I hated being so poor and having no reward for laboring in the fields.

Mother cooked, canned, and smoked or sun-dried everything edible that we could find, since we had no way to freeze or refrigerate food. After a hard winter our cupboard could be bare, and sometimes I'd arrive at school with no lunch. Of course I told the teacher that I had *forgotten* my lunch, rather than telling her the truth.

It was during one of these hungry times that Martha Maude invited me to walk downtown with her at lunchtime. She planned to buy a treat at Mr. Kelley's store. I thought my friend knew my financial situation and would buy something for me, too. When she did not, I asked Mr. Kelley if I could charge a candy bar and a soda. He asked my dad's name. When I told him, he said my credit was good. This was heady stuff for a 13-year-old.

Martha Maude kept inviting me to join her for lunch, so my debt began to increase. After about a month of lunches, I found myself two dollars in debt. Mr. Kelley said firmly, "No more credit for you, young lady. You need to pay back what you've spent."

I suddenly realized what I had done. It wasn't just me who was responsible for the debt—it was my dad's name that was on the line. My father was a strict disciplinarian, as he had to be to keep seven independent-minded kids in line, and I dreaded the punishment I was sure to receive. Desperately, I tried to think of a way to pay off my debt.

My mother noticed that I was unusually quiet when I got home from school that day. After I changed into my work clothes, she asked me what was wrong. I confessed to her about my debt and how I'd used Dad's name. My anguish poured out in stuttering words and sobs. "Oh, child, don't," she said soothingly. "We'll think of some-thing."

After school the next day, Mother instructed me to help Dad dig potatoes. I dragged my feet to the hilltop where he was working, and I saw that he had plowed deep to loosen the soil around the roots of the plants. Several feed sacks and one new bushel basket were set out at the beginning of the rows. Dad showed me how to get the biggest and best-formed potatoes, rub the dirt off, and place them, unbruised, into the basket. Dad dropped to his knees and began to fill one of the sacks with all sizes and shapes of potatoes. I wondered why my basket had to be so perfect. *Who is it for?* I wondered. *Probably for Grandma or some other special person.*

At sundown, we loaded my basket and several sacks of potatoes into the wagon and started for home. As we approached the lane to our house, Dad said, "Your mother tells me you owe Mr. Kelley some money."

Frightened, sad, and sorry, I began to babble. "I'm gonna pay him, Dad. . . . I just need more time. . . . I'll figure something out."

"I don't know how you think you can pay him. Nobody's hiring kids now. They're not even hiring grown people."

Nervously I blathered on. "I thought maybe I could take him some butter . . . or eggs . . . or maybe sweep out the store. . . ."

"Mr. Kelley told me this morning that a bushel of Irish potatoes will settle your bill. First thing in the morning I'll take him that basket you fixed. And don't you *ever* buy anything on credit again. Understood?"

"Yes, sir," I whispered, unable to say more.

That whole experience taught me some important lessons. Both my father and Mr. Kelley demonstrated the power of forgiveness. And Dad taught me that when you give, you always give your best. I also learned how important it is to think before I act, especially when someone else's name is on the line.

Who knew I could get all that from having lunch with Martha Maude?

God,
It's so easy to go astray in these years before adulthood. I want to make my own decisions. I want to prove to others that I am trustworthy and smart. But at the same time, these years are filled with pressures from friends to do what "everyone else is doing." I need your help with strength and courage to face my peers and honesty and wisdom to show my family.

My God shall supply all your need according to His riches in glory by Christ Jesus.

PHILIPPIANS 4:19 NKJV

Who Should I Be?

Everywhere you look they're telling us who to be! Magazines, television, movies, and of course, the biggest culprits of all, other kids!

First it was a certain kind of shoe. Everyone had them and if you didn't, well then you could just kiss being cool good-bye. Next it was a style of pants—until they got so baggy that the dress code had to ban them so they wouldn't start falling off the kids! It's just been one thing after another ever since junior high.

Sometimes I just pray to go back to elementary school where you could wear stretch pants and a Little Mermaid T-shirt that your grandmother had gotten you and nobody cared.

I've always had my own sense of fashion and style and what's "me" and what isn't. I love being like this and I thank the Lord every day! But that's made it really hard for me to fit in with my classmates.

It's like there is peer pressure about everything. First, you're supposed to dress like everybody else. Then you're supposed to drink if everyone else is, and you're supposed to have sex, too, if that's considered cool.

I'm sorry but I think most of that is just stupid. I don't smoke, drink, swear, or wear what everyone else wears. And you know what's cool? I may not have a lot of friends, but the ones I have like me for who I am—not because I'm their clone!

And you want to hear something funny? I've been wearing my hair in this really cool style I invented where I pin back one side in a certain way, and yesterday I saw that the whole cheerleading squad had their hair like that! My first thought was that I was going to change my style because I didn't want to be like them, but then I prayed and thought about it and realized that would be giving in to the pressure in some reverse way.

So I think I'll just go along and be me. That's just the way I like and respect myself!

K eep true, never be ashamed of doing right; decide on
   what you think is right and stick to it.
GEORGE ELIOT

Father,
Please help me to remember that when I'm in my 20s and 30s, it will be irrelevant where I bought my clothes growing up or how I styled my hair. It won't matter if I was popular or the captain of a sports team. All that will matter is what I learned. Please help me to gather knowledge from all my high-school experiences and help me to successfully transfer it to the real world. Amen.

If you gathered nothing in your youth,
how can you find anything in your old age?

Sirach 25:3

Fitting In

I've bought new clothes and restyled my hair. But it seems everyone still stares.

I've tried new sports and clubs. I've even acted dumb. But I still get the cold-shoulder snub.

No matter what I did I never seemed to fit. I was always a member of the "uncool kids."

It was only when I stopped experimenting and acted true to myself that my spirit felt free and my heart began to sing.

What's on Your Mind?

What tempts you the most? What is the most difficult thing for you to deal with? Is it peer pressure? Issues about sexuality? Drugs? Write down your biggest temptations in the space provided below.

_____

_____

_____

_____

_____

_____

Now, write a prayer for yourself that speaks from your heart. Ask God for the guidance you need to stay on the path that you know is right. Return to this prayer when you find yourself searching for the right direction for your life.

_____

_____

_____

_____

_____

_____

In God We Trust

I believe in the sun even when it does not shine. I believe in love even when I do not feel it. I believe in God even when he is silent.

AUTHOR UNKNOWN

Trust. One little word, one huge concept. Whom do you trust? Yourself? Your friends? Your parents? Your teachers? God? How do we learn trust? How do we regain trust once it's been lost? Sometimes, when times get rough, it is easy to lose sight of our faith, to lose our trust in anything and everything. Yet if we believe in God's wisdom, if we look for his light to brighten our path, then anything is possible.

These stories will take you on a journey to the very heart of trust, to the very heart of faith, and you will see how others have struggled and triumphed.

As you read this chapter, think about trust. It may be a small word, but its impact on our family, our relationships, our lives, and our faith is astonishing.

In the Shadow of Dad

My dad's a little bit famous. Some people know him on sight and ask for his autograph; other people don't even know his name. It's kind of weird, actually. When we go somewhere, we never know if we'll just be anonymous or if a busload of tourists will come up and start swarming our table at dinner.

Dad's not a rock star, unfortunately. He invented a cure for a disease that affects kids when they are really young. Sometimes parents come up and start crying and stuff and thanking him. They call him a saint.

I know he's a really good guy and all. But when I see him take a stranger's hand and smile and listen and give a hug, well, I'm sorry, Lord, but I get a little angry. You see, he's never been there for ME. How about inventing a cure for never spending any time with your kid? How about inventing a cure for not knowing how to be a real father? How about inventing a cure for always saying you'll be there and then never showing up? How about looking out for *me* for a change, God?

At our house, nobody ever noticed the kid—just the dad. I'd talk with God about it, then always feel guilty for thinking of myself when there were so many other kids out there who needed my dad. Did they need him more than I did? I prayed to understand. I prayed that just once I could trust my dad and believe that he was there for me.

I sort of started to fade into the woodwork. At home. At school. In my own mind. I always did well at school and in my other activities. I played saxophone really well and made the traveling soccer team every year. But Dad was the Big Guy. The famous guy. The guy who was saving lives.

Then one day, Mom insisted we clean the house because we were hosting our family Christmas celebration. It was my junior year. Of course, Dad never helped. I'd given up even hoping he'd be with us for Christmas.

I went into his study and sat down at his desk to complain to God. I wasn't even supposed to go in there, but I didn't care. There was a huge, messy pile of papers under the desk. I pulled them out and stared in stunned silence. I went through the endless pile. I couldn't believe it. And then I found the letter. I sat there for a very long time. My dad had saved every note I'd given him when I was little. Every single school picture. Every program from every concert he hadn't been able to attend. And he'd written me a ten-page letter explaining his work and how he hated it and loved it and couldn't NOT do it, even though he died a little bit each time he missed a part of my childhood.

I thanked God for giving me this gift of understanding. It was like a hole inside me was filled. It helped me see that I hadn't gotten such a bum deal in the dad department, that there were other ways to believe and trust in each other. And I saw that I did matter to Dad. I also came to see that God must've felt I could handle this—having a brilliant guy for a dad. God trusted me with this burden, this gift.

F or I, the Lord your God, hold your right hand;
  it is I who say to you, "Do not fear, I will help you."

ISAIAH 41:13

God,
Help me to avoid holding grudges and placing blame. Help me to find forgiveness in my heart and promise in the day. Let me be content with what I have and be thankful for what I'm given. Most of all, please remind me that my actions today can either be a source of pride or regret.

J esus said, 'You shall love the Lord your God
  with all your heart, with all your soul, with all your mind, and with all your strength.' This is the first commandment.

MARK 12:30 NKJV

One Awesome Miracle

My folks told me that high school was one of life's best experiences, so I was anxious to make the most of it. In my first year, I played on the tennis team, had a boyfriend, and went to school dances. I couldn't imagine that life could be any better. So when I was sitting in first-hour algebra class and felt a throbbing pain in my left knee, I figured it was nothing. Second hour I had PE. I plopped on the bench in the locker room and rubbed my knee. It felt unusually warm.

I asked the teacher if I could sit out, but she told me that unless I had a doctor's note, I had to join the rest of the class. That pretty much forced me to see my doctor, who sent me to a specialist. He bent my knee this way and that, sent me for an X ray, and then recommended an MRI.

I limped in for the follow-up appointment and sat there with my mom, studying the diplomas on the exam room wall. The doctor breezed in, shut the door behind him, and with little or no fanfare, said, "Your MRI shows a tumor." My jaw literally dropped. It had never occurred to me that I might have cancer.

As soon as we got home, my mom started our family's prayer chain. That's a good thing about having a big family—you can have someone praying for you around the clock. However, when she called our church's prayer chain, I was mad. I thought she was making too much out of it. Then, the Sunday before I went to the hospital, my pastor included me in his prayer. *Out loud.* In front of everyone. I was totally embarrassed. My face got so hot, my glasses fogged up.

Monday I was admitted to the University of Nebraska Medical Center, where I had more tests done. Tuesday I had a biopsy. Wednesday they told me I had osteosarcoma, a rare form of pediatric bone cancer. As awful as the news was, I believed God would be with me no matter what, so that helped me not to get too upset. Mom smiled at me and brushed my hair back. She didn't look well. Perhaps it was because she had a clue as to what I was about to go through.

The treatment for my cancer was aggressive and made me really sick for a long time. Fortunately I didn't need an amputation; instead they inserted an internal prosthesis. I spent 166 days in the hospital with 21 rounds of chemotherapy, 25 blood transfusions, and four infections. Through it all, the Lord helped me. Lying across the bed throwing up, sweating from a high fever, bald as a bat, with my leg aching, I *still* felt his presence. And I knew the whole time that I would get better.

Eventually, in the middle of my sophomore year, I left the hospital and got to go back to school. As thrilled as I was to be "normal" again, I resumed high school with a wig and a limp. For the first time, I felt different from my old friends. I had been through something incredibly overwhelming, and none of them understood. Emotionally distraught, I went back and forth between being angry with God for giving me cancer, then realizing that he loved me and I could trust him.

By the time my junior year started, I was feeling much better. I was not as close to God, though, because I didn't feel like I needed him as much. In January, I went back to the specialist for a routine follow-up visit. Again, he came into the room unceremoniously, and blurted, "Your CT scan shows six nodules on your lungs." Although I now knew that the first place osteosarcoma recurs is the lungs, I asked if it might be something else. Grimly, he informed me that the nodules were fluid-filled and looked like cancer.

This time I did not take it well. I cried for hours because, unlike the last time, I knew what lay ahead. And, worst of all, with a recurrence of osteosarcoma, my odds of survival dropped significantly. For the first time I thought I might actually die.

On the ride home, I leaned my head against the cold car window and thought about going through treatment again. I would lose my newly grown hair. Morbidly, I also thought about what would happen if I died. I wondered who would come to my funeral and what they would say. I realized I might never get married and have kids or go to college or even my senior prom.

That night in my room I prayed harder than I have ever prayed before. I got down on my knees and begged God with all my heart to let me live. Over and over I told him I couldn't handle having cancer again.

The next day, doctors at the university hospital did a biopsy of my right lung. Then they shipped me to intensive care, where I went in and out of consciousness. At one point I heard the surgeon tell my parents that he had to go back in and take another nodule because the frozen section he sent to the lab showed no sign of cancer. He wanted to take one more nodule and run additional testing.

But those results weren't any different. All the nodules they took from my right lung were benign. I tearfully thanked the Lord for giving me a second chance. Though I still had untested nodules on my left lung, I wasn't concerned. I *knew* God had healed me. When I went for a follow-up visit the next month, to everyone's surprise but mine, the nodules had all disappeared!

God poured out his love for me and made me whole, and this time I didn't forget him. I've been in remission for five years—I'm in my junior year at nursing school now—and every day I thank him for my own awesome miracle.

❖　　❖　　❖

God is our refuge and strength,
a very present help in trouble.
PSALM 46:1 NKJV

❖　　❖　　❖

Lord of all,
Please give me a sign that you exist. I feel as though there cannot possibly be a God since everything in my life is in shambles. Everyone tells me to have faith and be strong, but I'm afraid of what might happen in the future, and I'm afraid that you may not exist. Please, I will believe if I can just feel your strength, know your wisdom, and share your courage. Amen.

Unexpected Angels

We weren't drinking. We weren't on drugs. Everyone specu-
lated of course. But we were just in the wrong place at the
wrong time. The headlights came toward us—the other car
was on the wrong side of the road! I wasn't driving, but I
couldn't have done it any better. There just wasn't time to
do anything but scream. We all screamed. There were four
of us in the car. We were going to a mall near our little town.
Our parents were never keen on us driving on the two-lane
highway, but you couldn't get anywhere without driving on
one of the old roads.

When the car hit us, the sounds were deafening. Then
suddenly everything was quiet. *Well, I guess it's all over,* I
thought to myself. I didn't expect white lights. I didn't really
expect anything. Sure, I went to church with my family, but
who could believe all those stories of heaven and life after
death? Nope. I figured my time was up. Good-bye, everybody. No algebra test next week.

The silence was uncanny. I waited for shouting. Sirens.
Something. I opened my eyes. We were all still in the car.
Everyone had been wearing their seat belts. But my friends
still had their eyes closed. Then I heard the music. It
sounded sweet. Like elevator music, only it didn't make me
want to cringe. It made me feel—how do I describe it? It
made me feel full inside. Comfortable. There was a soft
rustling, then I saw some kind of creatures. Three of them—

one hovering over each of my friends. They all looked at me with eyes that were somehow sad yet not in a tragic kind of way. I closed my eyes and opened them again. The creatures were still there. Not creatures. Angels.

Then they were gone. And everything became very loud. I heard sirens and shouting, and I felt a lot of pain. My friends were all dead. I lived. Now, when I go to church, I choose to believe.

Father,
I trust you to bring guidance and comfort to my life, but sometimes I wonder if I will ever be able to live up to your standards. Am I good enough? Do I do enough kind deeds and live according to your word? Sometimes I think it's impossible to go even one day without violating your commandments. Please forgive me for my mistakes. I promise I will continue to live as faithfully as I can.

Looking for God

When I was little, I wouldn't have thought about looking for God. I thought he was a big man in white robes with a flowing white beard who sat on a beautiful throne somewhere in the clouds of heaven.

Then I got a little older and started to wonder about the "guy in the chair" theory. I started having all kinds of ideas about where God really lived. I thought maybe he had a condo in Hawaii; there aren't many places on earth more beautiful, and if I'd created all those oceans and stuff, I think I'd want to be able to surf on my waves whenever I wanted.

I'd tell the pastor my ideas, and he'd listen very patiently and smile and tell me to keep looking.

So I did. When I'd be riding in the backseat on the highway and a bus drove by us, I'd stare in all the windows. Sometimes I'd think I saw him.

It wasn't until I went away to college that I finally found God. I stayed up all night studying—an "all-nighter." I'd heard kids talk about it, but it was the first time I'd done it. I went outside for a walk to clear my head before going to get some breakfast. It was very early. Dawn. The sky was unbelievable—all the colors of the rainbow spread in a wash across the horizon. I watched in delight and then I knew. I knew that I was looking at God.

Later that year, I got a call to come home to my grandpa's bedside. He was 94 and dying. Grandpa was a cool guy and had always been a great friend of mine. I walked in to see him, and he smiled and took my hand. "He's here," Grandpa whispered. He died then with that peaceful smile on his face. I knew that he meant that God was with him.

It's happened to me numerous other times also. Once when I was cooking, of all things. I had great music on the stereo. My apartment was totally perfect for me. Some really good friends were coming for dinner. I was chopping vegetables for the salad, and there was God. The vegetables were his creation. The feeling of fullness within me was him.

And it happened once when I sang at my best friend's wedding. I guess I have a good voice because I'm always being asked to sing. I enjoy it but don't think about it much. I've never studied voice or anything. My best buddy's bride was coming down the aisle. She looked like an angel—all in white and veiled. I sang, and there he was. God was beside me, around me, with my friend and his bride.

I know now that these moments will follow me through my life as long as I never stop looking for God.

Jesus said, "I say to you, if you have faith as a mustard seed, you will say to this mountain, 'Move from here to there,' and it will move; and nothing will be impossible for you."

MATTHEW 17:20 NKJV

The Roots of Faith

My dad walked out on us during my junior year of high school. He just left. No words of explanation, no apologies, no good-byes. And just like that, my mom and I were all alone. I was so angry at my dad, I rejected everything that was his, including his religion. God didn't seem to be doing much for me, so why should I be praying to him? I didn't trust anyone or anything. Didn't believe in anything. Just life. And lots of time that seemed to be pretty bleak.

Then I met Jenny. She was beautiful, out of my league, and rather preppy for my taste, but there was just something about her. I was drawn to her. I went up to her at lunch and asked if I could buy her a milk. How lame could I be? She smiled and said no thanks. But that was the beginning.

We started talking every day. She asked me to go camping with her. What an offer! Of course I said yes! When I got to her house, I had to laugh when I realized she had meant go camping with her AND her family. How dense could I be? A girl like that doesn't go camping alone with a guy like me.

I'd already packed my stuff, so there wasn't any way I could get out of it. I could see her parents weren't too happy when they laid eyes on me. Her father took me aside and explained that I'd have my own tent and be expected to stay in it ALL NIGHT. I did my best "yes, sir," and we piled into their van.

We went up to the Redwoods, a part of northern California I'd never seen before. We got permission from her parents to take a walk early the next morning, before breakfast.

"We come here a lot," Jenny said. "I talk to God here. Isn't it incredible?" She looked at me with such a face—a face filled with wonder and belief and faith. How could I tell her I didn't believe in anything? Then I looked up. The sun was just beginning to shine through those magnificent trees. I can't describe to you what happened to me in that instant. Her face, and the sunlight, and those trees. Suddenly I was filled with the complete and utter certainty that all of it had come from something larger than myself. It was all God's work. And it was good.

Jenny and I never really dated after that. It just wasn't meant to be. But later, I came to feel she was some kind of messenger. She'd brought me back to the roots of my faith.

I thank You God for most this amazing day:
for the leaping greenly spirits of trees
and a blue tree dream of sky;
and for everything which is natural
which is infinite which is yes.
                    E. E. CUMMINGS

Sunday Morning Memories

Many of my childhood memories stem from a little brown church tucked amid evergreen trees a few miles from our home. It was a place to worship, sing, and pray. Not a rich, fancy church with luscious layers of velvet draped from high above in the rafters. Just a plain church with faithful Christians as strong and solid as the wooden pews.

Mom laid out the rules of proper conduct and would silently enforce them with a simple frown. Each Sunday in the car, she gave us a stern warning, reminding us how to behave.

As a kid, I found our church a bit mystical. Quiet and serene, the church was unlike any other place we visited. Hushed, gentle voices welcomed our family as we passed through the door on Sunday mornings.

Being a tomboy, I grumbled about having to wear a dress every week. Mom always stood her ground. "Put your dress on and look respectful when you enter God's house," she would say. It was a battle she never lost. We could not wear blue jeans or tennis shoes to church, and wearing a dress without a slip was considered downright disgraceful. Chewing gum, running, and goofing around were not tolerated at church either. Never.

Sitting still for the hour-long service is difficult for any kid, and I was no exception. With little to do, I often gazed around me and counted things. I knew there were three lambs in the stained-glass windows, 12 overhead lights, and 16 pews, 8 on each side of the wide red-carpeted center aisle. Our church was always spotless. The only dust I ever saw danced in midair in the rays of sunshine streaming through the stained-glass windows. Illuminated in the colored light, it glittered like teeny angels flitting to and fro. The pews were gleaming white, and on the back of each one, several hymnals were tucked into wooden holders.

My favorite part came early in the service. Standing, we turned to the correct page in the hymnal as instructed by the pastor. I can still hear Mom's voice, strong and clear, as I held the book in front of my nose, trying to follow along. Mom pointed the way when the first verse ended and then jumped back up to the top of the page for the second verse. The sudden shift always confused me. The old man who sat near the front every Sunday sang loud and low without ever opening a book. I wondered how he memorized the words to all the songs in that huge hymnal.

After the singing ended, we all bowed our heads to pray. It was usually a long prayer. Sometimes I took a quick look around to see if everyone had their eyes shut and their heads bowed. The adults always did. Spotting another kid peeking often made me giggle, but a gentle nudge from Mom's elbow settled me down.

The sermon was the longest and the hardest part to endure. It seemed as if the pastor would never stop talking. His voice melted into the walls as though it were a part of the church itself. Occasionally his words came out like thunder, and it seemed like a bolt of lightning struck as his hand rapped against the pulpit. Moments like those brought my full attention back to the kind old pastor's face as he once again lowered his voice and preached on. His words flowed through my ears, settling deep within my subconscious.

During those years of long sermons, with my skinny, scraped legs swinging beneath the pew, I had no idea of the wonderful gift my mom was giving me. Mom taught me to sit silently, and Sunday by Sunday, bit by bit, my impressionable young mind absorbed the words of the Bible, which provided me with a solid foundation. Those words and the lessons I learned began to surface in my teenage years. More than once they saved me from making some very bad decisions that could have changed my life entirely.

Until I married and had three children of my own, I failed to fully realize the precious gift Mom had shared with me. She helped give the gift of eternal life—a life with God and Jesus Christ, my savior. She set that solid foundation in my life, long before I was fully aware of it. Now it's my turn to pass this gift on to my children. I can only hope I do as fine a job as my mom did.

Unexpected Gifts

During World War II, we had many sad and fearful Christmases. Those were the times we mainly observed the holiday in our hearts. So after the war, in 1947, when we arrived in the refugee camp in Austria just a few weeks before Christmas, I wasn't expecting anything different. At age 11, I had become resigned to not having much.

The refugee camp, with its wooden barracks and dusty lanes, was pretty drab. But we had a warm place to sleep and warm food to eat, and we were grateful for that. We were given warm clothes, which had been donated to the refugee effort from various generous-minded countries like the United States, Canada, and Great Britain. We considered ourselves pretty fortunate. Plus, we had beautiful views available, since the camp was located in one of the most scenic areas of Austria-Carinthia.

As Christmas approached, the camp school I attended made plans to help us celebrate the holiday as a group. In the barracks where we lived, our private spaces were tiny cubicles for sleeping; families did not have room for individual celebrations. But the school had a large auditorium, where a donated Christmas tree was set up. We children created handmade ornaments, which we used to decorate the tree. There were even candles on the tree, to be lit on Christmas Eve—just like in Hungary, before the war. We stayed busy rehearsing a school play, to be presented on

Christmas Eve. I had a role as the angel who announces the birth of the Savior to the shepherds. I was very pleased and excited about the part.

On Christmas Eve afternoon, my grandparents and I decided to take a walk to the small town of Spittal, just a few miles away from the camp. Grandfather felt that even though we had no money to buy anything, taking in the Christmas sights and smells would be worth the walk. The town's many small shops were decorated with fir branches, and small trees in shop windows glowed with lit candles. People were hustling and bustling down the cobbled streets, getting last-minute things for the holiday and wishing each other *Fröliche Weihnachten* (Merry Christmas). We stopped in front of the bakery and inhaled the delicious smells coming out of it each time someone opened the door. I gazed at the Napoleons displayed in the window, my mouth watering. "Oh, they must taste so delicious," I said wistfully.

"And that poppy-seed cake looks wonderful, too," Grandmother sighed.

"Maybe this wasn't such a good idea," Grandfather said sadly. "Now everyone is hungry for something they cannot have."

"But who is to say that you cannot have a Napoleon or some of that poppy-seed cake?" a voice behind us asked. As I turned around, a woman in a fur coat and hat took my hand. "Come on, let's all go into the bakery."

"Oh, no!" I replied, trying to pull my hand out of hers. But she wouldn't let go, so we all followed her inside. The woman bought a large Napoleon square and a horseshoe-shaped cake just for us. "Fröliche Weihnachten," she called out merrily, then disappeared into a crowd of people. To me, she seemed like a Christmas angel in a fur coat!

On the way back to the refugee camp, as I sank my teeth into that delicious, custard-filled Napoleon and got powdered sugar all over myself, I felt very blessed. Although we lived in a refugee camp, my grandparents and I had much to be thankful for.

That evening, Christmas Eve, the candles on the community Christmas tree were lit, and all the adults came to watch our Christmas play, which went very nicely. Everyone remembered their lines, and the choir sang beautiful Hungarian Christmas songs. Many people had tears in their eyes. And if that wasn't enough, each of the children was given a present from underneath the tree.

When I opened mine, I found a pair of red fuzzy mittens and a matching scarf in the box. Inside one of the mittens there was a little note written in English: "Merry Christmas from Mary Anne in Buffalo, New York, United States of America." Imagine that! A gift from a girl all the way from America! I wondered how old she was, what she looked like, and what she liked to do. I couldn't help but think of her as I drifted off to sleep that night.

When I awoke on Christmas morning, it was already light out. I heard noises coming through the thin, wooden boards of the barrack.

"Good morning, sweetheart. Merry Christmas," Grandmother said.

"Why is there so much noise out there already?" I asked sleepily, rubbing my eyes.

"Well, I guess some early rising children are enjoying the newly fallen snow."

"Oh, did it snow?" I said, leaping from the cot and reaching for some warm clothes to put on. "How wonderful! Where is Grandfather?"

"He and some of the other men are shoveling paths so people can go for their breakfast."

Within seconds, I was out there, too, marveling at nature's power to turn a drab refugee camp into a pristine winter wonderland.

Soon, the surrounding snow-covered hills were filled with squealing Austrian children, sledding down those hills in their new Christmas sleds, or flying down on their new skis. Meanwhile, we built snow people, had snowball fights, and made snow angels, squealing with just as much delight. Nature's gift of snow was free for everyone to enjoy!

As I romped in the snow wearing my new scarf and mittens, I said a quick prayer of thanks. For those few days in 1947, it didn't matter that we were in a refugee camp. From the angel in fur who bought us pastries, to the candles on the Christmas tree, the joyful school play, the unexpected presents, and the fluffy white snow, God had made our holiday extra-special.

We seek help from friends and family,
which is good, but believe in God,
and he will provide the most
meaningful assistance.

Thank you for today, God. It is a beautiful day to just be happy. I am surrounded by loving family and supportive friends. I'm working hard to achieve good grades, and love is in the air! It is not often that everything seems in my favor, and I just wanted to take the opportunity to thank you for blessing me with so many gifts. Amen.

It's so easy to complain about
what you don't have and wish
for something more, but it takes a
true believer of God to make
the best of what you're given.

Parents Are People

I used to be pretty sure my parents didn't even belong to the human race. I mean they were okay when I was little. But then when I got to be a teenager, you'd think an iron gate had closed around me.

It was like they wanted to know EVERYTHING about EVERYTHING. They wanted to know where I was going all the time, who was going to be there, when I'd be home, and what we were going to do. I just wanted to scream!

The ONLY peace I got was when I did church stuff. So I went on a weekend retreat absolutely delighted to have two whole nights to myself. We were divided up into groups of four to share cabins. There was a "counselor" who stayed with us, but she was only 19 and pretty easygoing.

We were all up pretty late sitting on our bunks and talking in the dark. I started going off about my parents watching my every move. I was comparing them to the CIA when this girl on the bunk below me started to cry. Everyone tried to ignore it, but finally I couldn't stand it anymore. I leaned my head down to her bunk. "You okay?" I asked.

"I'm sorry," she said. "You must think I'm crazy. It's just—well, if I tell you, you WILL think I'm crazy. . . ."

We all encouraged her to talk. We were really curious.

"My parents tried too hard to be nice," she began. "They wanted to give me space and let me be 'free.' It was great at first. All my friends loved to come to my house since there were hardly any rules. Then one weekend my parents went away. My boyfriend came over and well, he sort of forced me to have sex with him. I didn't want to but I couldn't think of a way to get out of it. I got pregnant; then a month ago, I had a miscarriage. . . . Now I'm living with foster parents. So I guess when you started complaining . . . to me, your parents sound perfect!"

I got home and decided that maybe my parents ARE human after all. I try to remember that they're doing what's best for me, even if I don't always like it. And I try not to complain about them quite so much.

Everyone talks about the "joy" of the teen years, but I can't help but think if these are the best years, I'm certainly not looking forward to the years to come. God, please help me to see what is so wonderful about the world you've created. Help me to learn from my mistakes and those of others to make the rest of my years better.

Help me to learn not to just live with what I've been given but to improve upon it. Teach me to cope with a less than ideal family life and the stress of schoolwork—all while helping me to make the right decisions in my own social environments and relationships.

Please show me your world is not as bad as it sometimes seems.

In the Wheat Field

It had seemed like an unbearable, unending summer. When you're a teenager, summers should be filled with friends, fun, and playing in the sun. You should walk the midway at the county fair, go swimming at the local pool, double-date at the drive-in, and revel in the leisure of carefree days. But my summer was not about any of those things.

Instead, the summer of 1975, the year I became a senior in high school, had been a test of my faith and inner strength. My mother was dying and was scheduled to have her leg amputated. For the last two months, I'd seen her ankle rot away as her body grew weaker. It had been a painful and trying time for our whole family. I'd been praying to God to heal her, pleading with him to make her better. My mom and I didn't get along very well, and we needed time to heal our relationship. But, despite how much I prayed, it seemed like God wasn't listening to me.

I sat at the edge of my grandfather's wheat field in the hot Kansas haze and looked out over the stalks of grain standing listless in the still, dry air. Tears streamed down my cheeks as I shouted, "Are you real?" There was no answer. I poured my heart out to God, reminding him how he had promised to hear my prayers. Yet my mother was near death and about to lose her leg. I sat there for what seemed like hours, until my legs were cramped and my tears were spent. The heat made shimmering waves across the field, but not a drop of air stirred. My hair was plastered to my cheeks from the heat and my tears. With a sad certainty I finally made a decision: It seemed that no answer meant my faith was hollow. No answer meant there was no God. It hurt me to realize I had put my hope and trust in a God who didn't hear and didn't exist. It hurt that my heart had been deceived. In one final attempt to be heard, I yelled out to God, "Prove that you're real!"

It happened as quickly as the twinkling of an eye: The sky filled with golden color, and the wheat stalks became moving reeds of gold as they swayed in the cool breeze that suddenly blew past me. That was what my eyes saw and my skin felt. What happened in my heart is harder to explain. I had an overwhelming sense of the presence of God. A peace flooded my broken heart, convincing me that all was well and that God was not only real but also in control of all creation. I knew everything would be okay. I knew my mother would live, and I would have more time with her. I felt a peace I had never known before—peace in the knowledge that I would never again doubt the Lord.

I am 47 now, and that wheat field still stands in my memory as a place of holy reverence. The Lord did hear me cry out to him there, and he answered my prayers. My mother lived for 15 more years, and we were able to mend our rocky relationship. Since that summer, I've had many ups and downs in my Christian walk. But I have never doubted that the Lord is in control. Time and time again, he has made his presence known to me. I can feel him all around me, as vibrant and real as a cool, stirring breeze on a hot summer day.

When you examine the lives of the most influential people who have ever walked among us, you discover one thread that winds through them all. They have been aligned first with their spiritual nature and only then with their physical selves.

ALBERT EINSTEIN

Oh, taste and see that the Lord is good; blessed is the man who trusts in Him.

PSALM 34:8 NKJV

Danger in the Waves

The setting could not have been more beautiful. It was a bright April morning on Fripp Island, South Carolina. A group of us, all high school seniors only weeks from graduation, were enjoying a weekend together.

After a long bike ride on the quiet paths beneath the palms, my friends Kerrie and Beth and I were ready for a swim. Fripp Island is a private island with limited access, so there are no crowds. We had the whole stretch of beach to ourselves.

Though the sun was hot, the water was still cool in April, and Kerrie and I waded in slowly, gritting our teeth and laughing at ourselves as we tried to adjust. Beth had already plowed through the waves to beyond the breakers, oblivious to the chilly water. Kerrie and I grew concerned because we knew that Beth was not a strong swimmer and had, in fact, always been a little afraid of the water. We were surprised that she would go out so far alone.

Kerrie said Beth needed to come in closer to shore, so we called to her, but she didn't seem to hear us over the crashing of the waves. I strode out toward her, intending to convince her to head back to the shallows, but as I grew nearer I could hear her calling for help. I began to move quickly, concerned for Beth's fear but feeling none for myself. I was a confident swimmer, plus the water at that point was still shallow enough for us to stand. In the past, Beth had become frightened while swimming in a pool, so I assumed she just felt panicky because she was alone. It would be easy to take her by the hand and walk her back to the shore.

I made my way to Beth, grabbed her hand, soothed her, and tried to walk toward shore using my other hand to paddle. Though our feet could touch the ground, the water was chest deep, and the waves were frequent because the tide was coming in. After a while I was astonished to discover that while we hadn't moved out any deeper, neither had we made any progress toward the shore. By this time, Kerrie had come out to meet us. I told her what was happening, so she grabbed Beth's other hand, and both of us worked to pull Beth toward shore, without any success. We tried walking and then swimming but, despite our best efforts, we seemed to be staying in one spot.

To make matters worse, the waves were increasing in height and frequency. Soon we could touch bottom in the trough of the waves, but the crests of the waves lifted us off our feet. Some were even sloshing over our heads.

By now I was in a state of disbelief. Kerrie and I were both strong, experienced swimmers who felt at home in the ocean. Because I had grown up swimming in a lake near my house, I had never feared drowning. With the naïveté and confidence of the young, I had always assumed that I could swim myself to safety. Now, amazingly, Kerrie and I seemed unable even to walk Beth back to shore.

As more and more waves rolled over our heads, some caught us by surprise, causing us to cough and sputter. Beth's voice began to rise in panic. I started to realize the seriousness of our situation: If Beth became hysterical, all could be lost. Incredible as it was, we were facing the reality that the three of us might drown there together.

I began to pray aloud, shouting between the waves for God to help us. Kerrie and Beth now learned the depth of my fear, because though I was religious, I had always been private about my faith, never discussing it unless asked.

Soon after, an idea came to me. If we couldn't pull Beth out, maybe we could *push* her. I didn't realize until later that this was not the safest solution, but at the time it was the only thing I could think to do. I let go of Beth's hand and moved behind her, not even taking the time to tell the other two what I was doing. I planted my hands firmly on Beth's back and then shoved her with all my might. To my joy and relief, she shot forward with Kerrie still grasping her hand. I caught up with her, gave her another big shove, and again she moved forward. After a few more pushes, she was walking toward the beach on her own, yet I still kept giving her little pushes, unable to believe we had actually made it back and were now safe.

I was in a state of shock, not only because of what had happened, but because I had learned that it *could* happen. Before, I would have never believed that I could be in danger of drowning so near the shore.

Later, when looking back on the event, Kerrie and I realized that we could have easily left Beth and saved ourselves at any time, since after she was moved to safety, we had no trouble gaining shore ourselves. We were happy to realize that the thought of leaving Beth had never occurred to either of us. We also learned that our difficulty was increased because Beth, knowing little of moving in the water, had thought the best way to assist us was to hold herself stiff and straight with her knees locked.

Kerrie said she was amazed at how far Beth shot forward with my first push. "You must have had a great burst of adrenaline," she told me. But I knew where that strength really came from: It was entirely from God. When I called out to him for help, he heard me and answered my desperate prayer. During that April trip to the beach, I learned about many things: the fragility of life, the power of friendship, and the grace and strength of the Lord.

Look to the Lord and his strength; seek his face always. Remember the wonders he has done, his miracles, and the judgments he pronounced.

1 CHRONICLES 16:11–12 NIV

Thank you, God, for always being there to answer my prayers. I know sometimes I take your presence in my life for granted. I try to hide my faith from my friends because I don't want them to think I'm different. But I know my true friends would respect my relationship with you. Please help me to share you with my friends so that they may know the joy of loving you, too.

Who Knows God Best?

I grew up in a very religious home. My grandparents would NEVER miss church. We never ate a bite of food that hadn't been prayed over. If, heaven-forbid, we passed an accident on the highway, my mother would pull over and we would all say a prayer for the souls involved.

I felt I knew God and Jesus. I was confident in myself, my prayers, and my Lord.

I went to parochial school all through elementary and junior high. Our town was small, however, and we couldn't support a private high school, so in ninth grade I switched to public school.

All my friends did, too. So it wasn't like I didn't know anybody. But there were also lots of kids from around the area that I didn't know. We were the one high school for three counties.

I knew there would no longer be prayer at school. That was okay. I prayed on my own a lot by this time, and of course our whole family always went to church together. We spent Sunday together as a family. I loved it. It was so much a part of me!

Then I began to meet kids with totally different beliefs. I got to be friends with a girl in my homeroom. Priya's family was from India. At first we just talked about school stuff. Then one day, I invited Priya to spend Sunday with my family and me. She began talking with us about how lovely our church was and how different it was from hers. My parents listened and nodded and smiled while she explained the differences. I was starting to feel really funny about the whole thing.

Next thing I knew, I was invited to a Friday night potluck with another new friend. Sarah was Jewish. I knew that she always wore a Star of David and didn't eat cheeseburgers or pork chops, but that was about all I knew. When I asked my parents if I could go, I thought they'd be upset. But they looked at each other and smiled and nodded and sent me on my way.

The service was beautiful with lots of singing that I couldn't understand. But there was no mention of Jesus. "We don't believe he was the son of God," Sarah explained to me later. My mouth dropped open. Of course he was God's son. It was all I could do not to cry. I didn't know what to say in response.

I was so confused. Was everything I'd been taught just wrong? Were Sarah and her family wrong? And what about Priya?

Of course, I was old enough to know that there are many beliefs in the world. But still . . . I had been brought up so strongly to believe in OUR way. I prayed a lot about that. I went for a long walk. It was funny how I noticed all the people. There were couples I never would've put together in a million years. A little fat man happily holding hands with his tall, thin wife. Little old ladies with their various little old dogs. Dads with kids, moms walking with friends, families having picnics.

I don't know how to describe to you exactly what I was thinking. It was like God was showing me how we're all different, and yet we're all the same. And I came to understand and believe that it's okay. The important thing is to believe in whatever is right for you and to live a good life. I guess there are as many ways to find God as there are people in the world.

I still find him at our church, but I know that Sarah and Priya find him in different ways. He hears us all—I know it.

The multitude of those who believed were of one heart and one soul; neither did anyone say that any of the things he possessed was his own, but they all had things in common.

ACTS 4:32 NKJV

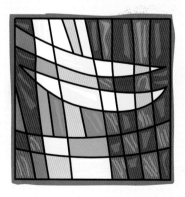

✤   ✤   ✤

I believe that God is in me
as the sun is in the color and fragrance of a flower—
the Light in my darkness,
the Voice in my silence.

HELEN KELLER

✤   ✤   ✤

Take comfort in the small miracles God gives us every day:
The sun will rise and set.
Someone will be born and another laid to rest.
Prayers will be said, and answers will be provided.
Rest assured that one day the sun will rise on you.
And it will be your prayers that are answered, too.

The Most Precious Angel

By the time I turned 14, I guess you could say I'd learned a lot about life, death, and adult weirdness. And about angels.

I was just seven when I had to learn my first hard lesson about life. My dad got really sick that year. He had to have surgery a bunch of times and really hated the fact that my mom had to support us. I think it was one of those "male" things. I was too young to understand why it finally got so bad that he reached the point of no return and took his own life. As if a seven-year-old could understand any of it, which I didn't. I only knew that I missed him a lot. So did my older sister, Angelina, and brother, Marco. What I understood most was that my mom was really sad.

I had happy memories of the years before my dad got sick and knew that he and my mom had been really happy. I guess that explains why I understood and wasn't upset when she met Kenneth and fell in love again. I wanted her to be happy, and he seemed like a nice man. The whole family thought he could be the answer to our mom's loneliness and be a loving fatherly figure, which we kids all wanted and needed.

We were wrong.

It went okay at first. He treated us really well, but then after the wedding he changed. He didn't have too much to do with me . . . maybe because I was the "spittin' image" of my dad. Or maybe he just didn't care. I still don't know. Finally my brother moved out, and eventually even my mother decided she just couldn't take it anymore. There was a long, problem-filled divorce, mainly about who got possession of the house we were building. We had to move away, but after some details were worked out, we got to move back home. That whole situation was another really hard lesson. Luckily, I got to stay in the same school during the moves, which made it easier.

I had also learned by my 14th birthday that guys are a lot of trouble . . . probably more than they're worth. It didn't take school to teach me that! But then I saw how lonely my mom was, and I realized she would soon be alone. Once I'm done with high school, I'm planning to go to college and become a journalist and writer. My brother was married and already gone, and my sister would be out of school and leaving soon, too.

"Dear God," I prayed every day, "please send someone who will make my mother happy." But if that was going to happen, I decided, she had to do her part.

"You need to be dating," I told her one day. "You've got to get out of this house." I don't know who was more sur-prised by what I said, mom or me. "You'll be okay," I assured her when she hesitated.

Believe me, though, she dated some guys that made me wonder what was wrong with me for ever suggesting it to her! But I kept praying, and one day she brought home someone different. His name was James Newcomb. The fact that he was so different actually scared me.

Whoa, I thought. *She's going to get hurt. Again.*

I tried talking to her. "I don't want you being with him," I said. "I've changed my mind about you going out."

"Give him a chance," my mother said.

Why should I? I asked myself. If you risk loving someone, you just wind up getting hurt. Or left.

But I did as she asked. Soon, my mother was beginning to smile. There was a twinkle in her eye. She was in love with James and he with her. I saw how happy he made her. . . and oh, how he treated her! He did lots of little things . . . sentimental and personal. If she said she liked something, he would get her a card or small gift that was a reminder of it. It told me he was truly paying attention. Most of all, though, he listened to her. And, surprise of all surprises, he even listened to me. And he didn't try to take my mother out of my life, either.

Not being listened to . . . or noticed . . . is the loneliest thing in the world. But James cared about me and what I felt and thought. He gave me a chance to speak my mind about everything and treated me like one of his own three children. It didn't take me long to figure out his love limits— there weren't any. He had enough love and kindness for all of us.

"Come with me to pick out your mother's ring," he invited me. "You know what she likes." No kid was ever happier at a wedding than I was at theirs.

I will always think of James as my father. We spend a lot of time together— sharing birthday parties and Sunday NASCAR races and ball games—and daily life that is so good, as life can only be when guided by an angel. Oh yes, James is an angel. What else could he be?

I have always believed in angels. It makes sense, really, when you think about it. God needs someone to help us out. If you are like me, though, your first thought when you hear "angels" is creatures with golden halos, long white robes tied with belts of sunflowers, wings lined with golden silk that sparkles in the sunlight, and beauty that can put a smile on even the saddest face.

But this angel, James, has black hair, a beard, and a mustache. He laughs a lot and likes to drive his new Camaro. He hides Christmas gifts—a sapphire ring for me—in a Cracker Jack box! He listens and—even more important—*remembers* what I say. If I talk about something important to me, he'll bring it up again weeks later, and he always shows that he cares about my opinions, feelings, and ideas. From the first day he walked into my life, he's made it better for me and my family. I thank God for him every day.

James has more than earned his angel wings, for he had a really tough job: gaining the love and affection of someone who's always been deathly scared of love. Now I'm not. Who but one of God's angels could make such a change happen?

Look around you. God's angels are everywhere. They could be homeless children on the streets or someone sitting next to you on a train or a bus. Or someone coming into your life as an answer to prayer to bring you a new chance. Treat every person as if he or she has some special meaning in your life, because it could really help you in the long run. Everyone is created for a special purpose. I've learned this from James . . . not from how I treat him, but how he treats my mom, me, and our whole family in little ways each day: with compassion, kindness, humor, respect, and attention.

As I'm learning through James, and because of how our family is doing these days, it just goes to show you that it's not the big things that mean the most, but the small ones. In the hands of an angel, they are more than big enough to change anyone's life.

For each whimper, there is compassion.
For each tear, there is comfort.
For each heartache, there is mercy.
And for each life, there is an angel,
taking instructions from God.

A Prayer of Chance

I couldn't have prayed any harder if someone had paid me to do it! All I wanted was for my cousin to come home safe. He was in the Army and had been stationed on the front lines of an area in conflict.

I'd always been taught to trust God and believe in the power of prayer, and I did. With my whole heart. I got friends together, and we held prayer vigils. If someone told me they were praying for the soldiers, I'd ask them to pray for Robert in particular. At one point, my dad took me aside and said "It's not a contest, you know: 'The one with the most prayers comes home.' It doesn't work like that." I guess he thought I was focusing too much on Robert instead of pray-ing for the safe return of all our soldiers. Still I prayed my own fervent pleas for Robert to come home.

Robbie had always been my favorite relative. He was the only one who didn't tease me about being the shortest guy. He was funny and nice and about the best baseball practice pitcher a hitter could ever hope for!

Yet in spite of my faith—in the face of all my prayer— we got the phone call saying that my cousin had been killed in action. I was devastated. I didn't wait to hear any of the details. I went to my room and began screaming at God. How could I be so forsaken? How could my faith have been so misplaced? I had trusted and believed.

Later, I learned that Robert had been killed while saving a village of women and children. If not for him and other members of his company, about 30 women and 45 children would have been gunned down by enemy fire.

It took a few weeks for me to understand that my prayers had been answered. Not in the way that I had wanted them to be, not in the way that I had prayed for it to work out for me and Robert and the rest of the family. But Robert had been where he was supposed to be; he'd done God's work. And that's what faith and prayer are all about. It just doesn't always work out the way we expect it to.

Why should you trust in a God that takes family members and friends away? Why should you believe in a God that allows buildings to fall at the hands of evil? Why should you have faith when so many daily life events cause chaos and discomfort?

Believe in him because you would not feel such pain if you had not been blessed with happiness first. Trust that he will replace the pain with a new source of joy.

Is Anything Too Small for God?

As children, we eagerly approach God with all our concerns, not stopping to contemplate how important they are. But as we get older, we start to wonder if the little things in our lives are really worth God's time. When I'm faced with a crisis, I like to look back to two childhood incidents. To me, they illustrate God's caring nature and his willingness to answer our prayers, whether our troubles are big or small.

When I was five years old, there was a fire in the forest behind our home. I was so young, it seemed as though the flames were coming dangerously close. Lying in bed that night, looking out at the stars, I prayed that the fire would not come near our house. I even asked God for a sign. If a certain star twinkled, everything would be all right. It did, and I drifted off to sleep.

The next morning, the fire had either burned itself out or been extinguished. That's when I learned my first lesson about answered prayer.

The second event happened when I was a teenager. After much discussion and a little arguing, I finally persuaded my father to let me get my ears pierced. As the holes in my ears healed, I searched for the perfect pair of earrings to wear, and I eventually decided on a pair of antique-looking beauties decorated with blue stones. Coming from such a poor family, I didn't have many pieces of jewelry, so I was quite proud of my new purchase.

One night I was out with some friends, riding around here and there, exploring city parks. When I got home, I realized I had lost one of my precious earrings. I was heartbroken, and I prayed that God would help me find it. It never occurred to me that God wouldn't care about a piece of costume jewelry; all I knew was that he had answered my prayers before, and I hoped he would answer this one, too.

My friends and I had been to so many different places that night, finding a tiny earring seemed out of the question. Yet I asked God to show me where to look. As I thought about it, I saw the earring lying on white gravel, around the bleachers at a ball park. There was only one place that fit this description, and the next day I talked my friends into taking me there. Even though the area was large, by the grace of God I found my earring!

Throughout the years, these two examples of answered prayer have helped sustain my faith. If I'm faced with a problem, a struggle, or fear, I know I can share my troubles with God and ask him for his guidance and help.

As an adult, there are times when I don't want to bother God with a prayer that might seem unimportant. Then my mind goes back to the earring, which I now wear on a chain. To me, it serves as a reminder that God cares about every issue in our lives, no matter how large or small.

❖ ❖ ❖

Know that whether it's a minuscule
thought or a monstrous concern,
the Lord is listening.

❖ ❖ ❖

Show me your faith without deeds,
and I will show you my faith by what I do.

JAMES 2:18 NIV

❖ ❖ ❖

I trust, Lord, that you have faith in me. But today I feel
unworthy of anything. I hate everything about myself, and I
just can't bring myself out of this funk. Everything I touch
seems destined for failure, and I have no confidence in my
abilities. God, please give me some encouragement and
bless me with praise so I can begin to pick myself up and
try again.

❖ ❖ ❖

If you do not stand firm in your faith,
you will not stand at all.

ISAIAH 7:9 NIV

I can do all things through Christ
who strengthens me.

PHILIPPIANS 4:13 NKJV

*It's difficult to have faith in
someone you cannot see or feel,
but watch a summer sunset or
the fury of a passing storm,
and the Lord will assure you
he is indeed for real.*

God gave burdens,
also shoulders.

YIDDISH PROVERB

Never Alone

In 1998, I was a senior at a high school in Pittsburgh, Pennsylvania. Several of us weren't doing very well in trigonometry, and our teacher had agreed to tutor us once a week in the evening after dinner. My mother picked me up at the school around 9:00.

One evening, my teacher had to leave our tutoring session a little early. I called my mother and asked her to pick me up before our regular time. As was customary for most students, I waited at the rear entrance of the school for my ride. Several of my classmates stood with me until their rides showed up. Soon, all the other students were gone. I was left alone in the building, except for the security guards stationed at their desks at the main entrance. In the evenings, the guards locked the rear doors from the outside. The only way in was through the main entrance at the front of the building.

Once I was alone I began to sing, periodically looking out the glass doors for my mother. Because I was alone, I sang very loudly. I was enjoying my time alone with God. *I'm never alone,* I sang. *I don't have to worry because I am never alone. He walks beside me all of the way. He guides my footsteps every day. Never alone, I don't have to worry because I am never alone.*

While singing, I saw a man walking back and forth near the rear entrance doors. He motioned for me to open them. I knew that he was too old to be a student, so I didn't let him in. He walked away, and I continued singing. Then the man reappeared. He paced back and forth in front of the doors a few times then walked away.

I kept right on singing. I could hear my voice echo through the hallway and bounce off the school walls. Then, suddenly, a rush of self-consciousness washed over me as I felt someone behind me. I stopped singing and turned around. It was the man who had wanted me to open the doors. He glanced at me strangely but said nothing. I turned around, embarrassed that he had heard me singing so loudly. His footsteps faded toward the front doorway. I didn't recall seeing that man before, and I wondered why security had let him in. Or had the man snuck into the building somehow?

A little nervous now, I continued singing, watching for my mother's car. A few moments later I saw the man on the street again at the rear entrance doors. Only this time he stopped right in front of the doors, reached into his coat, and pulled out a gun! He looked directly into my eyes. He didn't move, but held the gun so I could see it. Maybe it was 30 seconds or so, but it seemed like an eternity. The song died from my lips as I stood there in shock. I don't know what made me stand completely still, but in my mind all I kept thinking was, *He has a gun. Don't move.* We held each other's eyes just a few seconds longer, then suddenly he shoved his gun back in his coat and walked away. Shortly after that, my mother drove up, and I rushed to the car. It was then that the terror of what could have happened fully gripped me. I trembled as I told my mother what just occurred.

Then I realized why God had put that song in my heart. It was almost like a prayer I'd been singing over and over, without fully realizing it. God protected me through that song; I believe it saved my life. And now, if I'm ever feeling scared or lonely, I just think back to that night. Because that was when I learned that I am truly never alone.

God,
It is so comforting to know that you are always looking out for me. The world can be a scary place, but I know that I am never far from your loving gaze. Please continue to watch over me and fill my heart with your peace. Amen.

Be anxious for nothing, but in everything by prayer and supplication, with thanksgiving, let your requests be made known to God.

PHILIPPIANS 4:6 NKJV

What's on Your Mind?

Close your eyes and listen. What's it like to listen to the Lord rather than asking him for something? What happens when you are open to doing his work in his way? Try doing this for a week. Each night, write down your thoughts and feelings. What are you learning?

School Matters

I am always ready to learn; but I did not always like being taught.

WINSTON CHURCHILL

These are the best days of your life. Does it ever seem like you've heard that line from everyone you know? Your teachers have told you and your parents have told you and every relative you have has told you. So why does it seem like some days life couldn't get any worse? Your teachers and parents treat you like a child but expect you to be as responsible as an adult. Social situations at school can be downright painful. And everyone keeps talking to you about the future—as if you could possibly think past today!

However, even though it may not seem like it sometimes, you are standing on the threshold of great things. You're only years away from independence, from college, maybe from living away from home for the first time. Take advantage of this time. Remember that God is with you every step of the way. He's been by your side each year, grade by grade, and can always be counted on when you feel overwhelmed, lost, or alone.

Common Ground

I dreaded the next few hours. My school grades were hitting the floor, and I knew I was going to have to face my parents sooner or later. I was sure they would ground me, take away my computer and TV, and not allow me to use the phone for a month.

I decided to escape to a friend's house long enough for my parents to cool down once they saw the report card my school had mailed home. But as I dashed downstairs, my father was standing there waiting for me, holding the opened report card notice.

Prepared for the worst, I headed into the kitchen where my mom was waiting. I quietly asked what my punishment would be and was shocked when my dad came in and told me they had no plans to punish me. My mom simply smiled at me and said, "Let's go."

We got in the car and drove to my favorite restaurant—a steak house by the riverfront. I had no idea what was going on. We got a table and sat down. I just couldn't handle it anymore. "What's going on here?" I asked.

"We're going to have dinner," my dad responded. "And then the three of us are going to talk about you and your future. We only want the best for you. But you're going to have to start doing your part by getting better grades and devoting more time to your schoolwork."

Now I was really stumped. They wanted to TALK? That was it? No yelling? No punishment?

And we did talk, for three hours straight. When we finally got home, I actually felt great! In fact, I realized I had common ground with my parents: concern for the fate of my own future, to be exact. I also realized that I really liked my parents; they truly did have my best interests at heart.

What a concept, I thought. Talking to your parents. It was something I planned to do more often.

Lord,
When times are really tough and I feel alone and lost, help me to understand that my parents are not my enemies. Even when we argue and disagree, never let me forget that they care and that they are always looking out for me. And when I really feel like I cannot tell them what is going on in my life, let me remember that they, too, were my age once and that their concern for me comes from a place of wisdom, experience, and love. Thank you, Lord.

As you wrap up your duties of K through 12, remember your future is as bright as the star you set your sights upon.

Rapping Up an A

"There's no way I'm going to remember all this stuff, man. Biology is the bane of my existence," I lamented.

In case you haven't guessed, I'm a little dramatic. Not that I don't have reason to be. I have a biology quiz tomorrow, and I'm just not sure I'll pass it. My parents have already warned me that if I fail another biology quiz, I will be grounded for two weeks. They don't think I bother to study. The thing is, I do study. I just can't seem to remember everything.

My buddy Steve is helping me study, but he's one of those guys that already knows everything about biology and has a steel-trap mind, so he never has to study.

In fact, he's playing some video game while I'm over here trying to memorize the internal organs of an earthworm. Like I'm ever going to need to know that in real life anyway!

"Hey, man, put down that joystick and help me out. I'm dying over here," I yelled. "How do you just remember everything? Do you have a photographic memory or something?"

Steve put down the joystick and turned to look at me. "You've got to promise you won't make fun of me," he said. He waited for me to promise, then continued, "I memorize things by turning them into a song."

"Get serious, man, I can't flunk this quiz," I said.

"I am serious. You know how you can remember a song better than memorizing some list? Here, check this out."

Then he proceeded to show me a notebook full of his "biology raps." Yes, it was a little nerdy, but I had to admit it worked.

We had fun memorizing the songs that night. We never did find a word that rhymed with *mitochondria,* but armed with those catchy tunes I was ready.

And though I did get a little embarrassed when Jenny Mallory, the cutest girl in school, heard me humming a tune about an earthworm's lower intestine being used for digestin', I aced the quiz, passed biology, and developed a foolproof way to study for the rest of my high school and college days.

Why, Lord, do you make some people seem so naturally smart while I feel like I must struggle to even get a C? I know I've given up trying, but it just didn't seem like studying was working. I really want to get good grades so I can go to college and have a great career, but it's just so discouraging when I put the effort in and still see no change in my grades. Please bless me with patience to study, wisdom to learn, and strength to keep trying. Amen.

*A grade is nothing more than a goal
for you to exceed.*

The Unexpected Visit

Most of the kids at this school are white. It's a nice town—very open-minded. Everyone, no matter what religion or color, is welcome everywhere. Kids seem to hang out together and do stuff together.

Still, there is prejudice.

Look around you. It's lunchtime in the cafeteria. What do you see? (Besides the bad food, I mean!) See that table in the corner? Who's sitting there? The foreign exchange student from Germany, a couple of kids from India, and a kid who got an assigned seat for starting a food fight.

Now that table over there? Those are all the cheerleaders. They all sort of look alike, don't they? Their coloring, I mean. It's all pretty much white.

There's another table with the two American Indian students.

The Jewish kids have a table, and the black kids are all over there at those two tables on the side.

Why is this still happening? I really thought prejudice was a thing of the past. I bet you'd tell me you're not prejudiced. Maybe we all need to turn bright colors for a while. Will that help everyone see how ridiculous this is?

I just don't know what else to do. Maybe you should read my words a bit more. Think for yourselves. The only words you need are: people and peace. We're all people. We need to live in peace.

I can't stay. Not yet. But I'll be back. Every so often my Father in heaven sends me down to this lunchroom. He says that when I come down here and can't pick out any groups at the tables, then it will be time.

Good Luck!

Let us treat men and women well;
treat them as if they were real.
Perhaps they are.

RALPH WALDO EMERSON

Questions you won't be asked on your first job interview: What kind of shoes did you have in high school? Who were your friends? What was your most embarrassing moment in school? Did you have a boyfriend in high school? Have you ever been kissed?

Facing the End and Beginning Again

Life was so easy when I was a toddler.
I had no cares
    except, maybe, to find where Mom was.
But then it was off to the big yellow bus.
I was facing the end and beginning again.

Off to school I went.
And made lots of new friends.
Still not many cares
    except, maybe, where to play at recess.
But then it was time for the big junior high.
Facing the end and beginning again.

It was the first time I experienced being the "low person"
    in school.
Had to prove I was worthy of cliques and clubs.
Established myself and was uprooted again.
Off to the home of the big, bad seniors.
Facing the end and beginning again.

Now I'm a senior, and it's all about to change again.
But this time it's different—
More final, more done.
The friendships I formed over the years
    will be spread about at schools and jobs.
Opportunities will knock, and I'll be in charge.
Facing the end and beginning again.

I wish my peers wouldn't torment some of the less popular kids at school. They are often very cruel. I feel guilty for not standing up for those teased, but if I do, I'll just become one of the dorks and get teased, too. God, please forgive me for not speaking up, and give the victims of the cruelty courage to stand tall and not take it to heart.

Being popular isn't everything.
It won't get you a diploma.
It won't get you into college.
It won't get you a job.
It won't mean anything once you
leave the halls of high school behind.

Let no one despise your youth,
but be an example to the believers
in word, in conduct, in love, in spirit,
in faith, in purity.

1 TIMOTHY 4:12 NKJV

Making the Grade

All that mattered were my grades. I had to keep my grade point average up to get a scholarship. And I had to have a scholarship to be able to afford college. My mom had been on her own for a long time and hadn't been able to save much for college. She really wanted me to get a good education so I could get a good job and have a better life than hers. You know the story. So she kept telling me to study hard and keep up my grades.

I'm a decent student, but I'm not one of the brains. You know who they are—maybe you're one of them. I'm not putting them down. It's great. They were just born smarter and can get the grades without working so hard.

Now somebody like me—I'm pretty smart, I guess. But I have to work at it. I have to study like crazy. And this time, I just didn't take the time to study enough. I have a part-time job and also play softball on our church team. Pastor Bill has always been like a dad to me, so how could I tell him I was going to miss our big game so that I could study? I knew this test was important—pretty much our entire world history grade hinged on this timeline test.

I mostly prayed that it would work out. After all, I'm a good kid; I deserve good stuff. So I prayed a lot. But I didn't study nearly enough.

I thought my prayers were answered when Melody Menoff sat down next to me. She's one of those brainy kids, and she always holds up her paper to check her answers. It was pretty simple to just copy off her.

Too simple. I got caught. Got detention. Failed the test.

It ruined my grade point for the scholarship my mom was hoping I'd get. I'm going to go to community college now. That's actually fine with me.

I know the cheating was wrong and that God doesn't do stuff like that to answer prayers. But I do think my prayers were answered. I learned that I've got to think for myself and make choices. I should have missed the softball game, or I should've told my mom that I didn't mind going to community college. Either choice would've been better than the one I made. Next time, I think I'll pray for the wisdom to make the right choice.

❖   ❖   ❖

Dear God,

I'm so sorry I cheated on that big exam. No one found out, but I know you know, and I feel guilty. Please tell me what I should do—guide me in the right direction. I promise I won't cheat myself or others again; please forgive me for my wrongful actions. Amen.

❖   ❖   ❖

Cheating teaches you nothing but shame.

Lord,
Please help me to focus on my studies. It's so hard to dedicate myself to schoolwork with so many other pressures in my daily life. I'm distracted by thoughts about boys, upcoming parties and dances, and whether or not people think I'm cool. I know I am in school to learn. I really want to be successful, and I know I must be educated to do that, but sometimes it's so hard to juggle everything. Please give me guidance.

Wisdom is the principal thing; therefore get wisdom. And in all your getting, get understanding.
PROVERBS 4:7 NKJV

Dear God,
I think I'm in trouble. I have goofed off for much of my high school years because I didn't think I wanted to go to college. But now as I see all my friends filling out applications and making plans to live in dorms, I realize how foolish I've been. I don't know if there is any time to make up for my past mistakes, but I promise if I'm given a second chance I will use the opportunity wisely. Thank you and Amen.

Ms. Crabby's Class

Everyone hated her! Ms. Crabby wasn't really her name, of course, it was just what we called her. She never smiled! Everyone wondered if she even knew how. She wasn't that old yet, but you could see she was going to be one of those old women with the really deep frown lines between their eyes, from all her years of scowling.

I prayed and prayed that I would get the other ninth grade composition teacher, but the good Lord wasn't having it. On the first day of school, there I sat—placed smack in the front row of Ms. Crabby's class.

So I'd come home complaining day after day. The kids all came in ready to do battle, and she gave them a good show. She gave more detentions than any other teacher in the school. And she gave the most homework. I grumbled and whined. One night, my mom came into my room and asked me about Ms. Crabby. I gave her the usual rundown on why I hated her, why the whole school hated her.

"Why don't you try praying about it?" she suggested.

"Already did," I quickly replied. "Didn't do a darn bit of good."

"Well," she smiled, "did you pray about Ms. Crabby, or did you pray about yourself?" And off she went, claiming the dryer was buzzing.

It took a few days for me to get it. I mean of course I'd prayed about Ms. Crabby. I'd begged the Lord to get her out of my life! But a few days later, our priest was preaching about how you get back in life what you give out. If you give love, you get love, and if you're nasty, you get nasty stuff back. I nodded in agreement on that, thinking of Ms. Crabby.

Then I started thinking. *What if you refuse to give back the same stuff?* I mean, what if you give love to a nasty person? What will they do with that? After the service, I asked Father Clark.

"Why don't you try it?" he suggested.

So I began what I called "My Campaign of Nice." I started praying for Ms. Crabby to learn how to be happy, and I began being NICE to her. I smiled and always had my work done on time. I never talked out of turn during her class. My friends thought I'd gone nuts! At first, it was very discouraging. I began to feel my experiment was a complete failure. My last-ditch effort was on the last day of school before Christmas vacation. My mom had taken me shopping at one of those bath stores, and I had put together a basket of "happy" things that Mom said a woman would like—bath junk and stuff.

I hid it in my locker until the end of the day. I didn't want anyone to see me give Ms. Crabby a Christmas present. I ran into her room intending to just leave it on her desk, but she was there working. I set it down, said, "Merry Christmas," and started to run out.

She looked up, peering at me over the top of her half glasses. "Why?" was all she said.

"Huh?"

"Why would you give me a present?"

"It's Christmas," I said and tried to get to the door.

"This won't help your grade."

"I know. I just wanted to get you a present. To, um, to try and make you happy, I guess." And I walked away.

I didn't see her sit at her desk and cry, but she told me about it years later. For the rest of the year, everyone noticed that she was nicer. Two or three years later, the nickname Ms. Crabby had completely faded away.

I go to visit her now in her little apartment. She's long since retired, and now I'm the ninth grade composition teacher. We go for a walk in the park once a week. She loves to talk about the day I brought her the present. "It changed my world," she says and laughs.

She never told me why she was so crabby all those years. I guess it doesn't even matter. I'm just thankful I was able to do a little bit of God's good work. It changed both of our lives.

What should I do, Father, when I feel I am treated unfairly by one of my teachers? She is overly harsh and seems to expect more from me than any other student. Maybe it is because she suspects I am not working to my potential, but I really am trying. Help me to be the best student I can be, and please help her to see that I am trying.

❖   ❖   ❖

Remember, how you behave today will affect how you're remembered tomorrow.

Dress Code

I got suspended from school last month. My mother, bless her soul, almost had a heart attack when she got the phone call. I've always been a bit of a rebel, but basically I'm a good kid, and she knows it. She came to pick me up, and I was wearing this REALLY tight tube top, tiny little shorts, a bandanna on my head, and beach shoes. It was really hot outside, and I wanted to head right to the beach after school. Sure I know there's a dress code, but I didn't think anybody would really care about what I was wearing.

Mom was totally shocked. "What were you thinking? You know there are rules—there's a dress code for goodness sake!"

"I know, Mom, but it's really hot in class. There's no air-conditioning, and I couldn't take it another day."

She didn't say anything else—just looked at me with those "I'm really disappointed in you" eyes. That really got me. I don't want to be a disappointment.

It seemed like I'd been getting in trouble an awful lot lately. I know right from wrong, of course. I go to church; I've been listening to all the DARE lectures. I plan to wait until marriage for sex. It's nothing like that. It's just rules. I've always hated rules. It's like rules put me in a cage, and I can't rest until I get out.

When I got home I apologized to my mom and told her, "I just can't let those strangers tell me what to wear! I'm in charge of ME!"

"Yes you are, and I'm proud of you for saying that, feeling that, and knowing that. But they CAN tell you what to wear. There are lots of good rules, and it's important to know when to stand up and break a rule and when you need to let go and follow the rules."

I know the attitude I have is not a good one. It's getting me into trouble. I've been trying to thank God for giving me so many blessings—including the will to stand up to what I think is wrong. With my parents' guidance and the good Lord's help, I'm trying to learn where to draw the line.

I'm allowed to go back to school tomorrow. I plan to dress appropriately. I also plan to talk with the principal about starting a petition to change the dress code so we don't have to swelter when it's hot. Working to change the rules—YES! Breaking the rules? I don't plan to try that again.

I hate when my parents act like they understand what I'm going through every day. "I was a teenager once, too!" they say. But their generation didn't have to worry about date rape drugs and kids coming to school with guns and knives. Some things, of course, will always be the same, but I wish I could make my parents understand that sometimes school is a scary place. God, please help my parents see what I'm going through, and please provide me with strength as I head to the bus each day.

Brad

Brad, a lanky senior, loped into my English class 15 minutes late and slouched into an empty seat in the back row. His blue eyes darted around the classroom. He smirked and flipped his long blond hair out of his face.

"I hate English," he said, glaring at me, "but I need this class to graduate."

I smiled. "I'll try to make learning as painless as possible for you."

"Sure you will." He rested his head in his hands and burped.

Carlos, sitting in front of Brad, turned and frowned. "Knock it off."

Two of Brad's fingers burrowed into Carlos' back. "Who's gonna make me?" he sneered. "You, Carlos? You gonna make me?"

"That's enough, Brad," I said.

He rolled his eyes. "Anything you say, ma'am."

I passed out the class contracts and reviewed the assignments. "To earn an A, you must complete the course work, earn an A average on your tests, and do a creative project of your choice. Since this class covers the Bible as literature, your project must relate to the Bible. For a B . . ."

"What's for a C?" Brad interrupted.

"Complete the course work and earn a C average on tests."

"No project, right?"

I nodded.

"Put me down for a C."

The bell rang. On his way out, Brad shoved Carlos against the wall. "Don't mess with me," he threatened.

The fight in P.E. next period came as no surprise; neither did Brad's three-day suspension.

"What's the story on Brad Roberts?" I asked John, his counselor.

"Sad. His dad's dead. Mom's an alcoholic. He lives with his grandmother." John shook his head. "The kid's a real problem. Always picking fights. Academically, he's barely squeaking by. No motivation and a nasty attitude."

"Any chance to graduate?"

John shrugged. "Not short of a miracle, especially if I have to kick him out every other day for fighting."

At 1:00 that afternoon, two blue eyes met mine through a crack in the weathered door of Brad's house.

"What do you want?" Brad asked. "You ditchin' class?"

"It's my prep period. I came to talk."

"Yeah? What about?"

"You."

The chain clanked. Brad eased the door open. "You mind sittin' on the porch?" He motioned me to a faded patio chair, and he sat down on the rickety top step. "Well?"

"I'd like to see you graduate, Brad."

He scratched his head. "That it?"

"That's it—except that I'm willing to help." I leaned forward and looked him square in the face. "Do you think you can stop fighting long enough to make it happen?"

He looked down. "I gotta get to work, ma'am."

Thursday, Brad was back.

"Today we're doing journal writing," I said. "You may write about anything you want." I looked at Brad. "If you contracted for a C, one journal page is due at the end of class."

I was a little surprised later when I read what Brad had written. *I got a little sister, Karen,* he wrote. *She's 11. She's in Las Vegas with my aunt. I never get to see her. My mom's a drunk. That's why they took Karen away. I'm working two jobs. If I want to call Karen, I have to pay. I don't care about my mom, but I love my little sister. If I save up, Grandma lets me call Karen once a month and talk for a long time. I like to send Karen presents to make her happy. I'm saving for a real pretty Easter basket, for when she comes to Grandma's on Easter Sunday. Well, now you know. P.S. I don't have no idea where my mom is. She don't care nothing about me.*

The next day I watched Brad read my comments. *Come in after school if you'd like to talk,* I had written on his journal. He looked at me and nodded.

"Here I am," Brad announced. He straddled a chair and drummed his fingers on my desk. It took a little coaxing, but I finally got him to open up and start talking. I got the feeling no one had listened to him in a while, and he was nearly bursting from keeping so much inside.

"When she's around," Brad said about his mom, "she don't think of nobody but herself and where the next drink's comin' from. She's sick, and I s'pose I should feel sorry for her, but she took off and busted up the family. I have to take care of Grandma, Karen had to leave, and it's not fair. It's just not fair."

"I don't blame you for being angry, Brad. You got stuck with a lot of responsibility."

He looked out the window and then at me, his eyes brimming with tears. "The worst part is not seeing Karen," he said quietly. He wiped his eyes and brushed back a wisp of hair. He told me he was saving for a bus ticket so Karen could come home at Easter.

"She's lucky to have a brother like you," I said.

As the semester progressed, Brad and I met periodically to talk. He almost always brought up Karen, and he confessed to me how he liked to paint, a hobby I encouraged him to pursue. Gradually, he got into fewer fights and stopped getting suspended. He even started to study and got As and Bs on his tests.

"Can I change my contract?" he asked in class one day.

"Sure. What would you like to change it to?"

He winked. "How about an A?"

Carlos turned around and snickered. "You've got to be kidding."

"Nope," Brad said. "When are the projects due, ma'am?"

"In six weeks, on our final day of class."

"If *you're* doing a project, Roberts, you better get started," Carlos said with a laugh.

Six weeks later, in came Brad with a huge covered canvas in his arms.

"Where do I put this, ma'am? It's my Bible literature project."

"Why don't you set it against the wall, where everyone in all my classes can see it when they come in?" I walked back to join him. "What have you done?"

With great care, Brad uncovered his project—an oil painting of *The Last Supper*. Shafts of morning sunlight glinted across the rich, vibrant colors, bringing Jesus and his disciples to life. For a few moments, I couldn't speak.

"Do you like it?" Brad asked.

"It's a masterpiece, Brad. I'm so proud of you!"

He grinned. "Been working on it after my jobs," he said. "I just finished it last night, so some of the colors might be a little wet. Tell the kids not to touch it, okay? See you this afternoon." He turned to leave, then turned back around. "Oh," he said, "I might be a little late. My counselor wants to see me—he's got some vocational school stuff I asked for."

When Brad's classmates came into English that afternoon, they gathered in clusters at the front of the room so they could see the painting in its proper perspective.

"Wow! That's awesome! Who did that?" someone asked.

"Brad," I said.

"*Our* Brad?"

I nodded.

"Where is he?" Carlos asked. "I want to congratulate him."

"Me, too," other students echoed.

"He said he'd be a little late," I said. "Let's get started. We have a lot of projects to share."

A few minutes later, Brad walked into the room. All the seniors stood up and applauded.

A wide grin spread across Brad's face. "Thanks," he said.

"Give him an A+," Carlos suggested. "He earned it."

"What are you going to do with that fantastic painting, Brad?" another student asked.

Brad's lips quivered only slightly. "I'm saving it for my little sister, for when she comes again to see me graduate," he said.

He looked at me, and I smiled at him. "Thanks, ma'am," he whispered.

❖   ❖   ❖

How much better to get wisdom than gold! And to get understanding is to be chosen rather than silver.

PROVERBS 16:16 NKJV

❖   ❖   ❖

The wisdom that comes from heaven is first of all.

JAMES 3:17 LB

❖   ❖   ❖

I need your strength, good Lord. I'm heading into that part of the year when term papers and finals abound, and I am never able to keep my cool under the pressure. I can answer almost any question in class, but as soon as the test is in front of me I freeze. Please help me to retain all that I know and provide me with courage as I face the blank page.

Ivy League Rude

I was definitely going to a good college—a recognizable name, a place with great people from terrific families, a school that practically guaranteed a good job and a generous salary when I graduated.

Sure it would be expensive, so what? It wasn't my money. My parents could afford it. After all, I was an only child! They wanted the best for me.

I'd worked hard all these years and gotten good grades. Why else did I do it? It's not like I really cared if I got an A.

We'd had a workshop in filling out college applications, so most kids had applied at the same time. That meant that the letters started coming around the same time, too. The letters letting you know if you got accepted or rejected. Of course, I got accepted everywhere I had applied. Why not? It would just be a matter of choosing which school had the colors I liked best or something.

I brought my letters to school, and we were comparing notes in comp class. "How 'bout you, Marge?" I asked a shy girl who sat in the back. Mostly I just wanted to flaunt my Harvard acceptance letter.

"I'm going to the community college," she replied. "I want to stick around so I can live at home and help out my mom with my little sisters."

Yeah, sure, I thought. Probably couldn't get in anywhere. Probably doesn't have any money to go either. Oh, well.

As we left class, I noticed that Marge dumped a whole bunch of stuff in the trash. I knew I shouldn't look, but when did that ever stop me? I reached in and looked through her stuff. There was a letter that looked just like one of mine. It was from Harvard. I opened it up and read. It was an acceptance and full scholarship. Whoa.

It wasn't until Sunday—during my forced appearance at church with my family—that I began to really think about stuff. Marge could've gone to college anywhere she wanted. She CHOSE to stay with her mom and help out. Jeez, was I a selfish brat or what? I looked around. Hmmmm. How come I always seem to figure stuff out in church? Guess maybe I'd better start coming willingly. It seems to do me good.

I'm still going to Harvard. My mom and dad don't need me to help them out. But now I don't flaunt my blessings. I count them and give thanks.

❖   ❖   ❖

God,
I am proud of what I've achieved in school. I've worked hard and gotten good grades. But I'm ashamed to admit, I've forgotten to keep up my relationship with you. I've taken my blessings for granted. I haven't taken even a second out of my busy schedule to thank you for walking beside me every step of the way. So thank you. Amen.

Underneath It All

"No-o-o!" The high-pitched wail was so distressed it sent cold chills up and down my arms, even though it was September and the temperature was near 90 degrees. I knew immediately who it was . . . and I was pretty sure I knew who and what had caused her to scream.

Gritting my teeth, I walked across the playground. The hysterical sobbing continued. "Tony!" I said as calmly as I could manage, considering the commotion going on, "Give it back! Now!" The square-faced eighth-grade boy flushed a bright red and threw the wool ski cap he was holding back to its owner. The tiny kindergarten girl from whom he'd taken the cap was crying so hard she didn't even notice.

"Mandi," I said, bending down next to her. "Mandi, it's okay. Here . . . Tony gave your cap back." She snuffled a hiccup, grabbed the wool cap, and pulled it down over her fuzz-covered, nearly bald head. With shaking fingers clutched tight, she held on with a death grip, tears still running down her pale cheeks. Her huge blue eyes stared up at me from under the cap, and the terror there was very real . . . too real for a five-year-old.

"Mandi," I whispered, "you're such a pretty girl. Why don't you take your hat off today? It's too hot to wear it anyway." Mandi jammed the hat down to her eyebrows and shook her head. She crossed her arms and looked away, letting me know the discussion was at an end.

I sighed and turned to Tony. He squirmed a little and smiled up at me hopefully. "Sorry," he said, "I didn't know she was going to go crazy over that stupid hat."

"Leave her alone," I said, enunciating each word with great care so there would be no mistake. "Do not, under any circumstances, touch her or that cap again." I raised my eyebrows in an expression I saved only for special occasions. Tony nodded quickly. The look on his face was so sincere, I almost laughed. He wasn't a bad kid. I knew he was just a typical teenage boy... from his fashionably oversized denim shirt right down to his untied basketball shoes with fluorescent laces. And right now he'd agree to anything I said just to stay out of trouble. But I knew the minute I turned my back, all previous agreements went out the window.

I wondered if he'd be any different if he knew more about Mandi. What would he say if I told him that the little kindergartner riding the swings could tell him all he ever wanted to know about leukemia? That all summer, while he'd been playing baseball with his friends and jumping his bike over garbage cans in the backyard, she'd lain in a hospital bed struggling with chemotherapy treatments. Being constantly weak and sick to her stomach hadn't seemed to get her down, her mother told me, but Mandi cried big silent tears when her beautiful long blond hair began to fall out in clumps.

Now the disease was in remission. For the moment, Mandi had a future. But her main concern was that her hair was gone... her pretty hair. The day she got home from the hospital, she had found the winter cap in her dresser. She'd pulled it over her bare head, and there it stayed—despite pleading, cajoling, and even threats from the adults in her world. Even teasing from the older kids at school hadn't made a difference. I sighed and went over to sit on a bench. I'd learned long ago that life wasn't always fair, but knowing didn't make acceptance one bit easier.

A few minutes later, I noticed some kids clustered together and wondered what was going on. I saw Tony and was prepared to nail him to the wall this time if he'd dared to put a hand on Mandi's hat. He had. His face was redder than ever, and he squirmed when he saw me coming. As Mandi skipped past me, my plans for Tony changed—I saw a big hug in his future.

Mandi's eyes were filled with pride. A big smile dimpled her little cheeks. "Look!" she cried with delight. "I'm pretty!" The cap was gone. In its place, tied into a clumsy bow around her fuzzy head, was one of Tony's bright yellow shoelaces.

Growth occurs in many small steps.

H

He who reigns within himself and rules passions, desires, and fears is more than a king.

JOHN MILTON

Lord,
I pray today to ask for your help. I hate having to speak in front of my peers because they are always so judgmental. But today I have a presentation, and I have to stand up in front of the class. The thought sends chills down my spine, and I hope you will bless me with the confidence and poise to get through the project without too much harm to my ego. To know that I have you silently encouraging me will be all the strength I need. Thank you.

Everyone loves to tell a good story—and tales of high school embarrassment always keep a crowd's attention. In four or five years, you'll be sitting around a table with tears of laughter streaming down your face, talking about the day you walked off the school bus straight into the flagpole. So don't give it a second thought today.

What's on Your Mind?

Imagine your perfect school day. How does it start? What happens during the day? What do you have for lunch? How do you interact with teachers? With friends? What after-school activity do you participate in? Use the space below to describe your perfect day.

_____

_____

_____

_____

_____

Now, think about how you can make some or all of your dreams happen. What will you pray for? How will your prayers be answered?

_____

_____

_____

_____

_____

Dreaming Together

Once again, my parents were pressuring me to think about college prep classes and testing, and I didn't have the heart to tell them what I wanted.

Some of my friends had already decided on careers, and the ones who didn't have a say in it had already come to accept their parents' master plans for their lives. I, on the other hand, didn't want to go right to college. I wanted to travel in Europe, meet other young people from different backgrounds, and see what the world had to offer.

My parents wanted to send me to a great college to study law or medicine or something that would guarantee me a secure future. I had no interest in law or medicine. It wasn't that I didn't respect lawyers or doctors. I just knew in my soul that I didn't want to become either one. My dad especially would go ballistic if I told him I wanted to put off college, just for a year, so I could go to Europe and learn to speak Spanish, Italian, or French.

But when my mom and dad told me they wanted to go over application packages one night after dinner, I knew I had to take a stand. I had never been a super religious person, but I often prayed when I was confused, and this was one of those times. I sat in my bedroom and quietly talked with God about my dreams and goals; about how my parents sometimes thought they knew what was best for me better than I did; and about my fears of telling them the truth.

Then I just listened, not so much for a voice or anything but for a feeling. That's how God usually "talked" to me—with feelings. I got a distinct feeling of certainty about who I was and what I wanted. I decided I had to convey this to my parents without breaking their hearts.

I sat down that night, and before my dad could open the first college package, I stopped him gently. I told my parents everything that was in my heart: how much I loved them and wanted to please them and have their support; and how much I wanted to travel for a year. I even told them how I loved being around students from other cultures and learning their languages as well as helping them learn mine.

Maybe it was a little God work, or maybe it was just that my passion for what I wanted came across really strong. Maybe it was both. But my parents shocked me when they both smiled and suggested that I travel to Europe to look at schools there! My mom especially said she would miss me like crazy, but they both agreed they wanted what I wanted. My dad even came up with the great idea for me to look into some kind of exchange program, where I could stay with a host family and learn the culture directly!

For the rest of the night, the three of us dreamed dreams for me together. I don't know what I was afraid of. My parents had always been on my side. I just hadn't always believed it.

God,
I have my whole future ahead of me, and it scares me. But knowing that I always have you to turn to for guidance, wisdom, and direction makes the journey I am facing so much easier. Walk beside me as I take these shaky but exciting beginning steps on the path that will become my destiny. Amen.

Opportunities do not present themselves;
you must dig for them and claim them
as your own.

The keys to the world have been given to me now that I am nearing graduation. I pray for guidance to choose the proper door, knowledge to know if I make a mistake, confidence to know that I can recover from any errors, and courage to face any challenge. I know with your loving support, Lord, I can do anything I set my mind to. Amen.

I'm not afraid of storms, for I'm learning
how to sail my ship.

LOUISA MAY ALCOTT

The Faith to Follow Your Heart

It was four weeks until my high school graduation, and everyone wanted to tell me what to do! It was pretty ironic that right when I was preparing to strike out on my own, family and friends seemed compelled to insist that they knew what was best for me. It was really starting to drive me crazy!

The problem was that I wanted to be an actor. This was no secret—I had appeared in every high school production for the past four years. Everyone knew that I loved performing. It was my passion, my dream, and my talent. I had been accepted into a great college with a very prestigious theater arts program.

Now, all of a sudden, when it was nearly time for me to get my act together and take it on the road, everyone wanted to talk to me about practicality and being reasonable and not living in a world of dreams.

What?

All these years, I'd been taught to believe in myself. To believe in my dreams. To have faith that the Lord would help me to follow the proper path in life. I had spent hours in contemplation and prayer. I felt that being an actor was my calling. It was what I did best. I wasn't following foolish dreams; I was following my heart and my God.

Over the course of the summer, I began to falter in my faith and believe what people were telling me. The life of a performer was so uncertain, I should focus on something practical in school. By the time the fall rolled around, I had changed from a theater major to a science major. My parents were chemists and had always hoped that I would follow in their footsteps.

So I took tons of science classes. And I also appeared in all the college plays. I got okay grades in science and great grades in theater. After three years, I couldn't stand it—I quit college. I didn't know what I believed anymore, what I wanted, or what path had been set for me. I was confused and unhappy.

Every time I prayed and every time I looked within myself, I found the stage. Eventually, I realized that being an actor is who I am and what I need to do. I went back to college and finished with a degree in theater arts. I was offered an apprenticeship with a professional touring group performing Christian inspirational plays for teens.

I love my life again, and I love what I'm doing. And my favorite performance piece? It's the one I wrote entitled "Follow Your Heart."

In order to know what you want to be when you grow up, you have to know who you are now. What do you enjoy doing? What do you believe in? What do you stand for?

Credit Where Credit
Is Overdue

Last fall, my parents gave me a great gift: a credit card.
They gave it to me so I could get groceries for them or put
gas in the car—that type of thing. I was also allowed to use
it for my school clothes and supplies, as long as I paid the
balance off each month with my allowance.

At first, it was great. I could run errands and go to the
supermarket. I got to spend money that wasn't mine,
money that I didn't even have in my hand.

On Sundays, if someone forgot to bring the donuts
and coffee to youth group, I'd always volunteer to run out
and pick things up. Usually a couple of the other kids
would go with me, and we'd always get a few extras. It
was okay—I just put it on my credit card.

One month, I went to a big sale to shop for school
clothes. I had a certain monthly allowance I was given for
clothes, but with my credit card, I figured it didn't matter if I
spent a bit more.

I went a little crazy with the card at the shoe store the
following month and found myself praying that I'd somehow
come up with the extra cash. I knew prayer could
be powerful, so I just kept praying it would
all work out. If it didn't, I figured no big
deal; I'd just pay for it the next month.

My prayers didn't seem to be getting
answered, and I knew that I owed a lot of

money I didn't have. It would have to come out of my future months' allowance.

In June, Dad showed me my accounts. By pulling the money I owed from my future allowance, I had spent myself all the way to next January. I'd overspent by $600. And Dad had taken an extra 20 percent of that: $120!!! He said that was the amount of interest the credit card company would charge me in addition to the $600.

After I thought about it for a while, I decided that maybe my prayers HAD been answered after all. The good Lord (and my parents) taught me a great lesson in growing up. When I go to college in a few years, I won't take the credit card.

The love of money is at the root of all kinds of evil. And some people, craving money, have wandered from the faith and pierced themselves with many sorrows.

1 TIMOTHY 6:10 NLT

God,
I cannot wait to graduate. I'm eager to make decisions for myself: to pick my own classes if I decide to go to college or determine my career path if I enter the working world. The whole idea is so exciting I can hardly focus on my schoolwork. Please help me to concentrate on today's issues before worrying about tomorrow. You offer an awesome world of opportunity, and I can't wait to dive in.

Let Me Out of Here!

I'm a guidance counselor with our youth ministry program at church. The fall of my sophomore year, it seemed that all the other counselors and I could talk about was how we couldn't wait to "escape." We wanted out of our town, our houses, and our schedules! We wanted to be in charge of ourselves!

I cringed when I'd see something about someone my age in the paper or on the news. I still had a curfew, for goodness sake! Meanwhile, there were kids my age out there making headlines, doing good stuff in the world, and coming home whenever they wanted!

It was Reverend Bukowski who proposed "the experiment." Probably because we were driving her nuts with all our complaints. She arranged a weekend away for our parents. Those with younger siblings helped find friends for them to stay with. The idea was for us to spend the weekend alone. There were a few ground rules, which we grumbled about, but we knew they were necessary. The big one was that we couldn't have any parties. Reverend Bukowski was going to be checking on us from time to time to make sure we fulfilled our end of the bargain.

Contracts were drawn up, and the weekend came. We were psyched! A whole weekend alone! Cool! It was like an answer to our prayers. Or so we thought at first. Friday night was pretty much okay. I stayed up way too late watching television. I also ate every ounce of junk food I could find in the house. I fell asleep in front of the TV and woke up at around 7:00 A.M. with that nasty taste in my mouth from going to sleep without brushing my teeth. I climbed upstairs and went to bed.

Saturday morning I slept and slept. When I woke up at 1:00 in the afternoon, I was confused for a minute. I wondered where everyone was. Then I remembered! The house, my LIFE—it was all mine! I went downstairs. It did seem awfully quiet. There was no smell of coffee from the kitchen. No television on in the den. No phone ringing. Nothing. I poured a bowl of cereal and then discovered the awful truth. My mom hadn't bought groceries for me! There was no milk. So I sat at the table by myself eating dry cereal with my fingers. It was okay. At least no one was telling me what chores had to get done!

I have to admit, I was rather glad when Reverend Bukowski rang the doorbell at 9:00. I tried to get her to come in and chat for a while, but she declined. "Just checking in," she said.

By late Saturday night, as I sat on the couch, sick of television, and not any too thrilled with the box of cereal I'd just had for a late dinner, I began to feel like God was probably getting a good chuckle out of all this. I'd often heard the old adage: "Be careful what you pray for." And now here I was. I had just what I'd asked for, and it wasn't any fun at all.

Sunday dawned, and I slept half the day away since no one was around to wake me up for church. I had told myself that I would do no work all weekend, but I was tired of doing nothing so I headed out to the garage. My dad had the car engine torn up, trying to do some work. I began to tinker under the hood, thinking how surprised he'd be to come home and find the car fixed! I thought about my sister's laugh, my dad's look of pride, and my mom's cooking! Finally, I threw down the wrench, looked heavenward and declared, "Okay, I get it! I'm thankful for my family and for how we help each other get through life. I miss them!"

I know it will be different when I leave for college for real in a couple of years, but I learned something very important from the experiment. I learned to appreciate how my life is overflowing with some very special blessings. I'll never wish them away again.

✣   ✤   ✥

Don't be so worried about the future
that you forget to live in the present.

God's Green Earth

I grew up in God's country. In the heartland on a farm. We lived in a small town miles away from most of my classmates.

I hated it. I was always the "farm boy" or the "bus kid." I couldn't do anything in the fall except help with the harvest. Sometimes I had to miss school. When there was work to be done, it didn't matter whether there was an algebra test or a big dance. My parents couldn't afford to hire help, so us kids had to chip in whenever and wherever we were needed.

I couldn't wait to get out of that nowhere environment. I wanted to see what real living was like. I wanted to live in the middle of New York City with concrete and buildings and people everywhere!

Didn't I?

The summer before I started my freshman year of high school, my parents let me spend a month living with my cousins in New York. I was so excited—finally a chance to escape! I thought I would have the time of my life.

But I had trouble finding God. I had never realized that I always found him in the trees and the fields, in the sunrise and open spaces.

I felt hemmed in—like I had to bust up all the cement and find some grass or I'd go crazy. I was relieved when it was finally time for me to return home.

I always thought I'd be moving on after high school. Getting out of this "nowhere" town. But you know what? I've discovered that everything that is dear to me is right here. This isn't nowhere—it's everywhere.

Gotta go. It's harvest time, and Dad is calling for me to come and help.

❖   ❖   ❖

Package

I am a package
Being shipped across the country of life.

My destination:
To be loved for what's inside and
Accepted for who I am.

I've weighed too much and not enough
And I don't seem to belong to anyone.

The only countries I've seen are
Frustration, Disappointment, Confusion, and Hurt.

My box is so dented, warped, and ripped
That I'm afraid to move.

I am a package on the Journey
    of Life,
I only wish I knew which end is up.

Blind Spot

I winced as my daughter punched the last of her clothing into a suitcase.

"Mom, I'll send for my CDs, books, and whatever else when I know where we'll be."

"We" was my 17-year-old daughter, Sherry, and her 19-year-old boyfriend, Dommie. Music was always the biggest passion of Sherry's life. She had a summer job at Madcap Music. That's where she met Dommie. He was the soloist and lead guitar of Dommie and His Demons. When he sang to Sherry right there in the store, she flipped.

My daughter had always been levelheaded and sensible. But lately she had changed. Suddenly I didn't know her. And I was about to lose her.

"I'm meeting Dommie and the band at the bus terminal. Can you call me a cab, Mom?"

"Why don't I drive you?" I asked.

"Oh, Mom, I don't want any slurpy good-byes."

"I promise I won't be slurpy," I said, feeling that way already. I thought we had a close relationship and that I understood her. Apparently I was wrong.

I thought about Proverbs 22:6: "Train children in the right way, and when old, they will not stray." I wondered where I had gone wrong. At what point did my daughter become so distant from me? I didn't have any more time to ponder. Sherry was anxious to go.

"I'd simply die if I miss the bus, Mom. Simply die."

Was I that dramatic when I was her age? I couldn't recall.

As we got in the car, lightning illuminated the sky. Soon droplets of rain splattered on the windshield. Even though I had taught Sherry how to drive, she quickly became my mentor on the road. "There's a car coming up beside you, Mom. Watch out. He might cut you off."

Clearly, she didn't trust me behind the wheel. But I didn't mind. I was treasuring every moment I had with my child. Was there anything I could say to her now that I hadn't said already?

"Careful, Mom. Don't get too close to that car. You always told me not to tailgate."

"That's right, I did. You know we can follow cars too closely—and also people." Did I really expect her to get my message? We reached the access road to the bus terminal.

"Mom, what's the matter with you? You didn't even check your blind spot."

She was right. I hadn't. I was more preoccupied than I thought. I didn't want her to go.

"We all have blind spots," I said. "About things. About people. Sometimes even about ourselves."

I pulled up to the terminal. Sherry sighed in relief. I got out to hug her good-bye.

"I'll call you, Mom. Take care driving home."

I nodded as my tears mingled with the rain. "Look out for the blind spots," I called. I had done all I could. Now my daughter would have to live with her decisions.

The days dragged by. Silence filled the house. I yearned for some familiar sounds. Even though I could make a call whenever I wanted to now, I missed Sherry's constant chatter on the phone. I missed the incessant sound of CDs blaring through the house. I could watch TV at a normal volume now, but I wished I couldn't.

And the car. I didn't have to make an appointment to use it anymore. How I wished I did. It was the same way with the computer. I could get online whenever I felt like it. I just never felt like it.

What I *did* want was a phone call, an e-mail, a card, or a letter from my child, letting me know she was okay. None came. I waited anxiously for some small bit of correspondence.

I hoped she was in a nice hotel room. She had said she'd room with Dommie's girl singer. I was glad she hadn't said Dommie.

Since she didn't cook, meals would be a problem. It took a lot of money to eat out, and her babysitting money wouldn't last forever.

What would she do all day? Listen to the band practice? How long before that got old? At night the band would be performing. She'd be part of the audience—but for how long? Then what would she do?

I knew my daughter, or I thought I did. Were her feelings for Dommie enough to keep her happy otherwise? I wasn't really sure.

As the days became a week, the scenarios in my head became more serious. Was Sherry traveling from city to city? That might explain not hearing from her. Was she ill? In the hospital, maybe? Surely Dommie would let me know.

I couldn't believe she was so absorbed in her own world that she didn't even have time to contact her mom. But I didn't know what else to think. Then one evening I heard a key in the lock.

"Sherry?"

"Hi, Mom."

I hugged her as tears filled my eyes. Knowing how she disliked slurpy scenes, I let her go and smiled. "Welcome home. Did you come back to get the rest of your things? Can you stay a while?"

"Mom," Sherry said, flopping onto the couch. "I didn't call because I was afraid I'd start crying. I could have written, but I didn't know what to say. I'm not going back."

I sighed with relief.

"I'll tell you about it soon. But not right now. I just don't know how I could have been so dumb."

"You weren't dumb, honey, just starstruck by Dommie and his music. It happens." *And,* I thought silently, *when the reality of life sets in, sometimes things and people look different.*

"At the oddest times," Sherry told me, "I'd think about the last thing you said to me: 'Look out for the blind spots.' Then, one night when I was alone in the hotel, I remembered our drive to the terminal and the odd things you said. It took me a while to put it together, but I did have a blind spot about Dommie."

Right then I wanted to get super slurpy, but I didn't. Instead I thought of Proverbs 22:6 and realized that maybe I hadn't done such a bad job after all.

*The road ahead will be speckled with disappointment,
dotted with sadness, and even marked with failure.
Each speed bump in the path of life is a chance
to evaluate where you are, ensuring you
remain on the triumphant path.*

Pursue some path, however narrow and crooked,
in which you can walk with love and reverence.

HENRY DAVID THOREAU

Dear God,

The unknown is so scary. I don't know what to expect—of myself or of others. I don't know if I will be successful, if I'll be loved, or even if I'll be here tomorrow. Please, Lord, give me courage to face each day and help me remember you will be there through everything.

*The plans you make now for the road ahead
are not set in stone. If you feel you're headed
in the wrong direction, it's never too late to begin again.*

Growing Up

Throughout my childhood, I had many goals and dreams. Some of those goals—like becoming a ballerina—were replaced by other, more realistic goals as I got older. But one of my goals always remained the same: I wanted to be a grown-up.

I expected the transition from child to adult to be dramatic.

Maybe I'd get a congratulatory letter in the mail that read: "Congratulations! You are now a grown-up! Please enjoy being an adult!" At that moment, all the things my parents said I'd understand when I was a grown-up would be revealed to me. I'd feel confident and self-assured. I'd have the world all figured out.

It didn't happen like that.

It started one day in the fall when I was a junior in high school. I heard my parents screaming at each other in the backyard. I ran out to see what was going on. They were in the midst of a horrible fight about all kinds of things. That started happening a lot. Eventually, by having faith in each other and our family, they worked it out. But those few months made me see that my parents weren't perfect. They'd always seemed to have this perfect marriage and this perfect life. When I realized this wasn't the case, I felt betrayed. By God. By Mom and Dad. By life. Then I adjusted and thought, *Okay, so this is what it feels like to be all grown-up. Now I know that the world isn't always as sugar-coated as it seems.* So I crossed "Growing Up" off my list of things to do.

Turns out it didn't work quite like that. Not too long after, my favorite uncle got in serious trouble with the law. I went through all the same feelings again! "What's going on here, God?" I cried. Then I started to get it. This growing up thing was going to take a while.

When I reached my 30s, I really felt confident that I had it all under control. Then my mom passed away. It happened all over again. The anger, the hurt, the desire to turn back into a little kid. Only difference was, this time my faith was stronger.

So here's my analysis: This thing called "Growing Up" should just be called "Growing." It's not a thing to achieve. It's a process that never ends. I hope and pray that I'll always be growing, and I think it'll be okay. It's that faith in life and in the Lord that makes it all happen as it should.

God,

Life is funny. As I raced through all the challenges of school, I thought it would never end. Now as I sit at the fork in the road I wonder how I got here. It's amazing how quickly time has passed. I have mixed emotions, Father, on these final days of my childhood. I'm excited and afraid of the future, elated at my current success, and sad to see my school years behind me. Help me to make sense of my feelings and feel comfortable with myself.

As I look to the future, Lord, I am filled with aspirations, goals, desires, and determination. I am thankful you've allowed me to make it this far, and I want to ask for your help with my future endeavors. I do not expect to easily accomplish everything I set my heart on. But I am ready to face my future if you are willing to hold my hand along the way. Amen.

If one advances confidently in the direction of his dreams, and endeavors to live the life which he has imagined, he will meet with a success unexpected in common hours.

HENRY DAVID THOREAU

Life is like climbing a tree. Each branch will bring you closer to the top, but hasty decisions are more likely to make you fall.

Keep in mind that you may not be able to erase the mistakes of yesterday, but you always have a clean slate to work with tomorrow.

Change—I hate it! Every time I get accustomed to a situation it changes. I accepted junior high and then I became a dreaded freshman. Now that I've become a senior, the "top dog" in school, I have to start all over again in college. I'm afraid I won't be able to make friends or I won't be able to keep up with the classes and the homework. How will I work, go to classes, and keep in touch with all my friends? I was always scared with each new school and new situation as I grew up, but now I think I'm more afraid than ever. Everything I've known will change. Please help me believe in my abilities and provide me with the skills to adapt to such a massive change. Amen.

There are only four words you need to know, and you learned them in grade school: "I can do it."

What's on Your Mind?

It is a day in your life two years from now. Where are you? What are you doing? What have you been discussing with God? Have you met your own goals? Have you met God's expectations?

_____

_____

_____

Now, consider the same questions for five years from now.

_____

_____

_____

Now, try it for ten years from now.

_____

_____

_____

What goals have you or will you set to reach your future dreams? How will you pray about this? Do you have prayer requests? Prayers of thanks? What kind of spiritual life will help you get to where you want to be?

_____

_____

_____

Ellen F. Pill has contributed to several inspirational books, including *Blessed by an Angel*. Her stories and sentiments have also been published in *Whispers from Heaven* magazine and by American Greetings and Hallmark.

Marie D. Jones is an ordained minister and a contributing author to numerous books, including *Simple Truths: Teens, A Mother's Daily Prayer Book*, and *When You Lose Someone You Love: A Year of Comfort*.

Quotes compiled by Joan Loshek.

Other contributors:

Jennifer John Ouellette
Kristin Abraham
Bruce Adkins
Stephen Albrow
Marion F. Ash
Roy A. Borges
Jean Bowdy
Maureen Boyd Biro
Renie Burghardt
Tiffiny Carlson
Mary Chandler
Margaret Cheasebro
Linda Chiara
Jackie Clements-Marenda
Naoma Coffman
Barbara Davey
Sarah L. Dunning
Judie Gulley
Pamela M. Hall
Beatrice M. Hogg
Margaret Anne Huffman
Ellen Javernick

David L. Jenkins
Kevin Jordan & Vera Avery
Carol Kehlmeier
Tom R. Kovach
Cherie Kuranko
Sophia Mitra
Brandy Morris
Rose Moss
Meredith Napolitano
Jo Nathan
Belinda K. Nichols
Lorena O'Connor
Luis Perez, Jr.
Shad Powers
Heather Ray
Tom Rhodes
Michele D. Robertson
Ernest Shubird
Joyce Stark
Kristi Tullis
Josh Wright & Diane Nichols
Kevin Young